YOU ARE THAT

GANGAJI

YOU ARE THAT

EXPANDED COLLECTOR'S EDITION

SOUNDS TRUE
awakening wisdom

Sounds True, Inc.
Boulder, CO 80306

Printed in Canada

Book design by Karen Polaski

ISBN 978-1-59179-588-9

Library of Congress Cataloging-in-Publication Data

Gangaji.
  You Are That / Gangaji.
    p. cm.
  ISBN 978-1-59179-588-9 (hardcover)
  1. Spiritual life. 2. Self-realization—Religious aspects. I. Title.

BL624.G346 2007
294.5'44—dc22

                              2007005354

CONTENTS

*Blessings and gratitude to all those who transcribed tapes,
to Dan Hawthorne for formatting the original books and getting them
ready for press, to Eli Jaxon-Bear for his inspiration and consultation,
to Al Drucker for his invaluable editing suggestions, and especially to
Shanti Einolander for enthusiastically and tirelessly entering
the numerous changes while contributing to the overall book production.*

*Everlasting appreciation for Barbara Denempont.
Her clarity of leadership and supportive love have contributed to this
new edition in uncountable ways.*

Sri Ramana Maharshi

H.W.L. Poonja

For Beloved Papaji
Radiant manifestation of Self
whose recognition and confirmation
removed all pretense of doubt.
It is only through his grace that satsang
with Gangaji makes its appearance here
in consciousness.

FOREWORD

N o one has ever reported an end to realizing true self." These words of Gangaji will reverberate as you dive, or rather, float, into *You Are That*. With the turning of each page, the relaxation into true self becomes deeper and quieter; the movements of resistance, fewer. Reading this book will not be an exercise in acquiring knowledge. Rather, the experience will be the release of your imagined spiritual certainties. This release will sneak up on you. Just as your mind is busy trying to work some particular phrase, trying to hold it in a conceptual way, to "get it," the next words on the page will plunge you into quiet again. It is the opposite of reading a book for intellectual, emotional, or spiritual gain. It is instead the experience of reading a book in order to refresh yourself in what our teacher, Poonjaji, called, "the reservoir of nothingness."

And this is not, of course, the nothingness of a dark void. People will do anything to avoid their fear of such a void and, as Gangaji points out, "frantic mental activity is generated to fill [this] seeming void." The reservoir of nothingness refers instead to the incomparable respite from having to present something or someone to the world, from having to maintain any kind of image. It refers to the deep and consistent realm of simply being. When Gangaji, and before her, Nisargadatta (of the treasured collection of talks called *I Am That*), as well as countless other great teachers throughout time, refers to *that,* it is this ineffable, pure sense of being, the direct experience of existence pulsing in oneself and all things.

Yet Gangaji is a most contemporary teacher, well steeped, after many years of interacting with thousands of students, in the issues that arise for anyone turning to the simplicity of *being* from a complicated life of doing and having. Though her focus steadfastly remains on this simplicity of being, she also understands and addresses the disillusionment that comes from a life of grasping the things and experiences of the world, and the even more profound disillusionment that comes from trying to grasp spiritual experience. While acknowledging the journey of the modern seeker, who has likely traversed psychological as well as spiritual paths, she unfailingly points you back to stillness and to letting go of all spiritual strategies, even your most precious hopes of enlightenment: "That which you are is untouched by any idea of ignorance or enlightenment." Thus, she exhorts you to abandon your ideas for aggrandizing your spiritual persona, or else your turning to *satsang* would be "simply an exchange of trances."

Instead, Gangaji invites you to experience "true joy," a sense of well-being that is not dependent on comfort or possessions but on your stillness in the comings and goings of all phenomena, the stillness within your difficulties as well as your triumphs. And while many traditions have spoken of this stillness and have offered techniques and meditation practices to come to it, Gangaji says, as did Poonjaji, that these techniques and practices, though they have their uses for calming the mind, can also become mental traps if they engender the dualistic separation of *meditation* and *the rest of my life.* Gangaji suggests that you experience your *whole* life as a living meditation, a silent awareness in daily existence that requires nothing other than the recognition of its constancy to live in that experience. You will not need to add anything at all. You will not need to practice anything to enjoy that constancy. And in that silent awareness that is not trying to get somewhere else, not trying to get enlightened, not trying to get better, there is unmitigated peace, the true joy to which Gangaji refers.

It is so simple that it is easily overlooked. But the readiness to come to this simplicity, as Gangaji explains in this book, requires spiritual maturity. It is somewhat ironic that only with the deconstruction of one's various activities of acquisition—achievements, fulfillment of desires, acquiring of beliefs, practices, and spiritual experiences—that true maturity comes and is found in the surrendering of all acquisitions and experiences, leaving one with nowhere to stand. It is the maturity of confronting the question of who you would be if you were not the owner, the spouse, the adventurer, the parent, the lover, the spiritual seeker. It is the maturity of not needing to prove anything, proclaim cosmic insights, or be on your way to some greater goal. It is the maturity of being comfortable in your own skin, as is, and in the twinkling delight of knowing your own dear self—the stripped-down, bare-bones version—in what Gangaji beautifully describes as "the trembling shyness in the face of divinity."

Throughout this book, you will be in touch with this—your own dear self, shy in the face of divinity. You will experience what Gangaji speaks of as a living sutra, words that spring from silence and take you there. You will experience the quiet joy that comes not from unraveling a spiritual mystery but from living as one. I recommend that you keep this book by your bedside and dip into its exquisite reservoir of nothingness whenever you can. No matter what page you land on, you will be reminded that *you are that.*

—Catherine Ingram
Los Angeles, 2006

ABOUT THE BOOK

Meetings with Gangaji are public gatherings, open to everyone, in which Gangaji interacts with those asking questions or making comments.

You Are That contains selected excerpts from meetings held from 1993–1995 in various locations of northern India, Nepal, Bali, and the western United States, including Maui, Hawaii.

This newly revised edition comprises both original *You Are That* volumes, with additional material and chapters added from meetings held in Perth, Australia, in November of 2005.

WELCOME TO SATSANG

That which you yearn for, that which you hunger for, is that which is always present. That is who you truly are.

When I say "you," I am not referring to your body. Your body is in that. I am not referring to your thoughts. Your thoughts are in that. I am not referring to your emotions. Your emotions appear in and disappear in that. I am not speaking of your circumstances. Circumstances, too, appear in and disappear in that.

Bodies, thoughts, emotions, and circumstances change. They appear and disappear. They may be good or bad. They may be pleasing or displeasing. The truth of who you are is permanent and unmoving. The great, good news is that however you might *imagine* yourself, you can recognize who you truly are. Regardless of the experience of yourself as a body, or as the thought *I am this body,* you can receive the direct transmission of truth from your own self. That transmission is satsang. Satsang confirms your true identity as pure consciousness, free of all perceived constraints.

When this good news is heard, really heard, there is immeasurable opening. No one has ever reported an end to realizing true self. What does end is the preoccupation with imagining yourself to be some particular entity separate from boundless consciousness.

I do not have anything to teach you. Self-realization is not about learning. Self-realization is not something that can be captured in words. Although words will be used, no word that anyone has ever spoken has touched the glory of the true self. I am here to point you to that, to celebrate that, and to laugh at the very flimsy idea that something could ever really obstruct that.

I am not asking you to remember anything. I am not asking you to do anything or to get anything new. Nothing new is needed. I am asking you to realize you are already that which you want. And I am simply suggesting, as my teacher suggested to me, and as his teacher suggested to him, that you take one instant, one millisecond, to allow the activity of the mind to stop. In that millisecond, what a discovery is made! In that millisecond, you receive the invitation to surrender to what is revealed when there is no attention on body, thought, emotion, or circumstance.

This is a momentous instant! In this instant, the body is gone. In this instant of perfect silence, you discover what is permanently here, what has always been here, what is permanently you. This instant of silence is the invitation to true refuge, true retreat, true peace, regardless of comings and goings.

What an instant this is! There is no dwelling on the past, there is no speculating on the future, and there is no analyzing the present in relation to the past or the future. In this instant, there is no mental preoccupation. There is no conditioned existence. There is only pure, pristine consciousness. In this instant, you are in satsang.

Somehow, by some stroke of good luck, your individual consciousness has been called to satsang. You have heard the words that you are truth itself. Now you are free to discover yourself as truth. You are free to rest in that truth. You are free to be happy, regardless of bodies, thoughts, emotions, or circumstances. You are free to be who you truly are.

Welcome to satsang.

THE SEARCH FOR ENLIGHTENMENT

You have imagined yourself to be a body, and in this imagination, you are frantically trying to find the secret to the liberation of the body. Maybe you have studied Eastern spiritual traditions, or maybe you have studied Western spiritual traditions. Maybe you have been involved in certain activities of acquisition. All these *doing-to-get* activities are related to the liberation of your body.

Your body cannot be liberated. Your body is doomed to disappearance. Your body is bound by birth, hunger, disease, death, genetics, and environment. However, if you turn your face to that which permeates your body, that which surrounds your body, that which your body arises in, exists because of, and returns to, you meet freedom itself. This meeting is liberation.

People first come to the spiritual search from an egocentric idea of what will be attained. The beginning of the spiritual search is the positive aspect of ego: *I'm tired of suffering. I want to be happy. I hear happiness is the spiritual goal.* The thought *I want to be happy* comes from a developed ego, a functioning, integrated ego.

With courage and guidance, there arises the resolve to turn away from the forces that support ignorance and turn toward the forces that support enlightenment. All of this is immeasurably important.

The concept of enlightenment comes from the recognition or the insight, *My God, I have been living in ignorance. I want to leave ignorance.* This recognition is an evolutionary point in a lifestream.

The search for enlightenment takes innumerable forms. Perhaps first is the attempt to follow the codes and practices of religion. Usually next is the attempt to throw off the code of religion and live by a personal code. There may be superficial hope that in dressing or acting as the Buddhists or Hindus or Sufis dress and act, some of their attainment will transfer. However you have tried to get enlightenment, you have continually come to what appears to be a dead end. At this end, rather than experience the true *end,* you usually begin the search anew with a different code or religion, or a rebellion to all codes and religions.

You cannot find true happiness by *doing anything.* You can experience moments of happiness, certainly. But to recognize you are that which is happiness, you must abandon all vehicles of escape. The end must be experienced. Every *thing* must be given up.

What a surprise to realize that real happiness requires releasing everything! To receive ultimate attainment, finally you must stop trying to *get* anything. The idea of *you* must end. When you give up the idea of enlightenment, you realize what the idea of enlightenment points to.

If you can see that what you *thought* you wanted has not given you what it is you *really* want, then you are ready. You are mature. Maturity has little to do with age or education or spiritual practice. Maturity reflects ruthless intelligence in telling the truth. The truth is that no matter how much you have enjoyed your relations and circumstances, those things have not given you lasting fulfillment.

This recognition is a rude awakening, a disillusionment. Until disillusionment occurs, you wander through life in a trancelike state, attempting to grasp the things you want and reject the things you don't want in the hope of receiving happiness.

Through disillusionment and ruthless truthtelling, you can actually discover what you really want. If by luck what you really want is eternal truth, then have the courage to stop looking in any *thing* for eternal truth. Whether your search is in worldly things, philosophical things, or spiritual things, simply stop looking. When you stop looking, you can discover eternal truth. It takes less than an instant.

You are very lucky if you have the desire for truth, but in your search for truth, what is searched for is an image or an idea or a concept based on what you have been taught, what you read somewhere, what you imagine to be so, or what you remember from some glimpse in the past. These are all mental *things*. They may be beautiful things, but even the subtlest mental concepts are still things.

The great gift offered by my Master, Sri Poonjaji, and by his Master, Sri Ramana Maharshi, is the instruction to *be still*. To not look to the mind as the reference point of who you are.

What can be said about what is revealed in stillness? Much has been said that points to it. Nothing has been said that can touch true revelation. Words such as "infinity," "eternity," "grace," "self," "truth," "God," all point to that which is revealed in absolute stillness. Yet if the moment is conceived as some *thing,* then revelation also points away from truth.

That which you are is untouched by any idea of ignorance or enlightenment. While the concept of enlightenment points to freedom and the truth of your being, if you cling to the concept, you overlook what was present before you ever heard the word. You overlook what is present when your body is in the deepest sleep state. You overlook what remains when your body is long gone.

There comes an instant when, by some miraculous, mysterious grace, you are struck dumb of all words, all concepts, all searching, all striving, all identification. In that moment, an instant out of time, you realize that who you *really* are has never been touched by any concept. This very instant of realization is, in fact, what the concept of enlightenment points to.

The habits and tricks of mind are very strong, of course, and they may reappear. You may think, *Oh, I got it! I'm enlightened now.* This thought is already a trick of mind, based on the supposition that you are some entity separate from consciousness itself, separate from that which is revealed in the instant of the ceasing of mind activity. In thinking *I got it. I'm enlightened,* there must also follow *Oh, I lost it. I'm unenlightened.* You must have been through this many times. These concepts are opposite sides of the same coin, and they both lead to suffering. They both come from the thought *I am some thing, and enlightenment is some other thing I must get to be happy.*

Who you truly are has no need of, no desire for, and no fear of either ignorance or enlightenment. Who you are is free of all concepts. The concept of enlightenment points to realizing that. The concept of ignorance points to not realizing that. The moment you cling to any concept of ignorance or any concept of enlightenment as reality, you are already in the experience of ignorance again. Do you see how subtle the workings of the mind are?

Mind includes all thought, whether mental, physical, emotional, or circumstantial. All trickery of mind is based on the idea that you are a *thing.* You are no *thing* at all. Everything that appears, appears in the vastness of eternal truth. When you identify yourself as a thing—mental, physical, emotional, or circumstantial—and you believe this identification to be real, you overlook the reality of the vastness of being.

Realization is so utterly simple, and this simplicity is what has held it as the deepest secret, inherently protected by the corrupting power of the mind. All striving, all practicing, all comparing, and all codes are realized as irrelevant in the vastness of this utter simplicity. In the moment of realization, there is ultimate freedom. The radiance of eternal truth melts the mind into blissful submission to the unnameable. If you cling even slightly to any *thing,* then once again, the mind is caught in misidentification, and suffering is experienced.

The opportunity for your particular mindstream is to realize that you are the animating force that gives the mindstream its apparent power. This gift from Ramana, through Papaji, is the invitation to stop midstream and recognize who you are. This can be realized immediately in simply being still. You will never realize it by searching for it in thoughts. You may have intellectual understanding, but you will never be fully satisfied until you embrace the truth of who you are.

You cannot *make* stillness. You *are* stillness. Be who you are. Be still—absolutely, completely still—and see what is before any thought, concept, or image of who, what, when, how, or why.

Stillness is presence of being. You *are* that presence of being. Receive yourself. Drink yourself. Be nourished by yourself. Begin your exploration of the limitless wonder of yourself.

I do not mean explore your thoughts. You have explored your thoughts, and they have taken you as far as they can take you. I do not mean explore your emotions, your feelings, your sensations, or your circumstances. Explore your *self*—that which is before, during, and after all objects of awareness. THAT. That presence of being is who you are.

I am not attempting to teach you this. There is no way possible to teach who you are. There is no way possible to learn who you are. The message I bring is simply that in the heart of awareness, you recognize without a shadow of a doubt the truth of your own being.

All that is required for that recognition is to pull your attention back from the usual fixations and preoccupations. Let attention rest in the truth of satsang, formless and present as the core of being.

There is nothing that keeps you from the realization of your inherent, permanent, present freedom except your imagination that somebody or something is keeping you from that. Whether that somebody is called "me and my personality," or "them and what they did to me" or "what they might do to me" or "what they are doing to me," it is all just a story, an endless commentary based on nothing.

Someone once said in satsang, "Enlightenment is retroactive." It is true. You will see that your whole past is both perfect and nonexistent. Once you recognize the inherent, permanent truth at the core of all experiences, you will see that truth has always been present, and life has always been about that. Sometimes it has appeared in distorted, twisted, ugly, ignorant ways, but still your whole life has always been about that.

This is the divine birth present everywhere, in everyone. Not a special divine birth, but that which can never be separate from divinity. Birth, death, relationships, emptiness, fullness, existence, and nonexistence all come from the divine, exist because of the grace of the divine, and return finally into the divine.

❖

What is enlightenment? Is it every single moment keeping the awareness on awareness?

Enlightenment is a word that points to the recognition of totality as self. Unfortunately, the word "enlightenment" has become conceptualized as the experiential byproduct that results from that recognition. True enlightenment is not limited to any state of mind.

True enlightenment recognizes what is present before, during, and after any notion of enlightenment. That which is unaffected by either the state of enlightenment or the state of unenlightenment.

❖

Enlightenment, self-realization, is the answer to the question "Who am I?" But to aid in this discovery, it is extremely helpful to start telling the truth about what it is you mean when you say the word *I*.

I is the word we speak more than any other word. What are the typical definitions for *I?* The most obvious have to do with the body: *I* want some food. *I* need some sleep.

At a certain level of development, you begin to get in touch with another body, the emotional body: *I* feel angry. *I* feel happy.

Deeper than the physical and emotional bodies is the soul body. If you are lucky enough to get that far, it is extraordinary to be in touch with the soul as *I*. This is where most people stop inquiry, because the purity, luminosity, and radiance of the soul are quite exquisite. The soul as *I* doesn't exclude the body or the emotions; it is simply more pure.

But the soul as *I* is not the end of *I;* it's just the way in. If inquiry doesn't stop with the definition of soul as *I,* then it is possible to discover *I* as *everything, I* as *totality.* True *I* does not exclude the body, the emotions, or the soul. It permeates all of that because it sees all of that. It sees itself in all realms and domains. Self-realization is simply the realization of that.

Whatever role *I* may be playing as *me,* whatever feeling *I* may be having, whatever *I* as the body is doing, it is possible to see everything that appears in consciousness as oneself.

Maybe you have heard this before. Maybe you are thinking you know what I'm talking about. But you haven't really heard it before, because no one has yet said it. The truth of *I* has never really been said, and it has never really been heard, because whatever is said or heard still infers some kind of exclusion. Even the word "inclusion" somehow excludes exclusion.

What is it that can *really* include both inclusion and exclusion?

Yes! You catch it! That is who you are.

Certain words such as "awareness" get used, because awareness comes very close to it. However you are identifying yourself, awareness is always present. Throughout physical identification, emotional identification, soul identification, cosmic identification, or identification with the realms of hell, awareness is the constant.

Awareness is a good start, but what I have noticed in spiritual circles is that the recognition of oneself as awareness often shifts to identification with certain *states* of awareness. You might hear someone say, "I was in awareness most of the day, and then I lost it." This is not what I'm talking about. I'm speaking about what cannot be lost. I'm pointing to what is aware of losing what you thought was awareness.

If you have heard what I have to say, you already know that I don't put any stock in levels of enlightenment or levels of unenlightenment. This is neither my message nor my invitation. I really don't care what someone has realized or not realized. I don't care how good or bad you have been. That's not the point of our meeting. It is something much closer. The context of our meeting is only to discover the truth of *I*. Anything else is irrelevant. Anything else is just part of the texture and flavor of every aspect of being, the whole mandala. Yet all of it, every aspect, whether physical, emotional, joyful, difficult, or tedious, is valuable to the point of our meeting. All the willingness and all the resistance are welcome in true satsang.

I have never been in a meeting where I did not gain enormously by discovering myself again as you. I am not speaking to you from someplace other than you. We are speaking as one self. I see you as myself, not as someone that I have something to give to. Whenever I am with you, I am giving more of myself to myself, in whatever way it shows itself, and I invite you to play this way, too.

THE ONLY TRUE DESIRE

True desire is desire for reunion with God, desire for truth, desire for an end to suffering. This true desire is the core of all other distorted and misplaced desires.

If passion for truth is not recognized, then all the distorted imitations of true passion, all the other usual passions of greed, hate, lust, and envy, arise and lead to suffering.

Be honest with yourself. Ruthlessly honest. Ask yourself, *What do I want?*

Do you want to be free?

Do you really want to realize the absolute truth of who you are?

If you just want a nice spiritual high sometimes, you are welcome to it, of course. That is somewhat like putting your toe into the ocean. It feels very good, and the ocean doesn't mind if you just put your toe in. Yet you have the possibility of diving into the ocean of truth totally, with no hope of reemerging. Dive and see.

❖

I've heard you say put all your desires into the one desire for freedom.

Yes, that's right. Freedom is the true desire.

Well, what do I do with that?

What do you "do" with it?

Do I act on it or what?

If you put all your desires into this one desire, *it* does with *you,* totally. Freedom is vast. It is impossible for you to do anything with it.

Who you imagine yourself to be is annihilated by the revelation of freedom. You, as you have known yourself to be, are no more. You, as you have imagined yourself to be, are revealed to be nonexistent. There remains only the unimaginable truth of who you are.

Don't imagine that you will do something with freedom. This idea is the arrogance of egocentric mind. You will be enfolded in such an embrace that there is no thought of *you* left. Freedom is nothing that can be "done with." "Doing with" has to do with everything else. The power of mind can appear to do something with something. However, in true realization, all powers of mind are consumed by the source of mind.

Divine consummation is the feast of the divine on its soul.

Surrender! Let yourself be eaten by God however God pleases.

❖

Sometimes I feel like that desire just burns inside, and I want to bring it into everyday reality.

Give up the idea that your insatiable thirst and search for truth are separate from everyday reality. Relative reality appears in absolute reality. Everyday reality cannot be separate from the absolute.

There is no everyday life without truth. There is no appearance of any phenomenon without truth. All belongs to truth.

If you have the desire to realize the flame of truth, and you imagine that you can somehow put the flame aside until your life is convenient, you are tricking yourself with postponement, tricking yourself by keeping the illusion of separation active.

I go back and forth between external searching and going within. I feel I need something outside myself.

I, too, felt I needed something outside myself. I was not able to do it on my own. I knew intellectually that it's all within, but I wasn't experiencing it. So I met my teacher, Papaji. He appeared to be outside myself while saying, "I am within you!" This appearance occurred in my everyday life. Do you get the import of this?

If you have an insatiable thirst for truth, finally you will discover that distinctions of outside and inside are inaccurate. There is no outside separate from inside. These boundaries are mental boundaries. They appear to be real and are thought to be real, but in truth, they are not real.

I am on the apparent outside pointing to that which is both here in myself and here in you, that which is in every moment of your life. You will not find truth someplace else and then bring it back into your life. It is already present.

If you really have a thirst, you will see truth everywhere because it is all you will be looking for.

I want to be slain in the desire for truth. Please slay me.

The only thing that needs to be slain are your concepts.

Die to the habit of following any thought that defines who you are. Die to everything you have ever known about who you are.

If you don't follow thought, it can't stick anywhere; it can't continue. Realize what remains when there is no thought. This that remains has no need of a thought to be. It is before and after all thought, and has no use for the terms "inside" or "outside."

I don't use special magic here. If I did, then satsang would be simply an exchange of trances. Maybe you would feel good, and maybe there would be pleasant energy moving through the body, but personal identification would remain intact. Reality is much simpler. There is no need for special magic if what you are searching for is permanent and eternal truth located everywhere, in everything, with no possibility of being excluded from everyday life.

The truth is that no one can slay you. You can be invited into annihilation, into the ocean, or into satsang. By accepting that invitation, you discover you are beyond annihilation. Only *ideas* of who you are can be annihilated. By accepting the invitation, you realize you are the one who offers the invitation.

Is it time to accept your true self?

You have free choice. You are free to continue your personal trance, you are free to suffer, and you are free to put suffering behind you.

This is a moment of reckoning. Do not take this moment casually or trivially. Recognize that for whatever reason you are aware of the possibility of realizing the truth of yourself as limitless consciousness. This possibility has somehow penetrated your conditioned personal existence. What good luck!

❖

The habit of thinking is very strong. The pain and suffering are so very strong that nothing seems to penetrate.

Ask yourself, *What do I want? What do I really want?*

There's still a lot of wanting things to come out right.

When you say, "I want to end the suffering, and I know how the suffering should be ended . . . It will be ended if certain things turn out a certain way," then the habit of mind is fed. This statement ensures the habit of thinking and discussing.

When I say "thinking," I am not speaking of fresh insights. I am speaking of those same old thoughts that are thought and rethought over and over and are unnecessary mental agitation.

Who you are is wisdom itself, and wisdom is not found in obsessive thinking. You are intelligence itself. You are clarity itself. Relax and allow that to reveal itself. Allow clarity to surprisingly reveal itself, with no thought of how it should reveal itself, or what the revelation will be when it does reveal itself.

Obviously, you are free to continue the habit of commentary. You are free to discuss forever. The power of mind is a toy, and you are free to continue with it or to put it aside. In putting the habit aside, see what hasn't been played with, what hasn't been touched, what has never moved.

You are always free to pick up the mind and begin the play again. If you don't overlook for a moment what is before, during, and after all mind activity, unnecessary suffering is finished.

❖

There may be enormous pain in any individual life. Pain is part of the texture of life. When pain is met as it is, as simply pain, it can even be experienced as beautiful. It doesn't need to be anything different. When it is rejected and something "not painful" is reached for, pain is experienced as suffering.

The true spiritual quest is not necessarily comfortable. Many people begin the spiritual quest searching for comfort. However you begin it, what is finally revealed is a depth of being that leaves all notions of comfort and discomfort behind.

True joy includes both happiness and unhappiness. Recognize that, and you are no longer bound by grasping for pleasure and rejecting pain. True joy embraces all polarities, all action, and all inaction.

There comes a time to examine your life with ruthless honesty. Has true, deep desire really been touched by the accumulation of any object, physical, mental, or emotional? Speaking the truth is opening to the recognition that true fulfillment has nothing to do with circumstances. In the willingness for circumstances to be as they are, in that moment of stillness, you recognize what is untouched by any circumstance.

In that moment of humility, the arrogance *I know what it is I need to make me happy* is unmasked. Arrogance unmasked has no power. Recognize what has always been present, waiting to be seen.

What I am saying is very simple. I am saying you are already free. Who you are has always been awake. You have just been playing a game with yourself, and since you are who you are, this game is quite intense. For a moment, put the game aside.

I am not asking you to remember who you are. I am asking you to put everything aside and discover what has never really been forgotten. See what has always been present. Then this love affair, this true love, can reveal itself.

Self-love is not about liking the body or liking the personality. I am not speaking of the body or the personality. The body may be beautiful or ugly; it doesn't matter. In true self-love, what is loved is what is unaffected by evaluations of beauty, ugliness, or personality.

I am speaking of discovering who you truly are. In this discovery, you discover you are in love with that.

⊹

Do you desire things for the future at all, or is it a matter of riding the wave of the moment?

What I desire in this moment and in the future is your awakening. Please, satisfy this desire. Then I will leave you alone.

I desire this in past, present, and future. I have chosen to reincarnate in this moment only to fulfill this desire. Now what do you desire?

I desire to express myself.

You cannot truly express yourself until you first discover who you are. Before that discovery, you are just expressing some idea of yourself. Generally, in our culture, expressing yourself means saying what you think and feel. This is expressing thoughts and feelings. Discover who you are, and your expression *is* that.

❖

Is it greed or wisdom to want to be in your presence?

Maybe it is greed for wisdom.

There is nothing wrong with wanting to be in my presence. Through this desire, you may discover who I am. If you discover who I am, then you must, in that same instant, discover who you are. This is what your greed is for, what the yearning is for.

In conditioned existence, divine hunger gets funneled into distorted passions. This is then called greed and has a nasty connotation because distorted passions always lead to suffering. In the hunger to realize true self, wisdom itself is found. Then passions are no temptation. They are dull by comparison. Feeding the desire for truth reveals fulfillment. Lesser passions are never satisfied.

I don't want to remove your hunger. I want to feed it. I welcome your hunger for self-discovery. It is the desire for the true embrace.

Make your hunger an all-consuming desire to know your true self, to live that, to speak that, to give up the choice of any possibility of denying that. Yoke yourself to your hunger for truth.

Truth is being evoked in you. That evocation seems to come from me to you. In reality, what is calling for itself is also evoking itself. Follow your yearning to its source.

I welcome you in my presence. I recognize you. I know you to be my own self. I see that, I confirm that, and I point to the endless revelation of that, in sickness and in health, in pain and in pleasure.

It is through divine grace that satsang has arisen in your conscious-ness. The invitation is extended to never leave satsang. Leave behind all denial of satsang. Leave behind all denial of the truth you hunger for.

❖

Do you have any suggestions on how to cultivate more of the desire for liberation?

Honor it. Respect it. Do not trivialize it. Do not make it just another conversational topic. To recognize the truth of who you are is the most sacred, precious, unimaginable gift.

What a gift of this lifetime, in these times, that somehow true desire is revealed. The opportunity is to foster true desire, to let it live your life, to let it reveal its fulfillment. What a lucky birth. Don't squander the treasure of this birth.

❖

I'm feeling some appreciation for the statement I've heard you make: "Need nothing, and then see what happens." I could feel the parts of me that would resist even the idea of needing nothing. Then I heard something else coming from the core. You didn't say to "have" nothing. You said to "need" nothing.

Well, now I say, "have" nothing. Have nothing, need nothing, be noth-ing. That which has been feared the most—to be nothing, to be nobody, to have nothing at all—*be that,* and see if what you have feared the most does not hold the greatest gem.

❖

Could you speak about the contradiction between having desire for true self and the sense that there is a "me" here, particularly in regard to work and relationships?

You are true self. Everything is that.

If there is no desire for recognition of true self, then there is preoccupation with *me* and *my* work, *my* relationships, *my* eating, *my* sleeping, *my* acquiring, *my* losing, *my* victories, and *my* defeats. All of that is "me and my story." Suffering is the general condition of "my story."

In a very rare lifetime, there arises a desire for recognition of true self. When this divine desire appears, satsang appears. Satsang reveals that never, even for a moment, have you not been that true self.

Satsang is not an invitation to get more for "me." There are many opportunities in the world for that. Satsang is about the ending of the preoccupation with "me-ness." Mysteriously, in the ending of the personal story, you experience completion and fulfillment.

If there is no desire for true self, then it is not time to realize who you really are. Desire for true self arises mysteriously and unbidden. Who can say why? It has nothing to do with background, family, culture, race, or prior knowledge. It arises on its own.

We all know the hell of being tormented by personal desires. Perhaps now you recognize the exquisite torment of a true desire that calls you inward, calls you to silence, calls you to surrender all false, distorted desires.

You know the desire for more—more wealth, more food, more shelter, more experience. You know that there is never final satisfaction in following these objects of desire. There may be momentary satisfaction, and for that moment, there is desirelessness. What peace! What glory!

Because of mistaken identification, this peace is usually attributed to the acquisition of something. Finally, there is recognition that desire is never satisfied through acquisition and accumulation of objects. This recognition is maturity. Now you can finally ask yourself, *What do I really want? What is it that I truly want?*

You believed that you wanted more things, and you got more things. Eventually, there is a glimmer of understanding that things will never give you what you yearn for. Whether you have more and better things or whether you don't have them, things are secondary.

You believed that you wanted more personal power. Then you wanted more proof of personal power. You acquired proof of personal power, but personal power also didn't bring final satisfaction. No accumulation of objects has released you from the suffering of desiring.

What is it that you want, really, finally, so that with the last breath of your lifetime you can honestly say, "I received what it was I wanted"?

I ask you to consider who you are *really*. I promise that if this is deeply considered, your lifetime will not be a wasted lifetime. Your lifetime will not be lived in vain pursuit of false and misdirected desires. It will be lived as a celebration and an invitation. It will not be a lifetime of regret. It will be a lifetime of inspiration. It will be a lifetime that is a beacon.

By recognizing the depth of the answer to the question *Who am I?*, the fire of true identity will spread.

It has spread to you. Let it spread through you. Let it be revealed in you.

The Teacher / Student Relationship

I've tried to find enlightenment on my own and I've failed. Yet there seems to be something in you that has stabilized. I was wondering if you feel it's because of having had another person's help.

Before I met my teacher, I had tried as much as I knew socially, politically, and spiritually. In each case, I found the same basic knot of greed and insecurity, fear and hate. I was not satisfied, and in that dissatisfaction, I called out for help.

What happened in the relationship between you and Papaji?

First, I saw something in him that I had not seen before, something enormous and deep in a welcoming, down-to-earth, human form. In that meeting with him, I recognized something other than what my previous experience, desires, agenda, and planning had revealed.

I recognized that our meeting had mysteriously come from my cry for help. When I had prayed for help, I knew that I didn't know if enlightenment was real. Maybe it was just a story told to give hope so that we could be a little happier. If it was not real, I wanted to know that too. I wanted to know what was true.

I recognized that the meeting with Papaji had somehow manifested out of that prayer, so I paid close attention.

He literally grabbed me and shook me and said, "Don't miss this opportunity!" It was a shock, like a slap and an embrace at the same time. In an exquisite embrace, what has never been experienced before is experienced, and a different dimension of possibility comes into awareness.

Papaji said, "Stop! Put down every strategy. Put away everything you have ever learned. Forget every technique. Be absolutely still."

I listened to him.

I really can't say what I experienced in that moment. I have tried many times. Whatever I say is still not what I experienced. Whatever I say creates a limited image. I can only call it grace.

I wrote him a letter today, saying:

First your grace reveals understanding.
Then your grace reveals experience.
Then your grace reveals realization.
In realization, experience and understanding
can come and go.
Realization is realizing what has always been.

In realization, what is realized is that which has always been stable. Then yes, this is stability.

Lastly, I said:

Finally, your grace reveals itself as all of life.

All of life, with nothing excluded. Not just the good part of life, but all of life.

❖

Are you a guru to us?

I am your own self. I am perceived as whatever you project onto me. You may see sister, mother, friend, or teacher. Someone even told me once that I was like a big food truck. A letter in satsang yesterday called me the mass murderer of the false self. There are also those who see me as the enemy.

Whatever is projected onto me, I know it to be just a projection. I am steady at the present knowing that I am your own self.

Project whatever you want as long as you hear what I'm saying. If you have to call me "guru" to hear what I'm saying, fine. So listen. The guru says, "I am your own self. I am not separate."

This is what Papaji said to me. I needed to hear him say it. Some will be able to hear truth from sister, mother, friend, or enemy.

❖

You say that a true teacher will point you to your true self. Do you mean in any tradition, whether it is Hindu, Christian, Buddhist, etc.?

Yes. The foundation of all religions is the mysterious, unknowable, ecstatic union with the divine. What gets built out of that foundation is a structure of tradition, a path, a way to get there.

There are people within all traditions who have been ostracized or were even burned or beheaded because they broke through the structure to arrive at union. When the tradition becomes the barrier, it must be broken through, regardless of consequences.

So the vehicle really isn't as important as arriving at that realization?

If it is the living truth, the vehicle *is* the arriving at that realization. It is the recognition of true self.

Christ said, "I and my Father are one." This recognition is that the vehicle, the teacher, the Father, the Mother, is none other than your own self—not metaphorically, but actually and literally. All is your own self, appearing in different forms, but realized as same self.

There are countless teachers, known and unknown, human and nonhuman, physical, mental, emotional, and astral. However, the *satguru,* the true teacher, is the teacher that points to the absolute end of the suffering of separation. The satguru points so clearly and with such strength that it is realized to be your own self, pointing to itself.

How can I know if a certain teacher is indeed the teacher that you speak of?

You know.

Your knowing has nothing to do with what anyone else says.

You are very lucky if you recognize your teacher right away, but instant recognition is not necessary.

There is nothing wrong with initial doubt and taking the time to check out an attraction. Ultimately, you know. Then the challenge is to surrender. The challenge is to honor what you know beyond knowing, and to accept the knowing beyond any attempt to mentally prove it.

Ultimately, you must trust yourself. Some people fear to trust, and think, *Yes, I've made that mistake. I trusted myself and ended up losing all my money, or my job, or my position.* Truly trusting yourself takes no accounting of what appears to be lost in trusting. I am directing you to trust the deepest intuitive knowing within you, regardless of the inconvenience.

You might begin with relative trust, but if you honor the trust you have, if you follow it, and if you are willing to be both uncomfortable and open, then relative trust can take you to absolute trust.

People might say they want a teacher, but often what they really want is some powerful person to do what *they* want done. When these people pray to God that *thy* will be done, what they really mean is *my* will be done.

When you get into relationship with your own self, appearing as teacher, it is usually quite ruthless. There is no possibility to own, to control, or to direct.

Many people go to Lucknow, India, to meet Papaji, and most of them see how astounding it is that this man is love itself. He wants nothing from anyone except their own happiness, and whatever level of happiness is wanted, he will meet that. He wants you to be happy. How could he not? He is your own self.

People who look deeper get to experience the endless depth of a raging tiger who will destroy your suffering, blessedly and ruthlessly. He is absolutely loving. Still wanting nothing from you, he will search out the last little corner of hidden identification with the ego and rip it out by the heart.

This is what I call a teacher. Anything else is just child's play—playing a game of awakening, while always attempting to maintain control.

❖

Isn't there a danger of getting attached to a master?

The danger is in getting detached from the master. There will be many temptations to attempt to detach yourself. Becoming attached is the good luck.

This question arises primarily for Westerners. In the West we have a strong idea of independence. In the East the strong idea is of dependence. Both these ideas are just concepts, still within the realm of the mind.

If you have met a true master, you will find it is impossible to adopt either stance. You are not allowed to imagine yourself as either dependent or independent.

The true master is first found in your core. This is the satguru. The true teacher exists in the core of all being. In the core of your being is something stronger and deeper than any thought or emotion, and this something must be followed.

It is essential to recognize the master, which is alive within you. Nothing is possible before that. Before that recognition, you remain at the whim of society, culture, family, and all other conditioning agents. If the meeting with the master within is a strong, true meeting, you recognize that regardless of what happens, you must follow that. If you lose your reputation, you must follow that. If you lose your status, your family, even your happiness, you must follow that. At the risk of losing your life, you follow that.

When a physical manifestation of that internal meeting is needed, it appears. If you recognize your satguru in external form, you are very lucky. Your luck is a measure of your surrender to the master within. Then the more challenging surrender, the heart surrender, begins.

I never planned on having a guru. How could I have imagined such luck? I could not have. I came out of a particular culture, and I imagined my teacher to be somewhat like a guardian angel. I wanted my angel to just hold me and rock me. Of course, when I met my master, he did hold me and rock me in the embrace of truth.

The holding and rocking is the initial meeting. Then the master reveals itself to be not separate from life itself. Life does not always hold you and rock you. Life slams you against the wall. Life gives you everything, and then life takes everything back. A true master is as relentless as life itself. In the relationship with life, the satguru, you are tempted to run away. Do not run. Do not attempt to become unattached.

In the initial embrace, recognize what can never be taken away.

Once Papaji said to me, "If God itself comes down and says to you, 'You are not free, you are not realized,' then turn your back."

God itself may come down and say, "No, not you," and in your surrender to the satguru, you realize that this, too, is only the working of the conditioned mind.

When I speak of surrendering to the teacher, I am not suggesting you accept all opinions, beliefs, or preferences that may arise in the teacher's mind. To surrender to the teacher is to steadfastly surrender to the truth the teacher reveals. The particular form through which it makes itself thoroughly known to you (in my case, Papaji) is to be treasured and honored as the embodiment of that which is revealed.

Be attached in love, as you are eternally attached in reality.

When someone described what they experienced after you left last night, you said, "Well, then don't let me leave." It shook me because I, too, had let you leave; and I realized that if I let you leave, I let myself leave. It's all the same thing.

You imagined that I left. Leaving is only in the imagination. Me leaving, you leaving—it is all imagination.

Then I must have been aware of my imaginings, instead of who I am.

Yes, isn't that the condition? It is believed that what is seen with the eyes is reality. The conviction is that what is felt through the senses is reality. As you know, what you see and feel changes. All of that changes in *you*. You are the constant. In either limited awareness or unlimited awareness, awareness is always present, and awareness is who you are.

I won't let you leave anymore.

I could never possibly go anywhere.

What a relief, isn't it? We are deeply conditioned by the belief in appearance as reality. Suffering arises from the belief in apparent separateness and apparent comings and goings. So deep is the conditioning that apparent leaving plays an important part in true spiritual understanding.

After I had met and been with Papaji, and it was time to return to the United States, I went to his home at seven o'clock in the morning and said, "I can't leave. There is no way I can go."

He said, "That's right. There is no possible way you can go."

I knew there was nothing else I could say to him in that moment, and I also knew that I was definitely going to experience getting on the plane later in the day. It was quite clear that some experience of staying rather than going was not what he was pointing me toward.

For a time after I returned to the States, I experienced an intense longing, and there was a strong tendency to run from that longing. I felt that I had to go back to India where he was.

Through grace, I stopped my attempts to return to some place, and instead I dove directly into the longing. In the direct experience of longing I realized, *I have not gone! Papaji is here! The truth of Papaji's being and the truth of my being are the same. Same being!*

✦

What is this magic chemistry of being with someone who is teaching you? There is such a special energy.

Yes, absolutely special. You are with someone who does not believe for a moment that you are separate, regardless of appearance, feelings, thoughts, attraction, or repulsion. This is nectar. It is what you know in your heart of hearts to be true. Being with someone in this special way is satsang.

Will it jump from you to me, or do I have to work for it?

It is contagious! You don't have to work for it. What you have to do is listen, and that doesn't mean that you listen when you are in formal satsang, and then stop listening when you walk out the door. Listen twenty-four hours a day, and from that, true hearing happens quite naturally.

✦

Could you comment on your experience or knowledge of the male teacher and female student relationship, especially when it is sexual?

Whatever the gender combination, it is similar to the relationship of parent and child. In the intimate relationship of student and teacher, it is possible to recognize your spiritual parent and receive the true parenting that had never been offered before.

If our parents had been enlightened, the relationship of teacher and student would not be needed. We have not had enlightened parents. We have had parents who passed on to us what was passed on to them, which was misery and suffering. False aspirations based on attainment, defense of what was attained and grasping for what was not attained, have been our legacy.

The opportunity to receive the transmission of truth is the promise of the teacher and student relationship. It is a precious, rare, secret, subtle relationship, and like the parent and child relationship, it is often misused. Even if the teacher has realized a great deal, emanates *shakti*, and speaks wisdom, if there is any unburned residue of misery and abuse that was passed on to the teacher by his or her parents—or teacher—then the legacy of abuse will continue.

⟡

Tomatoes were once believed to be poisonous until a courageous soul publicly ate one. Then the paper tiger, the lie, was clearly exposed. I have asked you for guidance and help, yet I am unable to fully trust you. My lifelong core issue about trust and the inability to discriminate has surfaced, waving its demon banner. Where and how does foolish blind trust meet discrimination? I cannot override the good-sense safety mechanism, so I ask you to show me a tomato or some way through this.

I have shown you a tomato. I have offered you a tomato. I have opened a tomato. I have swallowed a tomato. I have pushed a tomato into your mouth. I have watched you go through your fear of poisoning from this tomato.

I am not asking you to trust me. Just check out what I say. Is this poison I offer you or nectar of truth?

I am not asking you to follow me. I am not asking you to obey me. I am not asking you to think I am the greatest. Just check out what I say. How can you know if you don't check it out?

I am asking you to trust that which reveals itself within you when you let go of every idea of yourself. Let every idea go. If you let all ideas go, in an instant you will see that your idea of Gangaji is not here either. Let ideas of Gangaji go. Let ideas of yourself go. Be willing to be nothing for an instant, and see what cannot be let go.

Have some distrust of your perpetual distrusting. Then see for yourself. No one can carry you to this. You are already this. If you wait for me to carry you, or for someone who looks more like what you think the carrier should look like, you will be waiting forever.

Postponement is a trick of the mind. I remember many years ago seeing Ramana's picture in spiritual bookstores. First, I was struck by the beauty in his eyes. Second, I saw his physical posture, and I thought, *Well, slumping like that can't be right, so I am not going to read what he says.* Shockingly, I thought that his posture actually meant something, because at that time I was very interested in the body and the pursuit of perfection of the body. I found something seemingly imperfect in a holy man's posture, and I used that as a way to postpone realizing the truth that so clearly radiated from his eyes.

Beware of these mental tricks. They are the poison of the myth of the perfected form. You have already eaten this poison and it is still gnawing at you. Spit it out. Then you will see perfection regardless of form. You will see through form. You will have no problem with form.

Do you understand how this poison is so prevalent in your life? People come to Colorado and are upset that it is dry. People go to Maui and are upset that it is humid. This upsetness is the result of poison. In being poisoned, you miss the *manna,* the power, the *darshan,* the emanations of grace that are being given wherever you are. Don't miss what is radiating everywhere. Don't continue to be sickened by mental poison. Look deeper than that, and you cannot miss the resplendence.

Don't trust me. Don't even trust that there *is* a me. Go all the way with this distrust, and then distrust will help you. Don't trust what you see. Don't trust what you feel. Don't trust what you believe. Don't trust what you experience. Cast it all aside.

What remains? What is completely untouched by your trust or distrust?

I am very happy to welcome that here.

❖

I have a general feeling of fear or mistrust arising in me, but it's not about you.

Fear or mistrust arises. Do you trust your story about the fear and the mistrust that arises? If you do, it is misplaced trust.

I don't really trust anything.

If you don't really trust anything, what is left?

The unknown. And I'm tired of being told to jump into the unknown. I've done that before, and I've gotten slammed.

You are lying. Maybe you have thought about the unknown. Maybe you have imagined the unknown, but you have never done this before. It cannot be done.

Those thoughts *are* untrustworthy. Give up everything, including trust and distrust. Give up both polarities, the whole coin, the whole package.

I am speaking of what has never, ever, been known. I am speaking of what is unknowable. Not unknown until you know it, but *unknowable*.

I'm laughing because, despite all the times I have trusted things that have turned out to hurt me, here I am with what is most likely the one thing I could have ever trusted, and it's comical what comes up.

What have you trusted that has hurt you? Some person? Some idea about what that person should give you?

It has been on many levels, even theories and teachings.

Especially theories and teachings! Those are words. Those are concepts. Even if words are pristine and accurate, they are usually heard through the filters of conditioned mind. Then you trust as a child hearing a Sunday school story trusts that God is in the sky and will come down from the sky and pick him up. There is a great sense of betrayal when the child realizes that God does not drop from the sky to rescue him.

Throw these stories away. It is time to grow up and stop wasting your life by pinning your hopes on some story. You have been continually let down. That betrayal is called suffering or neurosis, and in extreme cases, psychosis.

Here is the opportunity to put every concept aside, however elevated, however sublime, however true. In that nakedness, in true nakedness, there is no waiting for some theory or philosophy or image to come to the rescue. Be totally naked, and speak from that.

There is that which is totally, permanently present and has always been so. It can't be given to you. No one owns it to give it to you. No one can own it. You *are* it.

I don't want to foster your hopes that I, Gangaji, will give it to you. What a joke! How can I give you what you already are? If you imagine that I will give it to you, then you will be afraid that I might take it away.

You might be able to stop me dead in my tracks, though.

That would be wonderful. Then I will have done my job, but to do my job is not up to me.

Is it up to me?

Yes! It is up to you. I am waiting on you to do my job. You can catch this fire. Catching fire is possible because already within you the fire is burning. Whether it is a small, smoldering ember, or whether it is blazing, you can recognize it is burning. Recognize the fire and fan it so that it burns up everything—all coverings, all disguises, all masks—and you are left beautifully naked.

You fear nakedness; you fear being exposed, because mostly you are aware of the garments of shame, worthlessness, and inadequacy. You assume they are your nakedness, but they are like pieces of cloth covering true nakedness. When I say naked, I mean naked of *any* concept of who you are.

Remove the concept that you are your body. Remove it by asking truly, deeply, earnestly, alertly, and in surrender, *Who am I really?* Not who you have been taught you are, not who you have believed yourself to be. Who are you *really*, in truth?

No one can ask or answer this question for you. You cannot trust anyone to ask this question for you. No one can answer it for you; no one can live for you. You have to discover yourself. You have to see yourself. You have to live yourself. It is that simple.

Just for a moment, don't think about who you are. Don't think about what you need, or what you didn't get, or what you should get.

In this instant of not thinking, truth is evident.

The true teaching is everywhere. Just stop hoping for it to look a certain way, expecting it to speak or act a certain way, and you will hear it. It is everywhere. It is coming off every pine needle.

⟡

You just said that it comes off every pine needle, and in this beautiful setting, it is very easy to feel that. What about big cities and cancer-like developments? It seems much more difficult to feel it there.

When I was first with Papaji, we were in a humble room on the banks of the Ganga in India. The walls were mildewed, and yet I was struck by the beauty. Everything was shining. The quiet and the presence were all-pervasive. I thought to myself how ironic it is that in the West we have visions of God sitting on a golden throne in heaven. Here I was in a humble little room with strange smells and sounds coming up from the street and I realized, *Here is God. Here is God! This is heaven. I am in heaven, and who would have expected it in such a poor place?*

The next day he took us for a walk in the marketplace. Such sounds! Such smells! Such grabbing and screaming! Not aesthetically pleasing at all, and I wondered why he'd brought us there. It was so perfect back in that beautiful little room. I looked at him and wordlessly he said, *Here too.* In that instant, all noise was penetrated by eternal, abiding silence. The beauty was seen. Even the beggar whose body had been eaten away by leprosy was seen in his beauty.

Perhaps you realize the grace of a moment of beauty. To be true to that grace, you must explore it. See if it truly ends. Does it end when you step into downtown Denver or Manhattan? If true beauty appears to leave, be willing to retreat for a moment, one millisecond, and you will see that true beauty is everywhere, emanating from everything.

I understand that it seems harder to see beauty in rectangular buildings and in fearful, aggressive people rushing about. But if you stop in the midst of that, just for an instant, you will see that the buildings and the agitation cannot truly cover beauty. They can appear to. They can seem to. But they cannot truly hide it.

Honor the instant in your life when you recognize beauty to be the truth of who you are. If ever you assume it has been lost, honor that revelation by taking one millisecond to check.

It is very usual to honor thoughts, emotions, and feelings. Be unusual and honor that which is deeper than any thought, emotion, or feeling. Let your life be an unusual life of fulfillment, regardless of circumstances, regardless of moods, regardless of discomfort.

People overlook everlasting beauty because they desire to be somewhere different; somewhere they imagine circumstances to be better. Stop where you are and check.

Check deeper than the physical realm, deeper than the mental realm, deeper than the emotional realm. Then you are open to receiving teachings in all forms, pleasant or unpleasant. Then the satguru speaks to you always.

Satguru is the true guru, the real guru. The true guru comes in all forms and uses all forms. Satguru is your own self—as guru, as disciple, as giver, as receiver.

MEDITATION AND PRACTICE

What do you consider to be true meditation?

The purpose of meditation is to quiet the mind. In the quiet mind, conditioned responses are exposed and obliterated. Meditation allows the mind to release its fixation on objects and to rest in its source.

The quiet mind reveals that which is always silent, that which both activity and inactivity spring from and return to, that which the experience of ignorance and the experience of enlightenment spring from and return to.

That is your own self.

Often what gets called meditation is concentration practice. Like therapy, breath work, or yoga, concentration can be helpful. It has its place.

Discover what is beyond concentration. Discover what is no object of concentration but is silent awareness itself.

I am not against meditation and practice. I am against the separation of a meditation practice from life. When the separation between practice and life is recognized as illusory, then your whole life is meditation.

Life is silent awareness, and all the events of life appear and disappear in that silence. You are that silence.

❖

Do you feel that formalized meditation practices are at all useful in discovering this?

Meditation practice can be very useful for calming the mind and thereby experiencing relatively more peace. In time, however, the meditation practice usually becomes an obstacle, because then there are images of both "meditation" and "my life," as well as images of a "meditator" doing "a meditation." These images are mental traps.

Anything can be either useful or a hindrance. What has been useful can become a hindrance. What could have been a hindrance can become useful. It is not up to me to make this determination for anyone. Discover this for yourself.

The opportunity in this moment is to see for yourself if what I say is true, rather than just another theory to be agreed with or disagreed with. The opportunity is to allow your mind to be still for an instant, and then to speak from the experience of stillness.

In quieting the mind, there is the recognition of endlessness. There is, for an instant, the recognition of what has always been.

Endlessness does not come into being, or suddenly become endless. It is. It always is, whether you have an active mind or an inactive mind. The purpose of deactivating the mind is to realize that.

❖

Is it helpful to do things like visualization or bodywork to help move energy that seems stuck or held?

Finally, you are invited to step into the middle of the ocean. At that point, all that is helpful is to let go of everything. Every preconceived idea of what will get you somewhere is based on the assumption that you are not already there. You are already there. You are already that.

To immediately discover the truth, let go of every technique to get to truth. Whether it is peace of mind you want, or full, total realization of the truth of your being, let go of every concept that you are not truth. Let go of every concept that you have to do something to get truth, to realize truth. Let go of every concept of who you are, period, and see.

Is wanting to get rid of stuck energy the problem?

The problem is not with the stuck energy. A problem is created when you either deny something or wallow in that something.

Just for this instant, realize who you are.

Now what energy blockage touches that?

An energy blockage is like a bump on the earth. It is part of the physical terrain. In your willingness to be who you are, if only for one second, you will see that there is either physical release or not. Bumps are smoothed out or not. It doesn't matter.

In the past, I pursued different disciplines, both traditional and New Age. Although the highs had certainly been enjoyable, I wanted something that no formula had been able to reveal. I spent a lot of my time going around to teachers and workshops, and remained dissatisfied. Out of that dissatisfaction, I prayed to be delivered. I prayed to realize truth. I wanted truth more than I wanted comfort and pleasant experiences. I wanted truth beyond what my mind could deliver.

That prayer revealed itself in meeting my master, and his words to me were, "Give up every concept immediately, instantly."

I listened to him. Somehow, I had enough good sense to listen to him and not get into an internal discussion about *whys* and *buts* and *what-ifs.*

I simply heard what he said, and what is revealed is the limitless truth of one self. Not *me,* but one self, the *totality of being.* The *me* is lost in that. It is insignificant, a minor energy blockage, a bump on the earth.

How can one know the self without study?

What exactly do you mean when you say "self"?

Initially the small self, and then merging with the larger self.

What is the small self?

The form I chose to incarnate in.

Do you mean your body?

My body, personality, ego.

A body can be studied. A personality can be studied. What do you mean when you say "ego"?

Habits, imprinting.

Habits and imprinting can be studied, and the study can be useful. If there is identification with all those habits and all that imprinting as who you are, then the study is an obstruction.

   You spoke of merging with the larger self. What is the larger self that you merge with?

With what's infinite. I merge with what's everywhere.

If it is everywhere, aren't you already merged with it?

Maybe. Oh!

To mentally understand something is to objectify it, to particularize it, to categorize it, and to note its characteristics for storage in memory. Any "thing" can be studied. Anything that you objectify and believe to be separate can be studied as if it were separate. Totality of being cannot be studied.

   What is separate from totality that can study totality?

Maybe you can understand personality and bodily functions and natural laws. Self is the totality. Totality is no-thing in particular. The belief that to realize no-thing one must study is a big mistake, and an unnecessary waste of time.

If you believe that to recognize truth, you have to study some system about truth, then you are postponing realizing truth in this moment.

You are the totality. This that you are is much vaster than any one mindstream can understand.

The futile attempt to give characteristics to God, to no-thing, to truth, is a subtle mental diminishing of the totality of being, with gross results.

I ask you to consider, *who* is studying?

The objective would be to know it in a way that it would melt down and not be identified with.

What melts into what? First, in this moment, whether you have studied or not, ask yourself this question, *Who am I?*

Pay close attention. See if you can find any "thing" that can be studied, whether you call it big or small. This "I" that studies the self. Tell me, where is this "I"?

It's everywhere.

If it is everywhere, how can it be studied? What is separate from it to study it?

You can study something that you want to commit to memory. You can study to be a doctor, lawyer, mechanic, or singer. You can study to learn how to read and write. There is nothing wrong with studying. It is a great power of the mind.

Once the desire to realize who you truly are arises, then the habit of studying must be put aside for at least a moment. The habit of seeking yourself in categories and particularizations must be put aside.

Any spiritual study worth studying points to the fact that who you are cannot be studied. The truest teachings point to who you are as that which cannot be objectified and thereby cannot be learned.

Self-forgetting is an apparent mental veiling that gives rise to the mental activity of searching. The experience of self-forgetfulness is the source of all misery. There is great stress in attempting to remember who you truly are. How do we remember or know the self? The truth is, you cannot remember the self. The good news of that truth is that you also cannot truly forget the self. Stop searching in your memory and recognize what has been here all along.

In the instant of ending your search, all studies are released, as everything is released each night when you drop into deep sleep. In deep sleep there is sublime bliss. There is neither remembering nor forgetting. The opportunity in the waking state is to neither remember nor forget. See what is here when you stop looking for it.

Retreat. Retreat from all studies, all teachings, all conditioning, worldly or spiritual. Retreat from your name, your relationships, your past, your future, and your present. See that all relationships, names, form, past, and future arise in that. All come and go in that. That is permanent, eternal, and is present right here, right now.

Retreat is the open gateway. Walk through the open gate and recognize yourself.

❖

What is your own experience of developing *bodhicitta*, the "awake heart"?

Bodhicitta is not developed. It is *revealed* deeper and deeper. There is not for an instant any separation. You, me, it, them, *bodhi,* awake, ignorance, ego, mind, self, illusion—no separation. That is the absolute truth.

On the Buddhist path one generates bodhicitta. One way to generate bodhicitta is by the act of giving.

The antidote for the suffering generated by grasping is the act of giving. It is very useful medicine. However, this medicine also has its toxic side effects. If there is identification in the giving, there is ego-righteousness or spiritual delusion.

To discover and live bodhicitta, discover who you really are. An endless ocean of bodhicitta is discovered to be your true nature.

The essence of the Buddha's teachings is that you are not separate from the Buddha. What came after the Buddha were ways of figuring out how to get there, but trying to get there implies that you are not already inseparable from that.

I understand the dilemma. Obviously, the experience is that you are not that. This experience that you are separate from Buddha, from God, from truth, is an experience of suffering. It seems real and is believed to be real. Then all kinds of tasks, paths, and practices are performed to get through illusion to the truth of oneself.

It seems that revelation would be more of a receptive experience and generation would be more active, both waiting to achieve the full state of being.

If you are truly receptive, you need nothing. In needing nothing, revelation reveals itself. Not as something that was or is to come, but as itself, now and evermore. What you are calling "generation" is a slight misunderstanding.

Bodhicitta, Buddha-mind, or truth, is endlessly revealed, not generated. Generation is, by its meaning, a "bringing forth." It wasn't here and now it is.

Bodhicitta is eternally here. This is subtly but essentially different from something being generated. Generation requires concentration of effort; revelation requires receptivity. In receptivity there is no waiting. The instant there is true receptivity, there is overflowing bodhicitta.

Creative power is obvious, but that from which creative power comes, and that in which creative power rests, is the revelation. It can be named Eternity or it can be named Buddha. Whatever it is named is secondary to the truth that it is always fully present.

Do you understand? This is a very important point. Bodhicitta, like compassion or wisdom, is revealed through realizing what is eternally present.

Religions East and West have tried to teach compassion. Often, the result is suppression of the image of who you think yourself to be, which is bad and evil, layered over with other images of who you think you should be, which is good and just and kind. It takes enormous psychic effort to keep the dark side, the evil self, the negative mind, repressed.

The possibility is to realize what exists *before* good and evil, and in that, nothing is repressed. In that, both good and evil burn up. You realize yourself to be neither an evil person nor a good person.

When you are not in battle between generosity and selfishness, you are still. You are not defining yourself as either generous nor selfish. When you are not defining yourself, freedom is recognized. When there is no attention put on acting out or repressing any aspect of yourself, ironically, generosity is revealed to be your natural attribute.

Let me stress, I am in no way sanctioning acting out negativity. Be willing to directly experience what you fear to be your evil nature. By not moving to repress it *and* by not moving to act it out, negativity cannot survive.

Generating, focusing, or accomplishing involves volition of will.

Yes, that's right, the will to see what already is.

What needs no volition? What needs no creating? What needs no intending?

One has to sit, to meditate, and to reflect.

If what you mean by meditate is to immediately die to all form and to all thought, then yes, I agree. This is essential.

Whatever the practice has been—call it meditation or working in a store or being a parent—it has led you to a point of recognizing, *Aha! Here I am up against this dilemma again.* At this point, you have the possibility of being absolutely still, having no thought of Buddha, Christ, bodhicitta, meditation, goodness, or badness—an instant of no-mind. Discover what needs no practice to be.

An essential experience must occur, and I believe this is what you're referring to when you say one must sit. This essential experience comes most unexpectedly in the willingness to die. It comes in the willingness to not know what your relationships are, what your history is, or what your form is, much less all the permutations of that knowledge.

I am speaking of alertly not knowing anything, consciously not knowing anything.

In alert attention, your mind can become so calm that the idea of *you* or *mind* is simply no more.

❖

By the time the Buddha sat by the bodhi tree, he had tried many practices, and he had left them all behind. Regardless of what appeared to tempt him forward or backward into time, he remained still.

He died to any idea of who he was. His realization is not separate from your realization.

Permanence and Impermanence

've had experiences of awakening and bliss that lasted as long as two weeks. Yet how does one surrender or open to that state permanently?

First, a clear distinction must be made between what is permanent and what is impermanent.

If you link self-realization with a particular experience, then in your mind, realization is a thing. No *thing* is permanent.

Thoughts are impermanent. They appear and they disappear. At the very least, you know that they disappear every night when you fall into deep sleep.

All forms appear and disappear. Even the most sublime experiences are subtle form, and as form, they come and they go.

Maturity is the recognition that every *thing* comes and goes. This is the truth. At first it may seem to be a terrifying truth. There is no *thing* that will stay. Surrender in the face of this terror, and recognize the impossibility of holding on to anything. You cannot hold on to your own body. You cannot hold on to the most desired state. When you recognize the impossibility of holding on to anything, surrender is possible. In surrender, permanent presence of being is revealed.

As you say, awakening has been glimpsed. The experience of bliss that continued for some time is the result of that glimpse. The strong tendency is to attempt to cling to this sublime result. Don't you know this very well? As you feel the sweet experience ebbing or leaving, there may be panic, or a scrambling of mental activity in the attempt to keep it. Of course, as you scramble to keep it, the sweetness retreats much faster.

For a mindstream to recognize its source, an essential recognition must occur. If you try to cling to the result of that recognition, you overlook self-recognition now.

If you attempt to cling to a state of ecstasy, however sublime, you overlook what is deeper than ecstatic experience. And since no state can be clung to, disappointment is experienced again and again.

Why not cling to what is always here? This can be clung to. This is eternity itself, outside of time yet including time. Eternity does not come and go. It is not a thing. It is what all things, including all states, arise in. Bliss and not bliss, extraordinary and very ordinary, comfort and discomfort, appear here, in eternity. Eternity is your refuge. Recognize eternity within yourself.

Regardless of the state occurring, there is that which emanates quietness, openness, peace, and clarity. That is no-thing.

First recognize what is impermanent. I say every *thing* is impermanent, but you must discover this for yourself. When you really discover that everything is impermanent, you will immediately stop looking for permanence in things. Stop looking for permanence not only in gross things, but also in very subtle things such as ideas, states, and experiences.

The perpetuation of the cycle of suffering is accomplished by continuing to try to squeeze permanence out of something inherently impermanent.

❖

I'm unclear about the difference between an experience of that which is permanent and the permanence itself.

An experience is impermanent. There was a time when the experience didn't exist. At some time it appeared, and at some time it will disappear. An instant recognition of what is beyond experience, an enlightenment experience, is an instant of conscious no-experience.

There are many moments of no-experience in a lifetime or even in a day. Because our attention is usually fixated on experienced objects, the ground of awareness in which all experience of objects occurs is normally overlooked. Awareness overlooks itself.

Find awareness and you find permanence. How do you find awareness? By giving up the search for awareness as a thing, as an object.

Ask yourself, *who* is aware?

❖

I think I understand the knot that catches me, because what I'm trying to do is to make a concept out of what is permanent so that I can "get it."

Right now, find the *I* who is trying.

In the moment that you say that, it's obliterated.

Is it obliterated, or is it revealed to actually be imaginary?

It is gone. It was imaginary.

Then what needs to be held on to? Who can hold on to anything?

In this instant, nothing, nobody.

Excellent! This is the truth.

But I want to find some way to point myself there when I'm not here in satsang.

If at any moment you imagine you are separate from that permanent presence, see if you can find who is separate.

When the knot is recognized to be an impermanent figment of imagination, appearing and disappearing in permanent awareness, there is no knot left to be unraveled.

❖

You say if things or experiences come and go, then they are impermanent. My being in the state of openness also comes and goes.

The state of being open, meaning feeling open and then possibly thinking *I am open,* comes and goes. What does this feeling and this thought come and go in?

What all impermanent feelings and thoughts come and go in is more open than a feeling of being open.

Awareness is not limited to any particular state. True openness is so open that it includes states of not feeling open. It is not, I *feel* open and therefore I am open, but rather, I *is* openness and therefore everything is experienced.

Then by definition, if I have that glimpse, shouldn't I always be there?

You *are* always there.

But if that were so, I would be conscious there.

Consciously recognize where you always are. Self-recognition is not an attainment of a new state, although recognition does give rise to exquisite, sublime states.

There are traditions that will teach you attainments of states—great, powerful, yogic states. What I am pointing to is who you always are.

Anything attained was not here before attainment. What is permanent cannot be attained and cannot be lost.

You know that appearances cannot be trusted. Shadows cannot be trusted. Images cannot be trusted. That which you have assumed to be solid and real cannot be trusted to be solid and real. Anything that comes and goes, changes or vanishes, ultimately cannot be trusted except to come and go and change and vanish.

If you are searching for what is absolute, for what is permanent, then you must stop looking at what is relative and impermanent. Stopping the search reveals true self as no *where* in particular and no *body* in particular. You know yourself to be true, everlasting presence—here, now, and always.

❖

I'm always afraid of losing it, so I must be in the other state.

Conditioned experience alleges that you are in states. In truth, states and experiences are in you. They are impermanently in you.

You say "always afraid," but this is a lie. Can you honestly tell me that throughout your life experience there has never been one instant when fear was absent?

That's true. There have been many times when I did not feel fear.

Do you see that when you say "always afraid," you deny the truth? Can you ruthlessly tell the truth and recognize that your denial of even one instant of lack of fear perpetuates the cycle of misidentification and suffering? Do you recognize that fear is impermanent?

Yes.

Good. Now recognize what is exactly the same in the experience of "fear" and the experience of "no fear." Realize what is permanent.

❖

Experience itself comes from permanence, exists because of the grace of permanence, returns to permanence, and is therefore never separate from permanence. No thought, experience, sensation, or image you have ever had of yourself has ever been separate from the truth of who you are.

Releasing your attempt to define yourself in impermanent objects reveals the sublime secret. By giving up all definitions, self can find itself even in definition! Never lost, never obscured. Buddha in compassion, Buddha in anger. Christ in affirmation, Christ in denial. Then concepts like permanence and impermanence are irrelevant. These concepts, too, are just the play of mind.

What a secret! No mind can comprehend this secret.

NATURE OF MIND

The mind has to keep spinning to hold your view of reality together. Since personal reality is mind-created, it can be either a negative reality or a positive reality. You can view the world as enemy or you can view the world as friend.

A positive reality is much more pleasing, of course, than a negative reality. It is actually through a positive reality that you get glimmers of that which is beyond mind-created reality, that which has no need to be created by your mind, that in which all creation arises.

The readiness to discover what is before your personal reality, what is not contingent on your personal reality, what already is and does not need practice, support, or belief to be, is spiritual maturity.

Spiritual maturity allows satsang to appear in your mind. In your mind, you hear the call *Wake up! Wake up!*

Surrender to that call. Mental surrender is reflection, resting the mind, not thinking. To reflect means to give up all considerations, all computations, all measurements, and just be still. A reflective mind is alert yet at rest. A reflective mind is open. Then quite naturally, unexpectedly, and mysteriously, there arises that which is reflected upon.

I encourage you to reflect on truth, reflect on freedom, reflect on who you *truly* are. Reflect deeply and then more deeply. Insight and revelation arise quite naturally in reflection. Wisdom and clarity are natural byproducts of reflection, of not creating and not following mind activity.

All I am ever saying, regardless of whatever words I use, is to be still. Let all concepts rest and dissolve.

Be still, be quiet, and the glory and peace revealed are infinite. This is the message of my teacher's teacher, Ramana Maharshi, and the message of my teacher, Papaji, and the message of this life, Gangaji.

Silence is an opening in which the usual evaluation about past events, and speculation about future events, stops. When you let all mental activity stop, you make your mind available for the unknown, for your own self, your true self, your permanent self, your eternal self.

If you imagine anything stands between you and your true self, please, let us expose it and see the reality of it. Is it imaginary, or is it real?

It's my mind.

Where is your mind? Find it right now. If mind is the obstacle to knowing yourself, then we must see if mind is real or imagined.

I can't find it now. Where did it go?

Yes, where did it go? Where does the mind go in the moment of investigation?

It doesn't exist.

If something doesn't exist in one moment, and in another moment seems to exist, how reliable can it be?

It isn't reliable.

It is not even a reliable obstacle, is it?

I just keep believing in it somehow. I keep supporting it.

How?

By keeping it going.

What is this "it" that you keep going?

My mind, listening to it.

Where is this mind? Find it.

In substance, I can't.

When you stop assuming mind is some solid substance, what is it?

It's my thoughts.

When you look at this thought, *It's my thoughts,* what is there? What is there when you actually turn awareness directly toward thought?

Nothing.

If thought is insubstantial and is not there, what is there?

Feeling, emotion.

Find the feeling, the emotion, and tell me, what is there?

It's imagined.

Then what, in reality, *is* there?

Nothing.

And this "nothing"? What is this "nothing"?

   People have heard the word "nothing" and perhaps have all kinds of ideas about what "nothing" means, such as blankness, or some other concept of emptiness. I want to know, is this "nothing" truly nothing, or is it conscious, alive intelligence?

Sometimes it's intelligence.

If it is intelligence only sometimes, then it is not a reliable intelligence.

Yes, because much of the time it's clouded.

This that is aware of clouds and aware of some kind of intelligence that comes and goes, what is this?

That is who I am.

Yes! What you are telling me is that who you are is that which is aware when there are clouds, and that which is aware when there is clarity. Do I understand you correctly?

Yes, and I judge the clouds.

Is it awareness that judges the clouds, or is it that judgment appears in awareness as another cloud?

Judgment appears. I don't like it, and then I judge.

Disliking, aversion, and distaste appear. Is this the awareness that you have just said is who you are, or are these states simply phenomena appearing as another form of cloud?

They are another form of cloud. A state is not who I am.

Now you are speaking the truth. Just for a moment, be very still in this insight.

   This thing called mind that you have perceived as an obstacle, is this not just another phenomenon?

It is not who I am.

If I am hearing you correctly, you are saying that who you are is what is always present—that which is aware of judgment, aware of mind, aware of clouds—*awareness, period.*

Yes.

Awareness is always present. Everything else comes and goes in awareness.

I get angry that phenomena come and go.

Anger arises and again we have a layer of cloud. In the Hindu tradition, these layers are called the veils of Maya, because the mind, this cloud, has the capacity to appear to break into infinite particles.

My mind is very good at that.

The mind is a great power. The mind can imagine something to be so, and then quite clearly recognize it is not so. Isn't this a great power? This is the power of Maya, the power of illusion, the power of trance.

Yes, I see the trance more and more. I see the hypnotism.

Now see the seer.

Why does she feel so alone?

She? You must be seeing some object. Is "she" identification with some phenomenon arising in awareness, or is "she" awareness itself?

Some phenomenon.

Does awareness have gender?

No.

Correct! No gender. Does awareness have eyes?

Not really.

Does awareness have ears?

No.

Does awareness have form?

No.

The living truth is revealed when you see what is truly here. Nothing! Nobody! Is there ever a moment when this that has no eyes, no ears, no form, no gender, is not totally present?

No, it is always present!

What is always present is who you truly are. Correctly identify yourself as eternally present awareness and take refuge in that.

❖

I know in my mind that these formulations, this body, all these things that I do, are not the truth of who I am.

Knowing this intellectually is not sufficient.

I know that!

Stop knowing anything. Stop the search for intellectual understanding. Stop asking why. Every time *why* arises, it only takes you deeper into intellect. The only answer for *Why?* is *Why not?*

You are being called to that which is beyond mental knowledge. You are being called to direct experience. You are hungry for direct experience, and direct experience is not found in any formulation of intellect.

Be still, and then more still, and even more still.

Be still beyond belief. Then that which cannot be known reveals itself, both fresh and ancient, beyond any polarity of knowing or not knowing.

What is needed in stillness?

What survives stillness?

Stay here. Let stillness dissolve belief in any substantiality of independent existence.

Then there is no way to really know, because if you know, your mind is interpreting what consciousness is.

There is pure being, which is where individual being gets its power. There is pure consciousness, which is where limited, individual consciousness gets its power. Pure knowing is not *known,* nor is it storable by the mind, because it is bigger than what can be known from past memory or categories. It is immaculate. It leaves no tracks. It is what space is in, so it is even subtler than space.

❖

What about insights? Aren't they just thoughts?

Insightful, revelatory thought that is original and pure, coming directly from emptiness, is unmediated by conditioned mind. Insight is the holy child of the conscious union of the mind with its source. From that union spring sutra and scripture.

So these revelations are to be paid attention to?

Yes, they are beauty, and they reflect truth.

Speak them. Write them. Live them. This is what poetry is. This is what art is. This is what a true human life is.

In all the glory of the insights, that which is even more glorious—the source itself—is present always. Pay attention to that.

❖

I have some confusion about this idea that all is "that." There is thought, and then there is non-thought. There are these thoughts that are just noisy stuff, yet I keep coming back to the thought that even those are that.

Yes, absolutely.

So it's not necessarily a dilemma?

It is not necessarily a dilemma. The dilemma arises by following thoughts as if they were the limit of reality. They are not. They are waves in the ocean of consciousness. Our general condition is to focus on the waves as reality. Suffering is then experienced as one wave ends, or one wave is bigger, or one wave is something that another wave is not. In that suffering, what these waves or thoughts arise from, what they are composed of, is overlooked.

The teaching that comes from Ramana and Papaji is to allow the thoughts to stop. Be quiet. Be still. In stillness, the vastness of what is exists prior to thought, prior to wave, as well as after all thought, after all waves, and recognizes itself in its limitlessness.

We experience bondage only by our attention on these thoughts that are thought and rethought, and then considered to be reality. The thoughts themselves are nothing but electrical impulses, waves, limited reality. Yet these electrical impulses, these waves, this limited reality, are finally one with limitless absolute reality.

Individual consciousness is always one with pure, unlimited consciousness. Shift attention from wave, and ocean is realized. Shift attention back to wave and tell me, has ocean gone anywhere? Isn't ocean always present with or without wave? Isn't awareness always present with or without object (thought)?

Then even the experience of being bound is a thought, but is still unlimited consciousness?

Yes! The *experience* of being bound is not *really being bound*. The thought of bondage leads to the experience of suffering only because it is believed to be reality.

In the willingness to be still, no one can be found either bound or released from bondage. There is only indefinable, limitless consciousness, in which all definitions of bondage and liberation arise and end.

❖

It feels like without thought the body doesn't exist.

Excellent! That's right. The experience of body is the result of many past thoughts. These past thoughts have a momentum that will carry the body until its natural death. You don't have to continue to think to keep the body going. The body has its own momentum.

The body, as you have discovered, is only a thought body. It is a desire body arising from past desires. Let these desires go, and they are finished in their power to create future bodies.

In Eastern philosophy, self-realization is spoken of as the end of the cycle of rebirth. The cycle of rebirth is experienced each moment. Simply see that what is born dies, and recognize yourself to be the seeing itself. The body comes; the body goes. An emotion comes; an emotion goes. Strange phenomena come; strange phenomena go. See what everything comes and goes *in*. See what needs no momentum and no thought to be.

The ego is simply a thought based on the assumption that you are a particular body, and this is a lie. All assumptions that follow and support this initial, mistaken assumption are therefore also lies.

Let go of the practice of trying to hold the body together, of thinking your reality. This is the beginning. What is revealed is so secret that it cannot be spoken. If it is spoken, it is already a distortion of truth.

First, drop everything—just for an instant—and see if anything has been lost. Then speak from direct experience.

People are often worried that if they drop everything, they will lose their ability to function in the world. In general, however, acuity of both intellect and memory results from this release. When the mind is not forever chasing images and thoughts of the past, there is greater potentiality for pure intelligence to express itself easily.

Regardless of what I tell you, you will never know until you discover it for yourself, right? You will never know how delicious dessert tastes until you taste it. You can read it on the menu. You can look at the faces of your friends who have tasted it. You can hear their descriptions. But it is all secondhand.

The dessert is your own self. It is waiting to be eaten. When I say drop all concepts, actually what I am saying is to not pick up a concept. You don't even have to go through the effort of dropping anything. Don't pick up any concept, and then feast on this that you are.

✧

I have heard it said, "Mind is like a restless monkey—to overcome it, recite the sutras." Can any sutra really overcome the nature of mind?

A living sutra can. A living sutra appears in satsang, and satsang is occurring in the depths of your being.

The spring of living sutras is silence. If you surrender to silence, your mind will be tamed. Silence uses the mind to express itself in sutra.

Living truth, whether it comes from the historical Buddha or from the beggar on the street, is true nourishment. Drink it, digest it, and then the mind is blissfully subservient.

I once heard it said that religion is the tracks where something alive once passed. The tracks may emanate great power and truth. If the tracks can serve to inspire you to turn to truth, then they are to be honored. Follow the tracks to their source.

As a child, I used to recite a Christian prayer, and I found comfort in that prayer as I imagined an angel beside me and Jesus in heaven. Everything was in order and I would be taken care of. At a certain stage that comfort wasn't enough. I needed to enter heaven itself.

That prayer was a way of taming a child's mind. When childhood is finished, prayers from childhood are not enough. Finally, the one praying must be discovered.

Sutras arise from revelation. Realize yourself and you will recognize that Buddha is not someone separate from yourself. The Buddha's words, Christ's words, a saint's words, are all your words, your celebration, your devotion to eternal truth.

No one has ever measured the depth of silence.

Try. Turn your mind to measure the depth of silence. Silence is present right here, right now. Measure it. What blissful activity for the mind!

❖

Is there a difference between liberation and realization?

Within the apparent levels of mind, multiple differences, hierarchies, inner circles, outer circles, and levels of awakening appear. But when one awakens to what has always been awake, where can differences be found?

While there is no need to deny the experience of difference, it is the reality of difference that must be investigated.

Where do categories and levels exist? What is necessary for the maintenance of categories?

Where do the terms "liberation" and "realization" exist?

If your attention is pulled to categorization, you overlook what is not possible to categorize. If you imagine differences to be real rather than appearances in reality, you suffer unnecessarily. Discovering reality releases you from the bondage of differences.

I want to understand, to let go and let God.

Maybe you have studied metaphysics or practiced techniques and disciplines according to different religious dictates. Now you have to directly discover for yourself what is true.

For one moment, put all interpretations, speculations, and conclusions about reality aside. Let that which exists prior to any interpretation or conclusion reveal itself. Let that which is untouched by any categorization reveal itself.

For another moment, as an experiment, resist all temptation to define it, philosophize it, or know it. Just for a moment, rest in that, and see if your understanding can reach beyond definitions.

Is "being" really a dissolving?

Yes. A dissolving of all thoughts and all concepts. A dissolving of all ideas of who you are, who you might be someday, who you should be, or who you hope you can be.

✧

Could you explain what silence is?

There is no way to explain silence. Silence can only be experienced.

It is not something that you go to and get. If you go into nature or go into your room or close your eyes, you may feel quieter. In nature, or in a quiet place, you are not distracted by your usual worries. That peace of non-distraction points you to silence.

In silence, you recognize that any efforting arises out of silence and is actually searching for that silence.

If you tell the truth and are very attentive to silence, a profound discovery is revealed. You are home.

Many people stop at relative quiet, relative pleasure, relative comfort, relative happiness. Maybe you don't have a television in your house or you don't go to noisy places, but relative quiet is conditional. If by chance life flings you into the middle of downtown New York, where is the quiet? If it is relative, it is gone. Something else relative has displaced it. The lasting discovery of truth is in absolute, unconditional silence. Then, wherever you are, you know yourself to be the silence itself, absolutely.

✧

What I get from the silence is a deep sense of aloneness.

Yes, total aloneness. Aloneness is the truth. If you get that, then there is no question of a belief in an apparent "me" or an apparent "other." "Me" and "other" may appear, yet they are only appearances in the field of total aloneness.

True aloneness is all.

The mental definition or image of "alone" indicates something lonely, scary, needy—something in danger. That is not the direct experience of aloneness. The direct experience of true aloneness reflects deep peace and love.

❖

Yesterday after satsang, I stayed still. I said, "I'm going to follow what Gangaji says and be still." I really tasted that quiet. At the same time, perhaps because of those tastes, I was more aware than ever of my mental activity. There's nothing I'd like more than to be that kind of full stillness you're speaking of.

But I didn't say to get still or to make yourself still. I didn't say do stillness. I said be stillness.

I was doing the first three.

People often imagine that silence means an absence of noise and will attempt to suppress anything that seems to interrupt quiet. Stillness *is,* and being quiet is recognizing what is always still, regardless of events or commentary on events. Even what appears to be noise appears in silence. Return to that. Be that.

What a surprise, this stillness. In the midst of the turmoil, in the midst of all the mind activity, there is stillness. In the gap between thoughts, there is stillness. Before thought, there is stillness. After thought, there is stillness. No thought exists separate from stillness.

Be still. Taste stillness. *Be who you are.*

The challenge is then to recognize that stillness is always present. Simply check by turning your mind inward rather than pursuing its outward flow. Rather than effort to stop the mind's outward flow, rest your mind. Relax.

I am not anti-intellect, but I am suggesting that you give all thought activity a rest. Let the mind rest in its source. This rest is nourishment. Intellect is hungry for true nourishment.

At rest, individual consciousness expands and recognizes itself as not separate from the universal sea of consciousness. In stillness, there is no separation between "my mind" and "consciousness." Separation is experienced only when the thought, "my mind" is accepted as reality. Be still and see.

Be available for the unknown, for your own self, your true self, the eternal self.

Open your mind. Be available for what is unconceived, unimagined, unexpected, unnamed. Opening the mind immediately produces wonderful byproducts, but don't follow the byproducts. Following objects of experience is the great temptation of the mind.

❖

My mind still wants to figure it out.

A powerful intellect is a beautiful power, but realization is beyond the power of the intellect to grasp. Realize what gives the intellect its power, and the intellect is prostrate and humbled, floored at the feet of its source. In that prostration, the intellect serves, flowers, and sparkles.

This is the assignment: Speak what cannot be spoken. Speak what has never been spoken. What good use for the vocal cords, the intellect, and the life experience. Keep the mind totally at the feet of source so that it may serve that at a moment's notice, and the mind will be divinely used.

Thankfully, I finally don't know what to say.

That's a good beginning. You cannot know what to say. When you don't know what to say, your mind is humbled.

Don't know what to say. Stay right there.

I am not asking you to say something in particular. I want to hear what has never been said. I am not talking about words. I am talking about that which uses words. Let it speak for itself.

DEPTH OF SIMPLICITY

eality is not what you think is, not what you imagine is, and not what you have been told is. It is not what you believe is, not what you hope is, not what you fear is—but what simply *is*. What *is,* is beyond what can be thought.

To realize what *is,* there must be a ruthless investigation of what is transitory and what is immovable. When I speak of ruthlessness, I do not mean struggle or effort. True ruthlessness is effortless. It must be effortless. Relaxed and ruthless discipline is possible every instant.

I have wished for that kind of discipline.

Even wishing is too much effort. Wishing is a thought, a complication, and a postponement.

❖

Many people say enlightenment is difficult.

The great debate "Is awakening difficult or is it easy?" is similar to the debate "Is awakening gradual or is it sudden?" Every era will have a great debate, and the people who are debating are kept very busy. Being kept very busy, rather than just being right here, postpones awakening now.

Forget difficult and forget easy. Neither touches who you are. If it is neither difficult nor easy to discover who you are, if awakening is closer than either difficulty or ease, what then?

Who you are is out of measurement. I often point to the ease of awakening because I speak to many people who cling to the idea of its difficulty. If I meet someone clinging to an idea of ease—

You would say it's difficult.

Perhaps, because the solution is revealed when the hold on any idea is broken. When the internal discussion stops, the mind is quiet. In silence, where is difficulty; where is ease?

You have spoken of difficulty as the unwillingness to directly experience whatever is arising.

Yes, I have said that what makes anything difficult is if you are unwilling to fully experience it. What makes anything easy is if you are willing to fully experience everything.

What I am pointing to is immeasurably simple. It is more immediate than memory and closer to you than your own breath. Stop the breath, and it is still present. Breathe the breath, and it is present. Forget everything, and it is present. Remember anything, and it is present. Good experiences . . . *present*. Bad experiences . . . *present*. Denying . . . *present*. Affirming . . . *present*. Sublime discussion . . . *present*. Mundane discussion . . . *present*. All feelings, sensations, thoughts, emotions . . . *present*. No feelings, sensations, thoughts, emotions . . . *present*.

Do you see how simple? You are not separate from true self. Tell me any experience you have perceived where awareness has not been present. Just this simple recognition can end the habitual searching for yourself someplace else.

When searching is finished, the revelation of what has always been present is self-evident. It does not become present or grow to presence, but is simply always present.

❖

The truth seems too simple for my mind to grasp.

Stop looking in your mind for fulfillment. When your mind starts its habitual agitation, treat agitation as a dharma bell, and relax. You will not find yourself in your mind. Your mind is in yourself.

Awakening is experienced as complicated only because you believe depth is revealed in complication. When you are ready to be simple, you will put your ideas aside. You will stop stewing in complication.

If you have led a complicated life, begin right in the center of that complication, the very core, where there is nothing going on. If you like what is discovered in the core, if you are attracted to what is revealed, then bring all your complications to the core. Enormous complications may arise, but when complications meet simplicity, there is no match. Complications dissolve. Complication cannot fight true simplicity. Simplicity is too deep. It swallows up everything. Complications only arise as byproducts of mind activity. Simplicity is the emanation of truth.

I know that many people are afraid of simplicity. They have an idea or an image that simplicity will lead to stupidity.

Simplicity is not stupidity. It is the deepest wisdom.

I understand the fear of simplicity, but the fear only continues if it is fed with more complication. All that is required is the willingness to be still, to be who you are at the core. Not who you imagine yourself to be, not who you have been told you are. Any name is too complicated. Even the word "simple" is too complicated, because you might have some idea of what simple means, and any idea is too complicated.

Recognize the complication of picking up a name, picking up a past, picking up a future. Now put all names aside. Put me aside. Put you aside. Put time aside. Put complication aside. Put simple aside.

✧

How does one live in simplicity?

What is it that you really want? Not what you have been told that you want, and not what you think you should want, but what do you *really* want?

I want to be able to relax.

Wonderful. So relax.

(laughter)

Yes, like that! Easily, immediately. Laughter is the best method of relaxation. No one has to teach you how to laugh.

(more laughter)

That's perfect! It is the perfect, immediate yoga of relaxation. In this relaxation, what do you realize?

I feel an openness. Do I just come back to this every time I lose it?

The image or thought of leaving is a tensing of the mind. Obviously, tensing the mind is a strong habit that has been supported by family and teachers and culture for quite a long time.

When this habit arises, relax. In openness, there is no limit. Everything searched for in efforting with the mind is revealed in opening the mind.

This is a great secret, a great irony. All the searching, all the struggling, all the efforting to find your true self, is naturally revealed in open, relaxed simplicity. Keep laughing. There is no time to complicate matters when you are laughing.

Physical relaxation is very enjoyable and obviously supports deeper mental relaxation. For deeper mental relaxation, recognize that following a thought takes some effort, some attention.

Do not drift into a trance or fall asleep. Recognize where deep sleep and absolute wakefulness meet.

Usually in wakefulness we are conditioned to follow the thoughts *It is time to get up, time to remember "me" and "my story," what I'm supposed to do, what I didn't do, and what I should do better.*

This dialogue is usually called the waking state. In the state of deep sleep, all of that conversation is finished. There is no "me." There are no relationships. Bringing the pure presence of deep sleep together with absolute wakefulness allows the mind to rest while remaining alert. Reveal yourself to yourself as needing no thought to be, no name to be, no form to be.

I am pointing to intelligence in full potential, awake to itself. When attention is free and open, mind cannot veil the source of mind.

❖

Yesterday during the meditation a little click happened, and the "my's" and "me's" and "mine's" all disappeared.

A little click? This click is the end of the world!

There is just a resting happening—no fire, no explosions.

In the center of fire is a clear, empty core. That is peace. That is the *I* of the fire.

Somehow it seems so simple.

Yes. What is simpler than the clear core of fire? It is so simple, and yet there is no end to the colors that arise from it. There is no flame, no burning, no manifestation of fire, no form of life, without that which abides in the core of all things—the pure and simple presence of eternal being.

Awakening
in the Dream

Y ou are pure, uninterrupted consciousness, already whole, already free.

Somehow, in the play of yourself, of consciousness itself, a veiling of the inherent truth of freedom occurs. Consciousness somehow hides from itself and pretends it is lost. In a certain moment in the play, there arises the desire to end the game of hiding and begin being eternally found. The desire to be found is the desire to awaken in the dream.

I am not here to teach altered states or yogic powers, or even to teach techniques to overcome fear and despair. I am simply here as your own self to point to that which is found in the core of all being.

It is such a self-destructive, violent, greedy world that we live in. My question is, How do you live in this kind of world and not feel separate from it? How do you keep an inner balance, an inner peace?

The only way possible is to awaken to what is untouched by the world.

I'm trying, but it's hard.

If you are overly concerned with the world and its craziness "out there," you are overlooking the craziness, violence, suffering, separation, and absurdity within your own mind. It is easy to target "world" and its faults and its madness. In judging "world" to be separate from your own mind, there is massive denial.

Where is the horror within you? The willingness to stop looking outward is the willingness to awaken in the midst of a nightmare. Don't dissociate from the nightmare; awaken in it. Have you ever had the experience, while in the sleeping state, of awakening in a dream, in a nightmare?

Yes.

Excellent. Then you know the answer. Awaken in the nightmare in which you tell yourself about a world that is doing something to you, a world that is disturbing your peace.

Once you awaken, what's the next step after that?

Awaken and tell me. What good does it do for me to tell you the next step?

Your preoccupation is with the nightmare and how to escape from it. I am asking you to put aside all attempts to escape from the nightmare, and to awaken in it now. What you awaken to is that which has never been asleep.

You are exhausted from your attempt to flee the world. Your exhaustion is the signal that it is time to awaken. Awaken in this nightmare of demons who seem to be chasing you. Let the demons be liberated.

If you have the courage to turn and face the demons who seem about to get you, what a revelation! When you finally face your demons, you discover who they are, and you discover who you are.

❖

There is much communication these days about the dimensional shifting of Earth, planetary ascension, and things like that. Are there some things you'd like to say about that?

In this time of enormous change, a great opportunity is available to all. I have traveled the world over, speaking to people in many countries, and in every place I've been, I have seen a kindling of the desire to realize truth.

I don't pretend to know the outcome of humanity, but I can tell you there is a great quickening, and you are not separate from that quickening.

A particular mindset that is an enormous obstacle to realizing truth is the belief that realization is either something that happened to someone else in the past, or something that may happen to you some time in the future. If you give up both past and future as separate from right now, you can see what is possible in this moment.

I am not pointing you toward conceptual understanding. What is available is deeper than intellectual knowledge, and it is yours by birthright. It is yours because you are called to it, and that call has invited satsang into your consciousness.

Don't miss this opportunity. What great luck! In your lifetime, in this year, in this moment, you have the absolute potential and the capacity to realize who you are.

Don't waste time. Get to the core questions. Expose any latent beliefs in separation between you and God, you and true self.

You have a great role to play. It is time you play your role and stop rehearsing. Stop imagining what the lines are. Stop waiting for something in the future. The future is here now. This is your cue. You're on.

❖

I'm sitting at your feet today because I need your help. I'm willing to let this fire consume me completely.

Spiritual fire is your own true self, consuming the illusion of *I* as some *thing* separate from anything else. Just be as you are. There is no end to being who you are. There is no end to the depth of it and no end to the revelation of it. To simply, fully be is not learned or attained. All teachings and attainments come from the revelation of that which you are in truth.

What is so beautiful is that this process of revelation happens whether I call myself asleep or awake.

So don't call yourself either. Don't call yourself anything. As long as you call yourself asleep or awake, you are playing shallowly within the realms of the mind. Extremely shallow is *I am asleep.* Then you may drop into a more profound realm where a revelation occurs, *I am awake,* but pretty quickly you see the limit of any naming of I.

It is important to have the experience *I am awake,* but as it comes, let it go. This experience is just the springboard. *I am awake* is just the other side of *I am asleep, I am ignorant.*

Who is awake? *Who* is asleep?

This question plunges you into the depth of being where awake and asleep are left far behind. Don't play only in the shallows. The depth of being is calling you.

Sri Ramana said, "It is not the self that becomes realized. The self has always been realized." Realize the self is realized, and then self-exploration begins.

For someone who has relied on the workings of the intellect, to see deeper than intellect can be a great challenge. Many fears can arise: the fear of being stupid, the fear of going blank, the fear of being nothing, the fear of not existing.

Yes, don't exist. I recommend that you give up, if only for an instant, the struggle to exist.

I want to awaken, I want to realize myself, yet it seems there is a game plan here to survive, and if I'm going to survive, I have to play the game. Finding the time and the quiet to really do the internal work on myself is difficult.

Retreat from everything for five seconds. Close your eyes for five seconds. Drop everything, and just relax. Just be. Simply be.

Do not try to get something or get rid of something. Do not try to accomplish anything.

Just be immense simplicity.

If you are attracted to this simplicity, if simplicity reveals something that you have been searching for in either acquiring or accomplishing, then take the next step.

Discover where—in any moment—this that is revealed in these five seconds goes. What are its limits? What are its boundaries?

There are none.

Excellent.

That's not safe somehow.

Not safe? Do you imagine there is safety in doing what your culture says you should do, or in rebelling against cultural injunctions? There is safety only in boundless truth of being, because in this, there is no need of safety. This is foreground, background, above ground, below ground. This is the ground that is groundlessness.

We know that in the past, certain realized beings would shout the truth and then be shot down or burned at the stake. Yes, this can always happen. So what? You have tried to keep away from truth, to deny truth, and what are you left with? You may even have memories of being shot down or burned for daring to speak the truth, but look, you are still here. You are still here! Truth remains! Bodies can be shot or burned. Truth prevails.

Only your body needs safety, and of course there is finally no safety for any body. Eventually every body will be finished. Before your body is finished, recognize the truth of who you are. Then there is no need of safety.

Who you are has no need of anything. You are the fulfillment of all needs. Not your image of who you are, or your sense of who you are, or your feeling of who you are, or any idea of who you are. Those are all objects in the mind. You are the awareness that those mental objects appear in.

How did you find that realization?

I found that by looking into my teacher's eyes. I was attracted to truth, and I recognized I had done as much as I could do with my own ideas of how to find truth. I looked into his eyes, and in that meeting, the whole cosmos was revealed.

He stopped me in my tracks, and stopping me is his gift to you. He named me for the river Ganga because I met him on the banks of the holy Ganga. When he named me he said, "The Ganga must flow in the West." Now his body is too old to travel as much as he would like, so he uses the Ganga to flood the West.

I'm very moved. I feel like I want to be in satsang every night.

Yes. Very good. Not just every night, though—every moment! Never leave satsang. Satsang is the truth of your being. It is always with you.

You are saying, "I don't ever want to be separate from who I am." You *are* not ever separate from who you are.

✣

In the first satsang we had here, you asked me why I was here. I thought, This is real. This is not some new adventure. It is real.

In that first satsang, you heard from the depth of your being. Hearing occurs when all inner dialogue stops. By stopping all commentary and simply being here, you hear what could never have been heard before, no matter how many times certain words have been spoken.

Do you hear? If you do, you hear the heart speaking to itself purely and simply, penetrating all supposed barriers with its willingness.

If there is something at stake, some fear or belief that something has to be maintained, you will be too busy attending to that fear or belief to hear, too busy to recognize what is beyond fear or beliefs, too busy to realize what needs no maintenance to be.

You must have just said something important, because my heart's beating so strongly right now.

It is in what you heard.

Yes, but I don't know what.

Knowing cannot capture it.

I feel myself holding back.

Recognize where there is no holding back. Let the body get even tenser, and then in the midst of tension, recognize what is untouched by tension.

This opening is not physical, although there may be an enormous physical release as a byproduct. Recognize what is always open.

It's laughing and crying and . . . everything.

Yes. It is finally discovered in everything. It is in laughing, crying, joy, grief, ecstasy, sadness, emptiness, fullness, you, me, this, and that. It is even in past, present, and future.

When that which has never been contracted is recognized, an enormous physical, emotional, and mental release occurs. If you attempt to cling to any physical, emotional, or mental release, you once again overlook what is always open.

In the usual mode of conditioned identification, thoughts, feelings, and experiences are referenced for self-definition. These are traps.

You are the indefinable source of all feeling, all thought, and all experience.

Yes, the heart beats very rapidly in this revelation.

❖

What you are talking about right now, I've heard and I've read about many times. But as you were talking, I felt as if my whole body was burning.

Good! Until you burst into flames, you have not really heard. You may intellectually hear, but when you are really hearing, your mind catches fire. True hearing penetrates to the core.

❖

Gangaji, I really want to awaken, and I go in and out of how strong my desire is. Sometimes it's my total prayer, and then I become scared to do what I think I must do to awaken.

What must you do to awaken?

I don't really know. I know I've got a lot of ideas of what I think I have to do.

You need do nothing to awaken. Nothing! This is the last thing you expected! Spiritual seekers everywhere are scurrying to do something to get awakeness. Seekers are reading, efforting, and practicing to awaken. If it is as complicated as doing anything, then the implication is that you are separate from that which is eternally awake.

Don't do anything. Don't even *not do* anything. Be absolutely still. Let the activity of the mind retreat to the core of stillness. In being absolutely still, recognize what is absolutely still.

In stillness, there is no movement of the mind. In no movement of the mind, there is no mind. There is only that who you truly are.

When there is no movement of the mind, there is no trickery possible.

❖

I know I can't continue in the same way I have, that it's nonsense. My barrier seems to be the fear that I ultimately have to give up "I."

You do!

I know that, and my question is, Do I just sit with that?

Run headlong into that *I* that must be given up. Find it. Quickly. Where is it?

It's in my head.

Where in your head? In what part of your head is it hiding? Report from there immediately.

Can you find it? This *I* that has to be given up. Is it there?
Quickly!

I don't know. It's a bunch of thoughts. (laughter)

This is the joke! If all you can find is the thought of *I,* where is this *I* that must be given up?

I don't know. I've formulated it. I've—

In this instant, allow any one of those formulations to sink back into its place of origin.
What is lost?

Nothing is lost.

When a formulation arises, what is gained?

Nothing really.

Excellent.

I know that, and the mind still tries to formulate who I am.

The formulation *I know* has arisen. A knower has arisen as a formulation. Allow that formulation to dissolve back into its unformulated state. In ending the formulation *I know,* where is the "knower"?

It doesn't exist.

Has anything been lost in the dissolution of the thought of "knower"?

There's nothing lost.

There is nothing to lose. What is fear now?

Right now, nothing.

Be still then. Be quiet. Every time a formulation arises, even the concept that you have to get rid of the last formulation, recognize it as mind activity, as noise. Rather than embellish upon the previous formulation, let all mental activity cease.

Living life through formulation doesn't work, does it? You have tried endless amounts of formulas, but finally, you reach a certain point where you realize there is nothing to be gained by any formula of who you are. At that point, the grasping tendency of mind is naturally quieted. Mind can open; mind can rest.

Open mind is no different from pure consciousness. At the instant of opening, the truth of limitless consciousness is not veiled by mental formulation.

What is revealed?

Joy! Peace.

✥

I feel the stillness, but I still feel the tension, and I still don't feel awake.

Where do you check to see if you are awake?

Do you know somewhere? Oh, that would be great!

You are checking in sense impressions. You are checking in thoughts based on past conclusions. You are checking what changes to find what is changeless.

   You are the stillness that is eternally awake. Stillness is full, alive, limitless silence, true emptiness, boundless pure intelligence. You are describing a sense of separation from that. There is a you, and there is the stillness. Dive into that stillness and tell me, where are you and where is the stillness?

I definitely feel separate. I feel like there is the mind, and then there is the heart.

Yes, you *feel* separate. Let's examine your idea of what the mind is and the reality of your feeling.

   When you say "the mind," what do you mean?

It feels like tension.

If it feels like tension, relax. Now where is the mind? Is it there or is it gone? Is there a mind there unless you say there is?

I don't feel like I can consciously let go. It's like I have to do it by accident.

What you can consciously do is to notice how you are holding on. Relax. Unclench your mind. If you are waiting for an accident, well, yes,
you will relax when your body dies. The exciting prospect is that you
can relax now. You don't have to postpone it. You don't have to wait for
the great accident.

The thoughts *I feel this or that, and this or that therefore means . . .* are not
reality. If you don't follow those thoughts as if they were reality, where
is their power? When I speak of "mind," I mean all sensory experience
that ends in interpretation and conclusions.

It seems like there are two things going on right now. The mind is going
to town wanting to understand, yet I can feel in my being that there is no
way the mind will understand.

Once you know in your being that there is no way the mind will understand, then you are at the gate of surrender. At that gate, you can
stop following the impulse to understand with the mind. If you let the
struggle go, it is really over.

It just feels like an energy that's tensing.

Relax. Mentally relax. Tension arises in the attempt to cling to that energy as if the energy were who you are.

Now I am feeling it relax. The tension that I had when we started is gone.

Yes, but have *you* gone anywhere? Are you aware of the awareness of
feeling? Is *awareness* of feeling changed by whatever quality of feeling?

Tension comes and goes. Awareness is permanent. Recognition of
permanence heals the suffering of misidentification.

Who you truly are never moves. Therefore, it cannot be lost. You
cannot lose yourself. You can experience the loss of yourself if you conceptualize yourself as an "it." Regardless of the experience of feeling,
you are here always. Stop looking for an "it." Stop trying to find yourself in a particular feeling, and see what has never moved.

See that whoever you imagine yourself to be changes, comes and goes. Who you are is the permanence.

What a burden released! When this burden is released, your intellect, your memory, and your individual intelligence are used by truth in unknown and unexpected ways.

❖

Is awakening a gradual kind of deepening and returning to that place?

It has been gradual, hasn't it? How many moments of awakening have there been in your lifetime? So many precious moments in all kinds of circumstances.

There is an instant like a lightning bolt when what is realized, is realized to have always been present. This lightning bolt, this realization of what is and always has been, reveals what does not pass.

Ecstasy, laughter, and tears are all byproducts of that realization. If you try to cling to any byproduct, you will once again experience the cycle of loss and then search for release. Yet regardless of experience, what is always present *is always present*.

Is that realization with you around the clock?

Yes. It is myself. How could I not be with myself?

In your eyes, was it a gradual awakening?

In the moment that truth revealed itself, I realized it has always been.

If realization were of something new, then it would be subject to getting old. Something that is not here in one time must be subject to not being here in another time.

I realized that, in looking for true self, I had been overlooking true self. From that out-of-time realization, certain experiences occurred. Experiences occurred that I had never had before, and never could have imagined having. But realization is deeper than any experience. True self is the discovery of what is and has always been.

There are experiences of sadness, happiness, ignorance, and enlightenment. These experiences are all secondary to the truth of who you are. Throughout these experiences is underlying, abiding truth.

In your attachment to keeping certain experiences and getting rid of other experiences, you have simply overlooked abiding presence. In overlooking truth, there is suffering.

There is enormous pleasure in life, and there is enormous pain in life. In focusing on either the pleasure or the pain, what is overlooked is what is untouched by either pleasure or pain.

You can be happy, and you can be sad. You can be right, and you can be wrong. But without beingness itself, none of these can exist. First, primarily, foremost, and finally, there is beingness—before human being, before animal being, before plant being, before mineral being, before cosmic being—beingness has never gone anywhere.

Recognize yourself as the consciousness that pervades everything as beingness. What a treasure is revealed!

There is no grasping in this recognition. What could be grasped? You are overflowing. You have always been overflowing as the truth of universal *beingness.*

You may see what looks like people, trees, flowers, insects, angels, or demons, but in self-recognition, what is seen at the core of all these appearances is your own true self. What a meeting this is! Self to self.

❖

I've heard you speak before of "demons" that may arise as one begins to awaken. Can you explain what you mean by that?

As one begins to awaken out of the deep trance of misidentification, surrender to what is prior to all thought, feeling, emotion, and behavior is possible. By opening the gate of surrender, the suppressed subconscious beliefs, the demons that have been denied for aeons, often appear.

The ego is formulated by past thought. Its existence is predicated on a past. As you begin to awaken and relax and surrender into the truth of now, having nothing to do with the past, subconscious thought may appear.

My teacher, Sri Poonjaji, speaking in Hindu terms, said, "When you begin to awaken, all the gods and demons of your past come to reclaim you." If you recognize these gods and demons to be mind-created, what power can they have? Let them come. Latent tendencies arise to be burned up in the light of truth.

These tendencies, I notice, are so set from early childhood. Is it worthwhile to go into therapy to have a real look at why these wounds are there?

Whys are resolved through insight when you surrender to that which has no tendencies.

Therapeutic modalities can be helpful in bringing the mind to the gate of surrender if the therapist has directly experienced surrender. The appearance of previously denied or suppressed experiences and states is the opportunity to open to a greater depth of being. Insights as to why or when or how naturally follow true opening.

When you are willing to directly experience woundedness, with no idea of why or when or how, miraculously, you will discover that you are not wounded.

If the experience of the wound arises, do you dive into this wound?

Yes! Dive. Not into the *story* of the wound, but into the *experience* of woundedness. Let go of the story. The story is what keeps you feeling bound by experiences of being wounded.

I've been so curious about the story because I seem to find insight there. Is that the trap?

Direct experience brings enormous insight. Allow insights to come.

The secret is to not cling to any state. Let all states pass through you. States you have feared and states you have desired will pass through you. Don't attempt to cling to or reject any state, and in that, directly discover what they pass through.

So it's automatic that the insights are going to come?

The insights come with release. Insights within insights will come.

All is in your imagination!

Now isn't *that* a burden released?

Why do I keep waiting for the right moment, the right circumstance?

The right moment is this moment, wherever it reveals itself. Just in this moment, now, recognize *I* with no appendages, no predicates, no quali-fication, no measurement, and no particular location.

❖

I see my resolve rise and fall and ebb and flow, and I wonder whether resolve matters at all, as it relates to waking up.

Here is a story Papaji told:

An Indian princess was very interested in awakening, and every night she would slip away to visit her guru in his hut to hear divine teachings. Afterward, she would have to slip back into the palace because it was not allowed for women to go out alone at night, much less to meet with a guru for the purpose of awakening. It could cause a lot of trouble.

One day someone came to her brother and said, "I must tell you that your sister is dishonoring the family. She is having a love affair, and each night she slips out of the palace and goes to meet her lover."

The brother was incensed. So that night, he took his bow and arrow and followed her. He was going to kill her and her lover.

As he looked into the window of the guru's hut, the guru was saying to the princess, "Come very close to me. I'm going to whisper to you the very word that will finally dispel all illusion."

She went very near to him. The brother pulled the bow back and took careful aim. Just at that moment, the guru spoke the word and the brother awakened.

He had had no resolve to awaken. His resolve was actually negative and destructive. He was lucky beyond luck to be in the right place at the right time, even if for the wrong reasons.

At this moment, you are in the right place at the right time. Take aim with your attention, whatever your reasons for being here. Resolve is even more reliable than being in the right place at the right time. If you truly have total resolve, every place is the right place. Every word points to the secret word.

Ask yourself, *What is it I want? What is it I really want?* Recognize what is wanted, finally, when all is said and done. Be very truthful. At the point of asking yourself this question, don't be willing to lie even the smallest bit.

If what you want is some other relationship or some more money or a better something else, then ask yourself, *What will that give me?* When you get an answer to that, ask again, *And what will that give me?* If self-questioning reveals that what you finally want is truth, or peace, or freedom, then point all your desires into that one desire. Cash in all your other accounts. Put everything on the table for truth, including your body, your history, and all your relationships.

This is resolve. Anything less than this and you are somehow hedging. It is important to see if you are hedging. Now see what it is you really want and what you are willing to give for it. I suggest you give everything. It all belongs to that which you finally want anyway.

Give up every concept of ownership—your house, your mate, your children, your body, your mind, your fear, your courage, your life. Put it all on the table and then see. In other words, make yourself irresistible.

It is important to see if there is a lack of resolve. It is important to see if there is even a hint of nihilistic cynicism or falling out of love with truth. Recognize if anything is being held back. Everything that can be given, give. Give it all, and then you are left naked. In nakedness, you are unborn.

I find that resolve withers in the fear of the unknown.

It is not the unknown that you fear. Your fear arises from your imagination of what is in the unknown. You have some subtle image of what might lurk in the unknown.

There is no-thing there. It is unknown. Unknown is unconceptualized, unborn. Truth is unknown, unseen, uncharted.

Give up the lie that you can conceptualize this moment. What an unnecessary burden this lie is. One day the body is finished. At that time, where is your accumulation of concepts?

When you recognize the unknown to be here right now, you recognize pure potential. Before that recognition, there is speculation about what you should do, or what you could do, and there is obsessive rumination about what you did do. Put it all on the table at least for one instant. Then the unknown face reveals itself. See if the known can hold a candle to that.

❖

It's been very confronting to look honestly and assess where I am.

Yes, where are you? This is the question. When you really look, what do you find?

Well, I feel myself in you, and in this body of people.

Yes, you are not limited to your body. Excellent.

Now tell me, right now, in your experience, can you find a place where you are not?

(hesitation) No . . .

Why do you hesitate to shout what is true and self-evident? What do you gain from keeping this declaration hidden?

Realize that you are that which is everywhere, and you realize that any boundary that appears to separate you from anything else is illusory. A feeling or a thought of separation is illusion. As illusion, thoughts and feelings arise and disappear. You are that which does not arise and does not disappear. You are present regardless of thoughts and feelings.

Even if you sense separation, this sense cannot be perceived without your presence. Eventually this sense will disappear, and another will appear to take its place. Then this other sense will also disappear, and on and on. You are what is present when senses appear and what is present when all senses disappear.

I feel like I know it, but I don't feel like I'm able to live it.

You are absolutely able to live it. You *are* it. It may mean some discomfort, but so what? It may mean not always feeling a certain way, but so what? What is it you want, *really* want?

I would say I want a continuous state of grace and to extend love to all my brothers and sisters.

No state is continuous. If it is something that is not here now, it is already not continuous. If you are looking for that which is continuous, you have to see what has always been omnipresent, what is omni, eternal *presence*.

I welcome this.

"Welcome" means "Come in; the door is open." Don't close your door if a particular wind blows through that you don't like.

Once clarity has been revealed, once the essence of being is revealed as no-body in particular but that which is eternal and omnipresent, there is no more excuse for chasing the tail of illusion.

When you discover yourself to be that which cannot be limited to or separate from any particular, peace radiates to all particulars.

✦

Eternal truth is available to you. What animates this phenomenon speaking to you is no different from what animates the phenomenon called you.

Mine was not a particularly noble birth, and certainly not a particularly noble upbringing. Even though I am just like you, you can still, of course, imagine that I am different, that I am luckier, that I have better karma. I have had horrible karma, just like you. Yet I also have the wonderful karma to have satsang appear in my consciousness, just like you.

Don't make any more flimsy excuses or postpone awakening to some time "when things are better." It is here. It is now. It is you.

THE CHALLENGE
OF SURRENDER

There may be strategic impulses to protect, fight, pretend, deny, dismiss, trivialize, or indulge; but deeper than all of those is the call to just be. In surrender to being, an even deeper surrender is revealed.

Be. Be more. Discover if you can find a limit to being. For this discovery, you must surrender all ideas of who you are, where you are, how you are, what you are, when you are, and more. Surrender all ideas to pure beingness and then see.

The more you surrender, the more you are called to surrender. There is no landing strip where you say, "Now I am finished with surrender." You are called to surrender every possibility of landing—every concept of yourself, every concept of other, every concept of everything, every concept of nothing, and more.

Obviously, this is not a surrender in defeat. It is a victorious surrender. It is a surrender to peace—the peace that *is*. Surrender does not make peace or formulate peace. Surrender reveals the peace that *is*.

Surrender all for one instant, and see what remains.

There may be great fear that something will be lost in surrender. But tell the truth, what have you ever been able to keep? Finally, of course, you cannot keep your body. You cannot keep all your philosophies. All your neat, tidy conclusions are finally gone, nothing, less than dust.

I am not inviting you to surrender to me, Gangaji. I am not saying to surrender to your "higher" self. I am speaking of the surrender to truth, to that which holds all. Then everything is used as a signal for deeper surrender—good circumstances, bad circumstances, comfort, discomfort, beauty, and suffering. Fall deeper and deeper into surrender. No abiding anyplace, no landing anywhere.

✧

You use the word "surrender" a lot.

Yes, I love the word "surrender." It is my favorite word. Doesn't it strike terror in the mind? Oh, what sweet terror is this surrender.

What does it mean to surrender?

I can tell you what it doesn't mean to surrender. We can start there.

I do not mean surrender to your thoughts or your emotions, both of which you have been surrendering to. I do not mean surrender to particular circumstances. I mean surrender all thought, emotion, and circumstance to that which is bigger and deeper.

Surrender your identity. Surrender your suffering to that which is deeper than suffering, closer than identity.

Do you discover victory or defeat in this surrender?

Are you asking me?

Yes! Let's not pretend to be satisfied with theory!

I don't know how to answer.

The only way you can answer is by surrendering everything for one split second. Just a split second of absolute, complete surrender, and then tell me, is this victory or defeat?

Let go of the theory. Right now, give up your name, your history; give up your parents, your relations, or any possible future. Give it all up for one instant.

What is the result? What is the report from surrender?

It makes me think of—

Give that up too.

(laughing)

You're getting closer. You're showing the signs now. Thoughts fall away; laughter starts.

Give it all up for one split second. You are quite free to pick it all up again. Just for a second, put everything aside—very simply, very easily, very quickly. Tell me, in that split second, is anything wanted or needed?

It feels very spontaneous.

Yes, now even give up spontaneity. Give up any label of what it is. Give up any conclusion of what will be given if you surrender. Do you understand? Many people try to make a deal: *I'll surrender "if." I'll surrender if I get this, and this, and this.* I am encouraging unconditional surrender.

You may think that to surrender means losing something. In reality, all that is lost is the power of your thoughts, emotions, and circumstances to dictate a point of view about the reality of life. This is the most sublime victory. It cannot be understood. It cannot be imagined. But it *can* be directly experienced, and this is your opportunity. This is your time. This is your invitation to satsang.

How do I give it all up?

This is an essential question. Recognize how you have attempted to hold it all together. Then you will see that no attempt has ever been successful. Whatever the appearance of success, recognize it is finally impossible to hold it all together. Isn't that a relief?

There is a belief or a brainwashing that promises you that can hold it all together. It begins with the learning of your name. How many times did you have to hear your name before you learned to think, *Okay, yes, that is who I am.*

Your name is forgotten each night as you go to sleep, and has to be remembered each morning. Of course, you get very used to remembering, so that when you come out of the sleep state, your name arises and you easily slip it on. Your occupation is waiting and you slip on your occupation. Success, failure, worthlessness, and superiority are also waiting.

Now the question is how to remain naked.

See that everything you put on is illusion, is make-believe. You are not your name, however well you have memorized it. You are not success or failure, however thoroughly you have evaluated your circumstances. Recognize that it takes some degree of effort to recall your name and attach an evaluation, conclusion, or somebodyness. Simply see that you are, in fact, always naked. Recognize that illusion only *appears* to cover who you are. Realize the shining quality of pure presence that cannot be covered by your own or anyone else's name and form.

Do you know the story of the Emperor's new clothes? The Emperor walks through the streets naked under the delusion that he has many different, very fine outfits. Because he is the Emperor, everyone wants to keep him satisfied and happy. Almost all his subjects say, "Oh, beautiful new outfit. Yes, that is very nice." Except for one young innocent who truthfully says, "But wait, you don't really have anything on. You're actually naked!"

This is the teacher's purpose in your life. The teacher says, "You think you are dressed poorly or dressed well, but your nakedness shines through in its glory, its beauty."

Whatever you think you are clothed in is simply a thought, and it is a weighty, unnecessary thought. Whether you clothe yourself with a thought of rightness or wrongness, who you are is naked beauty, naked glory, pristine no-thingness. Stop thinking otherwise and see. Then you don't have to go to the trouble of letting it all go. You will recognize, *Ha! There is nothing here anyway. What I thought I could hold on to is simply a thought, and thoughts are made of nothing. They seem to be something, they may be experienced as something, but in reality, they are nothing.*

How to let it all go is a very good question. The only problem with the question is that it assumes there is something to let go of. This assumption is based on the naming process, the believing process, and the "acting as if" process. Don't "act as if." Don't name. Don't process. Just be.

Sri Ramana Maharshi often said, "Be as you are."

To be as you are is to be before naming, before clothing. Be that. The effort is in the naming and the clothing, the evaluation of what has been named and clothed, and the comparison of that with other names and clothes.

Be as you are, and you will see as I see. Then you will have a good, deep, serious laugh.

❖

I know that truth deeply, but to live it is a challenge for me.

Yes, surrender is a great challenge! Don't you like a challenge? Of course you do.

Of course I do.

Yes! This challenge goes against the whole tide of conditioning. This challenge is the invitation to satsang. Satsang is not an escape from challenge. It is a penetration into the depth and the core of experience to see what already exists, pure and unchallenged, with no need for defense, protection, or even maintenance. It is a penetration into the depths of yourself.

When you are ready to meet this challenge, you are finished with whining about *why* and *them* and *me* and *should have* and *could have*.

People sometimes have an infantile idea that a spiritual life is about learning something, after which you get a good grade, a good evaluation, and this proves you are very good. You graduate into the spiritual realm. And then you can go to sleep again.

A true spiritual life is the realization of the endless totality of being as discovered in the heart of emptiness. Every moment of every day is a vehicle for that realization. Good times are beautiful, pleasant vehicles. Bad times are horrible, unpleasant vehicles. Still, all is revered as the vehicle for self-realization.

I experience much frustration because I know of boundlessness but identify with the illusion so much of the time.

Just for a moment, acknowledge the sublime grace that allows you to say, with all clarity and without pretense, that you have experienced boundlessness. What a blessed life this is! What a graced life. Now give this grace more weight than you give the frustration.

If some previously suppressed or indulged tendency arises after this miraculous experience of boundlessness, how will it be met? In what context will it be viewed? The usual reaction is a scrambling of mental activity to either get something back or keep something away. In your case, frustration has arisen. Fine. Now frustration is the fire. Jump into the fire. Don't try to fix the frustration. Don't try to ignore it, overcome it, control it, or act it out. Directly experience frustration. Directly discover *who* is really frustrated.

I could be mistaken, but I feel like I've been sitting in this fire for a long time.

You are mistaken. To sit in this fire for even an instant reveals there is no entity suffering! There is only boundless freedom of being. So, if you feel you have sat in it for a while, recognize that you are sitting in some idea of it, usually coupled with the idea of getting out of it. All of this presupposes some entity located someplace.

Ask yourself, *What if, for every instant for the rest of the days of this particular experience of individuation, there is only total, absolute frustration?*

Do you see what a relief this is? For an instant, if you stop fighting it, you will see what exists in the core of frustration. Then you will directly discover the secret answer to *who* is frustrated.

Jump into the fire!

❖

I have a fear of selling out, which I feel I've done many times because normal life seems safer.

Your willingness to expose that fear, rather than pretend the sell-out is not possible, is your resolve to be vigilant. Willingness exposes everything. The challenge of surrender is now even greater, because the temptation is to identify and attempt to cling to wherever there are good feelings.

I've tried that and it doesn't feel good at all.

Wonderful! This is wisdom speaking. It truly doesn't feel good to identify anywhere. Fall into surrender. Fall into truth. Fall into true self, endlessly. As long as you possess a physical body in form, there will be some sense of identification. As long as this sense is present, surrender it to sublime truth. Then the sense that you are the body is a gift. Then you are constantly surrendering to the unknown fire, a deeper and bigger surrender, with bigger stakes. This is life really lived—not lived through some kind of image of security, but directly, openly, not knowing.

It feels like a tremendous gift.

It *is* a tremendous gift. It is a gift beyond value. Honor the gift. Do not treat it casually. It is sacred. It is holy. Don't diminish it in any way and see. Let this holy gift live the life you have called yours. Let the gift take over your life. Blessedly, it takes what has always been its. What was assumed to be yours is returned to its source.

The metaphor of Lucifer, God's very favorite angel, the angel of light, the angel of mind, is the story of *My, Me, Mine!—my power, my glory, my life, my actions, my attainments, my victories.* Finally, blessedly, the mind returns to its source.

Where does the mind get its power? When this is recognized, then Lucifer is no longer the devil, no longer in opposition, no longer in service to delusions of "me" and "mine." Then the mind can serve its source. Lucifer once again can serve God. The return is the surrender.

Let God have you. Give up every idea and every image of what God is. Stop placing a limitation on God. Let God have your life. It may not always be comfortable, but what is a life of comfort in comparison with this holy servitude?

Yes, don't sell your soul for comfort. It is a measly sell-out, and there is no rest in it. There may be a measure of momentary thrill, or a momentary cessation of pain, but you have done this too often. You know you will never be happy until you surrender all your unnecessary burdens. Why postpone? Any postponement is more unnecessary burden.

❖

I find myself donning a cloak of ignorance rather than living by what I know to be so obviously true.

Yes, you have the choice to lie and hide in the labyrinth of the mind. When you choose to not hide, you choose to discover who you are.

You have chosen to hide from truth by assuming, believing, and practicing that you are your name, body, history, emotions, and thoughts. The willingness to see is the willingness to give up the choice to lie, hide, or seek comfort in hope and belief. It is the willingness to experience the heart of annihilation. To see the outrageous truth that, even in the attempts to hide, nothing is truly hidden.

You have freedom of choice. For a long time you have chosen to hide and then chosen to deny the hiding. You have chosen to speak words and use concepts of freedom. Now you have the choice to be who you truly are. Realize who you are and you will finally realize divine choicelessness.

In your imagination you have a form, shape, characteristics, qualities, aspects, and these can be compared with other forms and shapes, past, present, and future. There is nothing wrong with imagination. It just doesn't have anything to do with who you truly are. Imagination is an enormous power, and from that power comes enormous experiences of pleasure and pain.

Finally, in a certain lifetime, there arises the desire to know who you really are. This is a very lucky lifetime. In that lifetime, satsang appears in your consciousness most unexpectedly. In satsang, you at least hear the words "It is absolutely possible for you, at this time, in this moment, to discover the truth of who you are, and to live out the rest of this lifetime in devotional service to that."

You have always been that. In this particular lifetime, you have the opportunity to discover what, in truth, you have always been. It is a sacred moment, a serious moment, and a joyous moment. It is a moment of choice.

I congratulate you. Somehow you are drawn to discover what gives mind, body, imagination, illusion, and the whole cosmos its power. In this discovery, don't wait for anyone or anything, because it is right here, right now.

❖

I had this thought: surrender to what? But I guess it is just to simply surrender.

Yes, surrender all your suffering. Surrender all your ideas of *not now, shouldn't be, not me, can't be, too simple.* Just surrender them and see. As an experiment, surrender your doubt.

What about resistance? What role does it play? Is there a way that it serves?

When you were a child, you played hide-and-seek, and at first you resisted being found. Then you began to recognize that you actually wanted to be found. Even though you may have thought you had the perfect hiding place, there is a great joy in being found. Maybe now you can recognize that this game is actually about being found. You only had thought it was about hiding. The prelude is to hide, but the real pinnacle of this game you have played on yourself is to be found. Then you are done with resistance.

Resistance may arise, but let it arise in the willingness to be found. There may be the temptation to stay hidden, but still you recognize there is something bigger in being found. Drop all your expectations of how you will be found, when you will be found, or what it will look like when you are found. To open your mind, your disguises, and your resistance is to announce the availability to be found.

Don't give resistance a thought. Don't speak about it. Don't get in a relationship with it. When you sense a contraction, let it be. When you conclude that it shouldn't be, or that it should be different, then resistance is given more strength. Let it be and it has no power.

You are welcomed to satsang in whatever state of mind. It doesn't matter. By obeying the urge to bolt, to close, or to dismiss, it is possible for you to discover your true self.

Be found. Be eternally found. Find yourself everywhere. This finding is a limitless revelation—so subtle, so immense, and so indescribable.

Surrender to being found?

Yes!

❖

My mind is quieter, but it wants to analyze and memorize. I tell myself to relax, be still, go deeper. I feel stuck, and then I start to feel separate. Please help me to finally surrender.

Help is here. You are never separate from help. Anytime you ask for help, help presents itself. It is beautifully humbling to ask for help. It is good to give up your idea of independence. Just say "Please help," and you will see instantly that every enlightened being in every realm, known and unknown, from all the dimensions charted and uncharted, is immediately supporting, helping, reminding, pushing, pulling, embracing, holding, shaking, or doing whatever is needed. Your plea for help cuts through all past arrogance. You are helped immediately because you are calling to the truth of yourself.

I know surrender is present now, but I also know that I'm very afraid of it. It's like I'm halfway to being fed, and then I open my mouth and say, "Don't feed me."

You opened your mouth, but then you closed your mind. You know the mind is closed if immediately you have an idea or image of what help should look like, when it will come, how long it will take, what it should do, and what it should not do. Isn't this the same old story? The replaying of this same old story is not truly asking for help. Help is not separate from the willingness to receive. The most profound help is already present, just waiting to be called, just waiting to be invited, just waiting for you to finish this tedious game of hiding.

I haven't been able to just accept that the truth will have me.

You are wanted totally, completely, by your own self. Freedom wants you as its own.

I am never speaking of freedom of the body, or any image you have that you've named "me." The body is not free and doesn't need to be free. I am not speaking of emotional freedom. I am not speaking of the freedom to do what you want to do. I am speaking of freedom that is already free, silence that is already silent, happiness that is already happy. While you tell your story of unworthiness, already within you is an ocean of happiness. It is calling you. Open your mind and see.

❖

You told me to relax completely, and now my fear is that life will be like it was before.

Then you are not relaxed. You are still chewing on doubt. It takes effort to follow the thought of doubt, and then the thoughts that follow those thoughts. Obviously, pretty soon you will not be relaxed.

To mentally relax, let go of all lines and ropes back into the past. Where is *before* in a still mind? To remember what it was like *before* requires some effort. See what it is like right now.

I am not saying you have to spend your life completely relaxed. You are free! You are free to struggle. You are free to be tense. You are free to follow all doubts. You are free to endlessly doubt. And you are free to just relax and be who you are. Perhaps you have overlooked that you can relax. You can let your thoughts cease, and you can see what reveals itself.

You will see that you cannot be like you were before, because what you imagined you were like, you were not anyway! See what is right now, and see that you have always been that.

❖

I was going to tell you how much I truly want realization, but upon radically honest inspection, I find that I cannot say anything except "Help." I want to want reality, but find myself this morning face-to-face with my conditioning and the desires of lifetimes.

This is an important moment. You hear about enlightenment, or you hear about the possibility of realization, and you say, "Oh, yes. I want that. Great. That sounds wonderful . . . and then I'll be happy all the time. Then people will respect me. Then people will love me. Then people will give me what I want. Yes, I want that!"

This is all right. This is the way it must be at first. There must be some appeal through the ego. But as you are drawn deeper into the truth of what keeps you unhappy, into what keeps propelling you through incarnation after incarnation of searching for happiness, there arises discriminating wisdom. It is at this point that true choice is possible.

When you are face-to-face with conditioning, the choice is real.

I often hear people speak from a kind of spiritual trance: "It's all taken care of anyway. It's not my doing. I have no choice." This is conceptual garbage. You have absolute choice. You are consciousness itself. How can you not have choice? You have the choice to deny yourself, and you have the choice to affirm yourself. You have the choice to turn from yourself, and you have the choice to surrender to yourself. You have the choice to know who you are.

You have the choice to continue to say you have no choice. Just don't expect me to believe or accept it. It is a childlike idea of choicelessness. First make the choice. Then maybe you can say you have no choice, but not before. Before that choice is made, the rest is just a theory of not having choice, a safety zone, and a very flimsy excuse to suffer.

Ask yourself, *What do I really want?* When the pleasures of the senses arise, you can ask yourself deeper, *What will they give me? What is it that I want from them?* If, in fact, what you are searching for are beauty, peace, love, and truth—good. You don't have to go anywhere for that. Face any desire or temptation and it will burn in the facing. All is burned in that.

If what you want is more excitement, more stimulation, more imagery, more fantasy, then follow those desires, and report back to me the result.

❖

What would be the first step in controlling desires?

I appreciate the question, but instead of controlling desires, I suggest you surrender to that from which the desire arises. In order to discover where the desire arises, you have to turn right into the desire. The usual mental activity is to be either very afraid of our desires or very in love with them. The usual is to indulge desires and, through indulgence, to finally discover that indulgence doesn't make for satisfaction. Indulgence makes for dissatisfaction. With indulgence, the demon of desire grows ever larger.

Some have also attempted to repress desires, and this repression usually leads to rigidity and covert indulgence.

Here, I am asking you to simply meet the very core of the desire itself.

Some desires will kill you if you meet them.

No. They may kill you if you indulge them.

That's not what you're speaking of?

I am not speaking of indulging. Do not move one iota either toward the desire or against the desire, but actually trace the desire back, with your consciousness, to where it arises.

You may have had an overwhelming desire for alcohol or sex or some other activity that produces pleasure. So you have pursued alcohol or sex or whatever. You have pursued it, and you have pursued it, and you have realized that the pursuit is killing you spiritually, emotionally, and physically. What I am speaking of is stopping the pursuit and stopping any rejection of the pursuit, and meeting the actual experience of desire.

Why don't you do it right now, and then see what the answer is. Then we are not speaking theoretically.

When you say to go toward it —

I believe you are misunderstanding "meet" as "going toward," or feeding the desire, or giving it what you imagine it craves. I am not saying to *give* it anything. I am saying to stop all giving, stop all taking away, and be naked in the power arising. In that nakedness, without moving the slightest to feed, give, reject, ignore, or control, discover directly what is at the core of the desire, what is the root of it. In that, you discover directly what it is you really desire, having nothing to do with alcohol or sex or any other pleasure.

I can't figure it out.

The deepest teaching from Ramana directs us to *be still*. In being still, there may arise a momentum of past desires that have been previously either indulged or rejected. Both indulging and rejecting are egocentric activities and generate further karma, further suffering. In being still, you are finally naked in the direct experience of desire without moving the slightest to take care of that desire or to cover it.

I am speaking of a great burning, a great, intense fire. This fire burns away all that covers what is permanently, eternally desireless, in bliss. Be naked in the flaming consummation with yourself as love and fulfillment.

When I speak of surrender, I am not speaking of indulgence, acting out, or giving in to. Indulging desires can kill you. It has killed you over and over. Rejecting, ignoring, and controlling desires also has killed you over and over. Now you can face this death directly. You have learned from many millions of years of evolution about the feeding and rejecting of desires. This is known. Since it is known, you can now put it aside. What has not been experienced? What is unknown?

I am directing you to the very core of your being. So what will it be? It is up to you.

Is the first step, then, just meditating or sitting with the desire?

You have already taken the first step by questioning what to do about these desires. In your mature recognition of actions taken toward desire or against desire, you have discovered what these actions have led to. Feeding, indulging, and repressing are attempts to handle or take care of desires. The direction I am speaking of is inward to the source of the arising—into the fire and through the fire, not feeding it and not putting it out. Go directly into it and discover what it really is. *Reality* is our concern here. What is this really? Who am I really?

For this meeting you can have no reference to past thoughts, activities, or conclusions. You must be absolutely still. Stillness means that all activity of the mind ceases. Then direct experience reveals what is. There is nothing to do. Just simply stop doing what you have been doing, and reality is immediate.

✥

After having experienced awakening, and then the deepening of that awakening, unconscious habits that are harmful or stupid are still manifesting in my life. What do I do?

Isn't it obvious? Stop them. Anything harmful or stupid, stop immediately. When it is obvious, there is no excuse, and this in itself is the deepening. Don't give yourself any excuses. Be finished with stupidity and harmfulness. When stupidity arises from past actions, past choices, past desires, it is obvious if you are willing for it to be obvious. If you are willing to see, you are willing to not go to sleep to what is harmful and stupid. You are willing to feel it, to experience the enormous, omni-directional pain of it. It is not just in you or in some other. It is omni-directional.

This is excruciating. It must be excruciating. The willingness for total surrender and sensitivity is the willingness to not allow anything to pass unseen.

You have spent many years denying what is obvious. Our whole culture is built on this denial and deflection. Our subculture in particular, out of some desire for personal freedom and to break out of the bondage of the generation before us, has spent years denying what is obviously stupid.

Now be still and tell the truth. At this point no one can tell you this truth. No one can tell you to do one particular action and to not do some other particular action. It is simply obvious as it arises. No matter what story or justification you are telling yourself, the willingness to see what is stupid reveals the possibility of surrendering to what is *not* stupid, which is pure, eternal intelligence.

You now have the opportunity, totally and fully, to experience the impulse either to deny the stupidity or to indulge the stupidity by acting it out. This impulse, when it is directly and totally experienced, burns up the stupidity! In this burning, there is, as you say, a deepening.

You can expect these old habits to arise. They have been fed and nurtured and practiced for a very long time. They know where to get a good meal. You must expect them to show up, and they know how to tug at your heartstrings and at your neck. These are the tricks of the mind. Now the trickster has been exposed. Awakening is the realization that in either denying impulses or following impulses, one continues to sleepwalk.

I am not here to teach you some kind of code of conduct. You don't need me to teach you that. You have tried many codes of conduct unsuccessfully. The latest code of conduct just has to get shoved aside for the next code of conduct. Realization of who you are is not about a code of conduct. It is simply about recognizing what is obvious and what is stupid. I am speaking of basic maturity.

You are no longer a child, and you will not find fulfillment in the attempt to return to childhood. Recognize and feel the excruciating impulse to act out something very stupid or to repress that acting out, which is also very stupid. In that simple recognition is the great opportunity to directly experience whatever arises. Then even these past impulses, these latent tendencies, this subconscious material, are vehicles for deepening surrender.

People often ask me about addictions, which all stem from a deep yearning and the impulse to find some substance or some thing to quench it. The impulse is itself the yearning for fulfillment. I always counsel to jump directly into the fire of yearning. This jump is neither acting out the impulse nor denying the impulse. In each arising of these impulses is the deepest, most profound opportunity to burn away layers of misidentification and suffering.

You know the moments in which you have felt or thought, *I must not feel this, or I will go crazy. I must do that. I must have this. If I just have it one more time, then I'll be satiated.*

Stop this sell-out. Even though all of society supports this sell-out, and many people are making a fortune on this sell-out—stop. This is very, very simple. It doesn't need extensive analysis.

This is the challenge of surrender. Whatever you think I mean by surrender, I mean something deeper. Please understand that true surrender is neither repressing, denying, ignoring, acting out, nor discharging. Surrender is the willingness to be crucified.

Some impulses are extremely strong. Some of them are biochemical. Some have been practiced and worshipped. In the surrender to the crucifixion of the moment, there is resurrection. As soon as there is total surrender, you discover that when everything is lost, everything is found. The very peace and bliss that you have unsuccessfully been seeking in habitual, harmful activities is realized. Not by following the habit, and not by denying the habit, but by being willing to burn in the impulse with no movement of the mind in any direction.

❖

I have heard you speak of resolve. Is there some difference between resolve and surrender?

Total surrender is effortless resolve. Resolve means being willing to see the slightest tendency to turn from truth. Resolve means being surrendered to seeing truth, rather than to seeing things look a particular way. Rather than seeing either enlightenment or ignorance, you are surrendered to simply seeing. Seeing deeper and deeper.

There is always more to see, and this is glorious. Glorious! Every instant, in every direction, life gives you the opportunity for deeper resolve, deeper surrender, deeper humbling.

This is the glory of limited perception. This is the glory of the conditioned existence. Because you have been conditioned to see things in a certain way, you now have the endless opportunity to see *through* the conditioning.

You may have aeons of latent tendencies and habits of mind that will come calling. Let them come! They are vehicles and gifts for deeper and deeper surrender, deeper humbling, deeper being swept off your feet, being floored. Always you can be more deeply prostrate at the endlessness of truth.

❖

I keep thinking I've got it, then I land flat on my face. Is there a point where surrender and resolve are finished?

No. Resolve, which is surrender, is gloriously necessary as long as there is breath in the body.

I tell you continually that beingness is naturally easy. However, it is only experienced as easy if you are true to the truth, not if you are true to particular phenomenal displays. Not if you are true to particular biochemical firings. If you are true to phenomena, then you will go the way conditioned existence has been going throughout time. I promise you this. But you don't have to rely on my promise. Simply tell the truth about your own experiences throughout time, and you will see that this is so. It is a hard truth because there is often an infantile idealization of the way things should be.

Hard truth, if met in the resolve to be absolutely true, is effortless. There is no effort. The effort, the struggle, and the experience of landing come from trying to cling to a certain phenomenon, or trying to get something again, or trying to get something someplace else. Whether it is the phenomenon called personal power, or the phenomenon called sexual excitement, or the phenomenon called spiritual power, it is all entrapment by the mind.

There is nothing wrong with phenomena. Some phenomena are quite delightful, and some phenomena are quite horrifying; but all phenomena are simply phenomena. If you attempt to cling to any of it, if you reach or grasp for any of it, you will experience yourself as bound. You will be following the mind, subtly or grossly. The value of satsang appearing in your consciousness again and again over time is to point to this very basic truth.

All the books and all the teachers always say the awakened being is very rare. This may have been true in your past, and in the collective past. Whether it remains true in the present and in the future is up to you, now. Self-realization takes a resolve so total it is unknown. When resolve is total, then resolve is ease of being.

Your life, as you live it now, is the reflection of what you really want. If what you really resolve is the surrender to truth, then you will live your lifetime in surrender to that, and not to some phenomenal display. If you surrender to the truth that no phenomenon has ever touched, you are free. Your life is then a beacon of freedom, a freedom having nothing to do with comforts or discomforts, likes or dislikes, excitement or dullness. True freedom. The truth of who you are is this freedom, and these phenomenal displays are simply masks, clothes, passing clouds, chemical or electrical moments.

The usual or normal pattern is to slip back into trance, to reincarnate into suffering. When what has been cast aside appears in another way, through another door, promising more glory, more beauty, more thrills, the temptation will be to say, "Oh, yes. I've waited for this forever. I'll get back to truth later."

Unswerving resolve is, in fact, the most extraordinary and the most unusual possibility for your life. You have the total support of all awakened being in all realms throughout time. Still, it is totally up to you. You are supported, you are cheered, you are shaken, you are cajoled, and still it is up to you.

True resolve is the most ruthless act of a lifetime. It is the willingness to die to all hope of pleasure. It is the willingness to surrender to truth. You can't surrender to truth so that you will get more pleasure. You have, of course, tried to make that deal, and what you have gotten is more suffering—perhaps with extreme pleasure—but finally, more suffering.

Expect the deepest, most thrilling displays of phenomenal temptation. Expect to arise what you have hungered for, what is latent in the most secret recesses of your mind. Whether it is a display of personal power, an appearance of the hungered-for soul mate, the winning of wealth, or some personal recognition, it will present itself because it all lies in wait as subconscious tendencies.

What makes resolve difficult is the attempt to also hold on to some idea of personal gratification. Ironically, this in itself is hell. When you are willing to face whatever temptation—horrible or exquisite—fully and completely, when you are willing to die to all fantasies of personal gratification, you discover gratification as who you are.

Expect to be pushed, pulled, and flipped, to be attacked from the side and the back, to be presented with flowers and sweets . . . and then to be clubbed. This is called *Leela,* God's theatre, God's dream. Leela plays very hard. If you are surrendered to truth, then this play will only push you deeper into truth. If you are, in fact, surrendered to some phenomenal experience, you will be pulled out of the experience of your own being as gratification itself and into the search for "more" or "different" or "better," which are the names of hell.

❖

It seems I've been given a very active mind. It's receiving and checking out so much, so many things, all the time. There is now a lot of attention being given to my music by a major producer, and this phenomenon you were speaking about is very big. There is "the big album," and all this attention and touring. I was just happy being here, and now it's "I'm getting there! I'm gonna get it!"

Many people before have fallen into this same trap of fame, money, and recognition. Use their fall as the encouragement for unswerving resolve.

Turn the active mind's attention to itself, and see what is discovered. Praise and adoration come and go. Hate and attack come and go. They are meaningless if your attention is on the truth of the bliss within you.

A current of bliss will reveal a river of bliss. A river of bliss will flow naturally into an ocean of bliss. An ocean of bliss lifts up into a sky of bliss. The sky of eternal self is truth. If life presents roses or if it presents ashes, attend to truth. You may like the roses and hate the ashes, but attend to truth.

I notice my mind is attending to all the phenomena that seem to be occurring in the moment.

What about truth?

Truth seems to be in acknowledging all the phenomena.

Where has that led you?

The mind is constantly commenting on what certain appearances mean.

This is all imagination. If you attend to truth, you are acknowledging what no phenomena have ever touched. You are acknowledging the truth of yourself. It doesn't mean you hate phenomena, and it doesn't mean you love phenomena. It means you are attending to truth.

Truth is permanent. Phenomena are impermanent. You know this essential distinction from your day-to-day experience. This is not esoteric. It is very concrete. Phenomena come and go. Thoughts come and go. Emotions come and go. People's responses come and go. Your attitude about yourself comes and goes. Good, bad, up, down, excited, flat; all of that comes and goes. Truth remains present, alive, available, blissful. Attend to truth, and phenomena are simply comings and goings. Not only are they simply comings and goings, they are actually vehicles for deeper realization of truth.

That's what I was referring to.

Phenomena are not vehicles for deeper realization of truth if you acknowledge phenomena rather than acknowledge truth.

Aren't they one and the same?

Have you realized that phenomena are nothing at all? Otherwise, you are using a spiritual concept to justify following phenomena, and then wondering why you keep suffering.

Using spiritual truth to serve egocentric understanding is a trick of the mind, and I see it in tragic ways. Forget any concept of "one and the same." If you are remembering it, you are using it as justification for following phenomena, and this is the trap.

Forget everything, and in that instant you will see what is permanent. Attend to that. Surrender to that. The mind cannot be busy then. The mind can only be busy with attending to phenomena. In the quieting of the mind, the deepest realization naturally appears because it is already here. In your attendance to phenomena, you overlook what, in fact, you hope phenomena will give you, or what you hope phenomena will keep away.

Surrender is a ruthless, unsentimental cut. The desire for this cut is why people traditionally retreat from the world of phenomena and live the life of a monk, a recluse. The world of phenomena that must be left is the world within your own mind. Surrender your interpretations, your measurements, and your qualifications for at least one instant. In that surrender, see what is available. Then you have the opportunity of free choice, of true intention.

I can guarantee you that many people want phenomena, and so they will spend however many lifetimes chasing phenomena. If what you want is truth, then take one instant to let go of everything you thought would give you truth, and experience what is already here. Then and only then do you have real choice.

Is the whole process just surrendering to what is?

Yes, and if you are to surrender to what is, first you must discover what *is*. Do you understand? What *is*, is truth. *Truth is permanent, eternal, unchanging presence.* If you are surrendering to phenomena and calling phenomena "just what is," then you are playing a nasty trick on yourself. Then you are biting the dog that will bite you back, because it looks like something soft and sweet.

I often hear, "Hey, I'm just going with what is, you know. Love the one you're with, right?" We have all tried that in the name of freedom, in the name of truth, in the name of choice, but secretly in the name of "I've gotta be me."

That is not what *is*. What *is*, is unchanging. It's true that all phenomena arise from that, exist never separate from that, and return to that. But in the deep disease of conditioned existence, attention has been paid only to phenomena, and in that, there is unnecessary suffering.

It is possible to stop unnecessary suffering. Only when truth is realized are phenomena no problem.

We are trained by what we hear people say. If we like what they are saying, if we resonate with the energy of it, or if nice things happen, then when they speak, we want to learn and remember what it is they are saying. We hold in our minds what we think it all must mean, and then we model our concepts after that. That is not what realization is about. Final truth has never been spoken and can never be spoken. What can be spoken comes and goes. I am speaking of what is in all the comings and goings. This that you truly are, *is*.

If for one instant you surrender to *is*-ness rather than surrendering to phenomena, then you honestly have a choice. It doesn't mean you are any less *is*-ness if you choose to follow phenomena. Maybe you like to suffer. Maybe you like drama more than peace. That is all right at certain stages, but you are here in satsang to discover the possibility of choosing truth—permanent, eternal, never-going-anywhere truth.

❖

I say a lot of things in satsang, but the truth is, I am really only saying one thing in as many different ways as this mindstream can conjure. What I am saying is simply to trust yourself.

When I say trust yourself, I mean to trust the truth of who you are. For this trust to be complete, you must first discover who you are. You cannot wait any longer, and you cannot rely on someone else's interpretation, whether mine, your parents', or your government's. You have to discover directly, for yourself, who you are. Then you have the opportunity to trust that discovery totally and completely. You can surrender all thoughts, all emotions, all interpretations of reality, and see what comes from that trust.

Gangaji . . . I surrender.

To declare this is to stand up, to stand away from the herd of self-hatred and self-doubt. Good. Your surrender is eternally accepted and celebrated.

Now, what has been lost in this surrender?

Judgment of others. Judgment of myself.

What is found?

What has always been here!

That's right! In surrender, what is found is what has always been here. Isn't it about time you surrender to what has always been here? What a victory this surrender is.

· I see your face opening and tears streaming. I don't know if these words even make sense to you. It doesn't matter. Something recognizes itself and shakes in that recognition. The byproduct of that recognition, the shaking and the tears and the declaration "I surrender," is a beautiful event.

There is no end to surrender. When you declare "I surrender," this is the beginning. The gate of surrender is wide open, and you are walking through the gate. Now it begins. What has always been here begins manifesting its eternity in the mindstream that has surrendered before it.

I just realized that you are constantly surrendering.

Yes!

That it's not as if you arrived anywhere.

I arrived nowhere, and I am finding no limits to this nowhere. Any time some semblance of arrival appears, I discover it to be nowhere, nothing. It is not something that *happened* to me one day. It is something that *is*.

The great fear of surrender is that some kind of nihilistic force will take over, some kind of brainwashing will come in, but it is obvious we all have already been brainwashed. That is the nature of conditioned existence.

Are you willing to surrender all conditioning? Not to substitute a new philosophy or a new point of view, but to surrender it all, so that what is before all points of view can be revealed.

It's always new!

That's right. Otherwise, realization is something that happened yesterday, in the past. Realization is absolutely new, and at the same time, it is seeing what has always been.

There is no end to surrender, no end to awareness, no end to being, no end to God, no end to truth, no end to who you are.

Exposing the Core of Suffering

ost people are firmly convinced that if they can get rid of their suffering, happiness will be achieved.

We have tried everything to get rid of suffering. We have gone everywhere to get rid of suffering. We have bought everything to get rid of it. We have ingested everything to get rid of it. Finally, when one has tried enough, there arises the possibility of spiritual maturity, the willingness to stop the futile attempt *to get rid of,* and instead, to actually experience suffering. In that momentous instant is the realization of what is beyond suffering, what is untouched by suffering. There is the realization of who one truly is.

❖

I am a person who has been politically involved most of my life. I am greatly concerned with human rights and fairness and justice. I have had the belief that if the murderous, greedy dictators would just get out of the way, then people could find the way to peace.

Then I came to a satsang where you talked about self-inquiry. You spoke about turning inward and focusing on the question "Who am I?" At that point the lights came on. "Who am I?" appeared everywhere. I see now that there is no solution in focusing on what is "out there." The only possibility for peace is within myself.

When your heart is open, your life is peace. Peace is willing to see everything. Be willing to see fully and completely every impulse of separation, acquisition, and greed. Be willing to see hate and war. The promise of this seeing is the end of the war.

When the personal war is ended, "your" life is not limited to the personal anymore. "Your" lifetime is then turned toward peace and reconciliation. Then "your" life is the resolution of these demanding questions of justice and human rights that you have had all your life. Your life is a life given to resolution.

Honor the life that is peace. Bow to the peaceful life. Support the peaceful life. Serve the peaceful life. Any time or any place you feel a wavering, call on all other servants of peace to remind you of what is always peacefully alive within you.

Most people come to spiritual or religious gatherings in search of personal enlightenment. That is how it begins. The lack of personal fulfillment serves as the grit that reveals self-hatred and the resulting mental/emotional war. By consciously facing suffering, by seeing it in all its horror, and by being willing to continue to see it as long as it is there, the horror can be finished.

We will see what happens when more people are willing to give up their personal wars. We have seen what has occurred when people are not willing to give them up, when they are only willing to attempt to change others. We have seen this over and over and over.

I am asking you to step away from the herd, to be exposed to all kinds of dangers and lack of safety. I am asking you for an instant of pure meditation, for one second of silence.

The herd is the activity of the mind. To know the peace that is permanently present, you must be willing to experience the exposure.

I want to live this lifetime open and exposed to everything that comes, never wavering in my devotion to peace for all beings.

I am happy to hear you speak like this, so truly, so clearly. It is time.

❖

I'm deeply concerned about the fact that twenty percent of the world's population consumes and accounts for eighty percent of the world's natural resources. I'm concerned about the fact that in the next century, the world's population is going to double and then quadruple.

Suffering is not limited to a group of people living in poverty or a group of people living in affluence. Suffering is almost universal.

If you are concerned with really getting to the root of the suffering, which, in the case that you describe, is manifested by the overwhelming impulse to consume and acquire, then let us have a dialogue. If you are just concerned with saying "Bad, bad, bad," then your finger-pointing is not different from any pretext for war throughout time. We can study history to see what these pretexts have in fact led to.

So please, tell me, what is it you really want?

Well, I'm concerned about the suffering that those facts end up generating.

If you are just concerned with the suffering that those facts reveal, you are quite possibly overlooking the root of suffering. Getting *this* particular group, which is doing *that,* to stop doing that will not touch the root of suffering. As long as the root remains, the suffering will break out again and again.

Well, then what do I do with all that information?

For a moment, drop all facts about everything. I guarantee you that everywhere you look, you can find some fact that points to suffering. It is very tempting to stop at the facts, and then gather more facts around that.

Going for the root of suffering does not excuse the greed and the acquisition and the consumption. But if you stop your investigation at the manifestation of suffering, if you want to merely chop off the fruit or the flower, then the root of suffering grows stronger. You must realize this from history.

Whenever revolution has arisen, even with pure idealism, whether it is political revolution, religious revolution, or ecological revolution, it has failed to eradicate suffering. Finally, the root of suffering must be exposed, and this exposure begins right where you stand.

I am not by any means against commitment to a cause. I am saying that, before you commit to anything, without pointing outward, discover the roots of greed, fear, hate, and aggression. Then whatever cause you champion, you champion from self-confidence. Then your cause is no more about changing facts and statistics. It is about exposing the root of suffering and revealing the source of happiness.

Thank you. I didn't know at the end of the question if I was really going to understand your answer.

I didn't know either. When there is no knowing what will be said and no knowing what will be understood, there is true speaking and true hearing.

I have a small amount of experience being involved in political groups. Once, I even went to jail for nonviolently protesting an action taken by the government. In my involvement, I discovered something very interesting. I discovered that the root of most political action is based on making somebody else wrong so that one's own enormous sense of emptiness, incompleteness, or wrongfulness doesn't have to be felt or experienced. I discovered within my own mind, and I observed in others, that there was primarily an investment in keeping the struggle going. Ironically, there was more energy directed to the struggle than to the resolution of the struggle.

Unfortunately, this same dynamic is present in most nations, most societies, most cultures, most subcultures, most religious groups, most families, and most individuals.

Most action of any kind is an attempt to run from the fear of being nothing. You secretly hope, *If I do this, then I will be something, and this something is worth something. That worth will, at least for a moment, make me forget that perhaps I am really nothing.*

The truth is that you really are nothing! Left unexperienced, this *nothing* is terrifying, and frantic mental activity is generated to fill the seeming void of nothingness. The sublime joke and the great discovery is that in the willingness to be nothing, you realize fulfillment; you realize inherent peace. Then there is no need for *them* to do something so that *you* can feel whole. Action that follows fulfillment is pure, spontaneous, creative, and intuitive, having nothing to do with any perceived lack. The commitment then is to peace and the overflowing of peace, however it overflows—spiritually, politically, through the arts, speaking, or in silence.

Once this discovery has been made, then yes, there can be enlightened politics, enlightened religions, enlightened families, enlightened relationships of all kinds.

The possibility in this lifetime, in this moment, now, is to expose the root of suffering. When the root is exposed to the light of truth, it cannot survive. Then the entire tree of *your suffering* is finished. Without the root, it cannot continue.

For many of us in this country of affluence, there is no real necessity to think about the next meal. There is no real necessity to worry about where you will sleep tonight or if someone will gun you down. So there is no longer any excuse to avoid this essential discovery. If you are distracted from this discovery, you are distracted by trivial matters.

Discover who you are, and let your life be lived from that discovery. Then we will see what becomes of the world.

❖

I have so much trouble accepting the suffering that is going on in the world, and I wonder if, in the state of true love, everything is seen as okay.

True acceptance does not condone starvation, hatred, or suffering. It sees *through* violent fragmentation to inherent wholeness. That seeing *through* serves the end of starvation, hatred, and suffering.

Not just the big suffering, but all the little things too?

Yes, the mundane suffering as well as the profound suffering. Part of the nature of true love is infinite compassion for suffering.

When you say "I have trouble with the suffering; I am suffering because of the suffering," who is this *I*? *Who* is suffering?

Sometimes I fall out of true knowing.

This *I* who falls out of and falls into true knowing, who is this *I*? Where is this *I*?

In my mind.

Where is this mind? Can you particularize this mind or this *I* as a separate entity? I know you can imagine it that way, but in looking directly at the imagination, is this *I* particularized from the totality of being?

No, it's not.

Excellent. You are not separate from the totality of being, as your toe is not separate from the totality of your body. If your toe hurts, you are aware of your toe hurting. True compassion recognizes the experience of hurting and attends to the hurt as best as possible. If the toe isn't attended to in its hurting, it may fester, and then maybe the foot or even the leg will have to suffer because of inattention to the toe.

True understanding does not mean neglect of the world. While your toe is not the totality of your body, it is also not separate from the totality of your body. Change the bandage. Use medicine. With compassion, attend to your true self however you appear—as other human, as other species, as the entire universe.

Compassion is an aspect of love, not a sentimental, judgmental story of love. It is not to say "bad" toe or "poor" toe or "wrong" toe or "stupid" toe. It is compassionate attention, which is love.

✧

A couple of satsangs ago, I asked a question about suffering. I don't remember what you said, but it really made me angry.

That happens sometimes.

What I thought was, "How dare you? How dare you take this away from me, and to take it away so easily!" But you know, I walked out of here with such a lightness that I had not ever really felt before. What I have found since then is joy . . . maybe the other side of suffering.

I wouldn't say that joy is the other side of suffering. That's really the good news about joy. When you experience joy directly, you can find no end to it, no limit to it, even no cause for it!

When you experience suffering directly, you find it is not even there!

This is *very* good news.

Yes, I've become much more available to the world.

Excellent.

I wrote in my journal this morning, asking where this longing has gone, this longing that's connected to the suffering. What I wrote was that it has turned into a simple prayer of thanks.

This is so beautiful, so immediate! This is the beginning. Surrender reveals the open mind, and the open mind is freed from the imagination of separation from pure, free consciousness, which is bliss.

I have heard it said that suffering is voluntary, and bliss is involuntary.

I like that! I would add that suffering has cause, and joy is causeless. If you assign a cause to joy, then there is suffering. Realize causeless joy. It is your inherent nature.

I am not speaking of a "la-la, ha-ha-ha" kind of joy. I am speaking of the joy that even allows unhappiness. I am speaking of the joy of being, the ease of being, not needing anything, not the right circumstance, not the preferred state—just pure being recognizing itself as consciousness and delighting in its discovery.

✧

I come from a background where a lot of attention is paid to suffering, and this week in satsang, I've been very emotional. It has undoubtedly been one of the richest weeks of my life, with a lot of pain and grief, incredible joy, and deeper understanding.

One of the things that happened that was so amazing was that I saw beyond the suffering to something so much bigger and higher. I don't really know what happened, but I hope I can come back to that. I saw suffering like a cloud, that there is really all this light and sky and so much beyond.

This is essential. Before an experience like this, everything spoken in satsang seems abstract or theoretical. In the midst of extreme emotionality, that which is untouched by any emotion revealed itself. You glimpsed the truth. This glimpse, this perception, is now in memory. Though you cannot get back to the experience, the memory of it is a testimonial.

Don't try to recapture that moment. Something in your personal identity has been cut now. Some identification with feelings, circumstances, or emotions as the limit of reality has been cut, and what is limitless has revealed itself.

You cannot get back to your true self, because you are *already* there. You are where your true self is.

I am very happy for you. It is a moment of great joy. It is the beautiful death knell of personal identification, a death that is a celebration of what is deathless.

⟡

I've been in the situation where I intuitively know the answer to all my questions. Recently, however, the questions are coming up, but there is no answer. There is only the recurrence of certain questions demanding an answer, and I notice I want to deny this.

Questions neither touch the true answer nor disturb it in any way. What a wonderful joke. If you deny the question, the question assumes the veil of projected reality. If you follow the question into metaphysical explanation and analysis, it assumes the veil of mental reality. If you give the question to the answer, the question is at rest. Then the question itself has been liberated, has been set free, and is no longer in the hungry ghost realm.

A memory is a hungry ghost, crying for liberation. Release the ghost.

It seems I experience peace, and then there is a sudden return to the suffering, and I wonder how I got back there.

There is peace, and then in peace, some memory of past suffering arises. Do not close the door of peace by attempting to keep any past memory locked in the realm of suffering. Suffering will keep knocking at the door. This is what I mean when I say "hungry ghost."

The moment of peace is an announcement of satsang. Peace welcomes all.

Welcome whatever arises, whatever its disguise, whatever its past association. Expect these past associations, these hungry ghosts, these latent tendencies, to arise. In fact, in your announcement of peace, this is the call for the past to be liberated. There is some past demon in some realm of memory that hears, "Ah, satsang. This is my chance. Maybe now I will be admitted into satsang."

I find myself efforting to stay in no-mind when it arises.

Your effort is the suffering! Recognize that your effort reveals a latent belief that no-mind is something that is not yours already. No-mind is truth, now. Everything appears in that. You cannot leave no-mind. You cannot leave yourself.

When one of these latent tendencies, thought forms, demons, or hungry ghosts appears, this is the opportunity to discover directly if there are any real limits to peace. Not what you have believed the limits to be or what you have imagined has taken you from peace, but really, what are the limits of peace? There is no need to war against your experience of non-peace. Invite everything that arises to peace. That which arises and is welcomed to satsang will either disappear or be revealed, in reality, as peace itself.

❖

I judge myself for having thoughts, yet I'm afraid to stop judging them.

Afraid that you will then be a bad person?

My judgment is that I already am a bad person.

We are taught that we are essentially bad, essentially savage, and that we must learn to be good. Obviously, many things must be learned. Conditioning itself is no problem. When conditioning is overlaid, however, with the belief that you are essentially bad, there is enormous, unnecessary suffering.

Our parents taught us this way. Their parents taught them the same way. It is certainly the way our schools teach us. It is the way our politicians speak to us, and it is the consensual belief. You believe that the Buddha is essentially good. You believe that Christ is essentially good. But there is still the belief that you are basically bad. You believe this because you have bad thoughts. You have negative emotions. You have done bad things. These are the proof that you are bad, and you suffer with this proof.

This is the trap, and within that belief is a deep unwillingness to experience the internal violence, to uncover the root of the badness, and to directly experience the badness that you imagine yourself to be.

I see that every time I judge someone or something, it is a thought in my own mind. I recognize that, and I judge the judging.

I am not saying there is anything wrong with judgment. Obviously, judgments are also a part of life, and if you see something as bad, you must acknowledge that you see it as bad. You do not want to get into philosophical numbness. You know there are occasions where you must shout out, "This is bad. This is wrong. Stop!"

What I am addressing is the internal litany that you practice weekly, daily, or hourly. In the avoidance of direct experience, what is felt as bad within your own mind is left untransformed. It is left as some seed of self-hatred, some sense of worthlessness. You have a deep-seated belief that you must continually think to do the right thing and then to analyze every act, because, obviously, if you don't, your badness will slip through.

There is nothing wrong with the intention to stop contributing to the badness of the world, except that it keeps you in your mind. It keeps you judging, and then judging the judgments—and through judgment, you perpetuate self-hatred.

Now is the opportunity to open your mind totally to all the negativity that you have ever acted out or ever thought. Horrible thoughts can arise in the mind, and yes, you must take responsibility for that. To take responsibility is to stop the mental traps—*I am bad. I shouldn't think that. I've got to practice being good.* Taking responsibility is being willing to really experience the enormous pain of negativity and hatred. Ruthlessly and unsentimentally experience the pain. Be still in the core of the pain.

You feel you have done horrible things, hurtful things, mean-spirited things, nasty things, maybe even evil things. Out of your unwillingness to directly experience the hurt of these actions, the tendency to hurt remains hidden in the mind. The tendency festers for a while and then erupts in some negative thought or emotion or action.

Experience the pain. Maybe you haven't been able to before. Maybe as a child you couldn't, you didn't have the resources or the maturity, but now you can. Have the willingness to meet the pain that you have been unwilling to meet.

It is very easy to tell stories of how we have been hurt, but you have hurt at least as much as you have been hurt. And, anyway, it is finally the same hurt.

Feel the suffering that you have caused. Whatever you have done to someone else, you have done to yourself, and in denying that, you give suffering power for future suffering. When you experience the pain of the suffering that you have caused, you know without a doubt that you have done it to yourself. This in itself is a revelation. In that, you discover what is underneath the pain.

The cause of pain is ignorance. At some time you believed you needed to get something for yourself, and this belief led to greed and lust and hate and violence. In that feeling of need is the germ, the kernel, of yearning for true self. When you are willing to experience it all the way to the core, you will see that all this hurt that was done to you, and that you have done to others, has all been based on ignorance. It has been based on the mistaken misconception that I am not. Experience not-ness to realize *I am*. *I am* is pure, untainted being, naturally cleansed of the past in its own self-recognition. It is the doorway to self-realization. True self is nothing that can be purified, for it is nothing that can be dirtied.

To meet your subconscious beliefs, to keep the door open to meet your karma, to experience it all fully, is to release the past and offer it freedom.

❖

I see people who are pretending to be open and to have fun when they are really suffering.

Yes, this pretense is denial of suffering, and pretense itself is suffering. Both the denial of suffering and the entertaining of suffering lead to more suffering. I am not speaking of putting on a happy face. I am speaking of no face. When there is no face, then you do see falseness. You do see pretense. You do see suffering. And, more importantly, you see what is forever deeper than pretense or suffering. You see natural goodness shining through all the masks of suffering.

Do you catch this?

The doubts come in.

When doubts come, invite doubts to doubtlessness. The secret is neither to try to overcome doubts nor to indulge them, push them aside, or deny them. Invite them to satsang, and then you will see the particular habit of doubting, and more important what is at the root of doubting.

Inviting doubt into the limitless truth of being is a way of recognizing vastness, of being no-body. In the vastness, in totality, the suffering of another is not separate from your own suffering. It appears in you.

I doubt that I am strong enough or big enough to discover what you suggest.

Your doubt is your slave collar. Unlock the slave collar by questioning, now, as we meet, who it is that needs to be big and strong.

Now?

Yes. Now. Who is not big enough or strong enough?

. . . There is no one—just space—just vastness.

Where is doubt in this?

Nowhere.

❖

Gangaji, it seems that I can use the experience of separation as a signpost that I've turned my back on myself.

Yes! This is the dharma bell ringing. If you are experiencing separation, suffering, holding on to or rejecting pain, you can ask yourself, *What is really going on here? Who is suffering? Who is separate?* Then the experience and perception of duality, the illusion itself, are vehicles that point to truth. Nothing needs to be rejected. If the experience of separation arises, it, too, can drive you deeper into the truth that is before and beyond any idea of separation or union.

❖

Will you speak about the distinction between pain and suffering, and the role of suffering on the path to enlightenment?

Pain is simply pain, sensations in the physical or emotional body. Suffering is in time and has with it some story line about the pain. The story line generates strands and permutations—who caused the pain, why, when, how, and on and on. There can be an enormous investment in the story and, therefore, a reluctance to let it all go. If you were to let it go, it would mean that all those hours, years, and lifetimes with the preoccupation of "What about me?" would be finished. Finished, with no return on the investment. All of the story gets its life force from this resistance to let it go.

When the story of pain is released, pain can be experienced as it is.

How do I let the story go?

Open the mind to experience. Experience whatever comes up without filtering or judging. As the mind is opened, concepts are dropped. Opening the mind to pain, or any other physical, emotional, or mental phenomenon, can reveal what is at the core of all phenomena. Pain, experienced with no story line, reveals Buddha-nature.

Suffering reveals nothing except more story about pain. Suffering is justification, blame, sentimentalizing, and dramatization of pain.

By opening the mind, pain is discovered to be no *thing*. This no-thing that appeared as pain is absolute. It is intelligence, clarity, joy, and peace. The truth of yourself is discovered in the core of pain. Pain is potentially a vehicle for revealing truth. If the story of the pain is followed, the vehicle is overlooked, and then pain is wasted as more investment in unnecessary suffering.

Certainly all of us have experienced pain of one kind or another— emotional, physical, personal, and worldly pain. If you have had the experience of surrendering in the moment that pain arises, not resisting it but actually opening to it, then you have discovered peace in the midst of pain. In this discovery, you are no longer preoccupied with personal suffering.

When you are willing to end your personal suffering, you are willing to experience pain beyond any idea of "your" pain. You are willing to experience your neighbor's pain, your parent's pain, your child's pain, the pain of the whole universe, and in that, there is less denial of pain and less dramatization of pain. Then the thoughts circulating around the avoidance of pain and the acquisition of agents of pleasure (in the hope of some insurance against pain) lose their power. When you are willing to open, you are willing to *be* fully. Then pain is to be bowed to as simply truth appearing as pain, as God appearing as pain.

❖

I know now that I'm not this body, yet I have a problem with migraine headaches, and I still want that pain to go away.

Well, stop wanting it to go away.

I've done that too.

What you have done is to stop wanting the pain to go away so that it would go away!

You're right, but nothing works.

Have you tried letting the pain be?

What I've gotten to now is that I can still be joyful and alive even with a headache. But I still hate the pain. It hurts, and it does kind of get in the way.

Many bodies have conditions that hurt. Some bodies hurt more than other bodies. If you experience hurt totally, you discover what is closer than the body, closer than the hurt. Rest in that. The pain comes, the pain goes, and you rest in that which is closer. Don't struggle any more with trying to do something with pain. Tend the body, but if your body will not be tended with its migraines, rest in what does not come and go. Give up the struggle.

The body will have better days and worse days. This is the nature of bodies. But that which doesn't go away has no judgment of good days and bad days.

Rest in that where there is no judgment. Especially on a bad day for the body, rest in that. Then you will see. Without looking for it, you will see that even pain has beauty. Even that which you hate, at its core, is beauty.

One day you may even thank this gift. You may say, "I am grateful for this gift that has forced me to see in pain what I imagined was some-place else." If you imagine that truth is only present in good physical feeling or good emotional feeling, it is a limited truth.

There was a time when Ramana's body was being eaten by vermin. At some point, maggots and vermin will eat your body also. Before that time arises, discover yourself not to be limited to your body. You are not separate from your body, and you are not limited to it. You can discover immediately, instantly, what is eternal. Not by doing anything but by just being. Discover if there are limits to being.

❖

Pain is a very strong energy, and sometimes it can even feel almost like bliss.

When you know the core of pain, you know the secret of pain. In that instant, you know bliss. There is only the core there. Everything else is imaginary.

❖

I experience chronic pain almost on a daily basis. What do I do when pain comes again and again?

Do you hold the notion that pain shouldn't come again? When this thought is seen and finished, where is the record of pain coming and going?

Awareness is the record.

Does awareness have the judgment "Oh, no, not again"?

I suppose not.

Pain is pain, and in itself, pain is no problem. You have somehow been taught that you have to escape pain. Aversion to pain is deeply embedded in the DNA, in the genetic code. Can you give up what you have been taught about pain?

Then is pain just a thought?

It is a word defining a range of sensation from slightly uncomfortable to horribly intense. For a moment, let's keep the definition. Let the definition be a useful vehicle in the dynamic of pain versus pleasure. To cut this dynamic, *be* pain totally, even for an instant. Be that which you are running from.

Then meeting pain is a skillful means for realizing truth. Isn't that interesting? Your biggest enemy turns out to be your great ally. It has been calling you, calling you, all these years chasing you, no matter what you did. Clearly, there is some message being announced. Hear the message by being the messenger.

The Lakota Indian sun dance creates that experience of renouncing pain.

Renunciation has been practiced in many religious orders, and it often takes the form of self-flagellation. What I am speaking of is different from renunciation. I am not speaking of dramatizing or amping up the pain, and I am not speaking of overcoming the pain as in dissociation.

I am speaking of something more subtle. I am suggesting that you experience pain at its core. I am inviting you to discover what is revealed when physical or psychological pain is not fought or dramatized. When no strategy is followed, you discover what exists at the very core.

You have tortured yourself mentally and emotionally for a long time. Now turn to that tormentor and see who is there.

❖

I had a powerful experience with Papaji two years ago. It was the most beautiful experience I've ever had, but afterward it didn't come again. I tried this way and that way. I also tried not trying, but nothing helped me.

Last year I suffered a lot and felt that the hangover from this enlightenment experience was really too much.

So where does all that leave you?

Here.

Good. This is the place to be. Recognize that all your conclusions about that experience are in the past, and now that recognition is pointing you here. Now be here. Forget about any experience of anything, good or bad.

But I don't want to suffer.

As long as you say "I don't want to suffer," you will suffer.

I don't understand.

When anything, even the deepest, darkest suffering, is experienced as it is, you are freed from the twin illusions of escape and safety. As long as you are unwilling to experience suffering, you will search endlessly for escape and safety, and you will suffer endlessly.

This you must understand, and you eventually will. You have rejected suffering, and you have run from this shadow and that shadow. Finally, you will say, "Well it's not working. I can want to not suffer over and over, and still I am suffering." In wanting to not suffer, your attention is on suffering. In wanting truth, in wanting freedom, in wanting to be here where you are, attention is placed on truth, freedom, and now. By not wanting to lose an experience, you lose it because your attention is placed on holding on to something rather than experiencing what is here.

The nature of all experience is to appear and disappear. Even the best experiences come and go, but the source of all experiences is present always.

For some instant in your meeting with Papaji, somehow any idea of what should be or what was, evaporated. From that instant, an exquisite, sensory byproduct arose, and you became infatuated with the byproduct. It felt very good. When it passed, as all experiences pass, you began to attempt to get it back. You discovered that grasping for the experience didn't work.

The truth is that when your desire is for truth, and you are willing to realize truth, you will open your heart totally to all suffering. You will open to your own personal suffering and the suffering of your spouse, your country, the whole cosmos. This is a conscious opening of the heart. You are making the declaration "I will not run."

Do not open your heart to suffering so that you will not have to suffer. Do not open your heart to suffering so that you can dramatize yourself as a sufferer. Just be willing to be here where you are. When suffering arises, don't run from it, don't cling to it, don't deny it, don't repress it, don't indulge it, and don't act it out. If your mind can direct none of these actions, where is suffering?

This realization is simple beyond belief, but it is not simplistic. All the past complications of your life and everyone's life around you arise in this simplicity. In the willingness to discover, even in suffering, what is at the core, you discover what is beyond and closer than any experience. This discovery is what the words "enlightenment" and "freedom" point to. It is what can never be practiced, learned, or believed, because it is beyond and closer than any concept or idea in the mind.

What has happened to you is very important, but I caution you to not make a foolish conclusion from this experience.

I was merely looking for another way to experience enlightenment again, but without so much suffering.

There will always be another way. You can endlessly think, *I'll find another teacher. I'll find another country. I'll find another spot in nature. I'll find another lover. I'll find another job. I'll have another child. I'll get rid of this body. I'll take another body!* You will think of many, various strategies until finally, just as the Buddha did, you will say, "I will not move from here. I have tried all doctrines, all practices, all modes, and I find them all limited." Perhaps they each helped at a certain stage, but finally you refuse to move; you must be still.

If suffering comes, let suffering come. If suffering comes for a million years, let it come. In the willingness to let suffering come, a most extraordinary discovery reveals itself.

You are free. You are free to suffer endlessly, and you are free to stop. You are free to be here, unmoving, unflinching, neither denying nor indulging. You are free to be here absolutely and to discover the depths of here, the measurelessness of here. You are free to discover that when suffering is truly met and experienced all the way to the core, suffering itself becomes a celebration of freedom. The great, feared demon suffering is realized to be a manifestation of truth.

You must be willing to meet suffering in the dead of night, alone and forsaken in your mind by God, guru, society, and life. Forsaken in the dark of the night, in this era, the *Kali Yuga,* the "dark night." It is your opportunity, in this Dark Age, to meet this. It is the best of times for this meeting.

Once Papaji said, "Even if you have to go to hell to give satsang, you go, because in hell, satsang is appreciated; satsang can be heard."

Call suffering hell. Call suffering by whatever names you have given it. Meet it. Don't flinch; don't move; don't turn your face. You will discover in the core of suffering, pure, empty intelligence. Then you will recognize and embrace everything as that purity. Nothing is excluded—so-called ugly, so-called beautiful, so-called ordinary, or so-called extraordinary. Until then you are just chasing an idea of "better." If you are in satsang, then somehow the grace of Ramana and Ramana's awakening through Papaji has reached you. Somehow, mysterious grace has plucked you out to have these words and this presence revealed to you.

Hear this. It is given to you freely, no credentials asked. Ready or not, it is given to you. You are free to drink of it in unbelievable depth, and you are also free to cast it aside. The guru reveals the flame of the truth of self. Ignition is the guru's gift. That ignition has taken place. What is given is yourself—by yourself and to yourself—your true self.

DIRECT EXPERIENCE
REVEALS SELF

The projecting power of mind produces all bodies of mind—the mental body, emotional body, physical body, and circumstantial body. By perceptive consensus, these "bodies" are accepted as reality. Through self-inquiry—*Who am I?*—the thought *I*, or personal trance of reality conceived in the mental body, is revealed to be nonexistent. It is experienced as real, yet it is realized to be unreal, as a play or a movie is experienced as real, yet realized to be *just* a play or movie.

Now science has also demonstrated that when physical phenomena are investigated very closely, they are revealed to be not as they are normally perceived to be.

Self-inquiry is a spiritual investigation of the *I* that is perceived to be real—in other words, "me" and "my story." Spiritual investigation reveals that any perception of an entity separate from the totality of consciousness is a false perception. Spiritual investigation reveals self as limitless being, in truth unbound by any and all perceptions of bondage.

Circumstances rely on physical, mental, and emotional bodies for their perceived existence. How can circumstances be considered real when their components are recognized to be essentially nonexistent?

Paradoxically, in exquisite irony, by recognizing the essential unreality of what has been perceived as reality, there is a momentous release of deep love and compassion for all that is perceived!

By recognizing your essential nature to be that which is unchanging, the *experience* of life is totally altered. It is not altered by any attempt to alter, but by surrender to that unalterableness at the core of all guises of thought, emotion, and circumstance. It is not altered by the *cultivation* of love and compassion, but by the discovery that what is *revealed* at the core radiates love and compassion. Unimagined, unsentimental love is pulling one deeper into its embrace through every experience.

When the answer to the question *Who am I?* is experienced directly, the truth at the core of all form, whether physical, mental, emotional, or circumstantial, is revealed. The core is eternally present, regardless of body, regardless of experience. The core is the presence of being, radiating pure intelligence and joy of itself.

✧

How do I discover that core of all being?

For direct self-inquiry, do not be distracted by the periphery, the story, the energetic field of phenomena.

Your story about sadness or any phenomenon is based on the experience of your ancestors, your culture, or your personal history. Your story is unreliable because it is based on a conditioned viewpoint.

You know that past conclusions are unreliable because they can change so quickly. The very obvious example of a mirage in the desert. Thinking someone is your friend when they are not your friend, or thinking someone is your enemy when they are not your enemy. Thinking you are brilliant one day, and stupid the next day. Understand that these stories all come from conditioning.

Everyone is searching for what is absolutely reliable. Absolute reliability can be discovered because it exists as the core of any phenomenon, whether body, thought, emotion, or circumstance.

To discover the absolute core of any state, be absolutely still as a state appears or disappears. Be unmoving. When the conditioned tendencies to move away from a state or toward a state arise, relax your mind. Surrender the activity of mind to what is before and after all activity of mind.

Surrender is new for me. As I surrender I find that my sadness is one of the things I hold on to most tightly. I've practiced sadness for a long time, and I'm afraid to leave it behind. I'm afraid, as I surrender, that I might not have that sadness to give import and meaning to me and my life.

That's right. You won't.

I'll miss it.

Are you sure? I don't believe that you will.

It takes some courage to leave it behind.

It takes the courage to be free. It takes the courage to leave behind what was known, which is how you have defined yourself and how you have defended that definition. About your sadness, you might have believed, *Ah, this is deep. This is not trivial.*

The sadness isn't deep?

No, and if you are willing to directly experience the sadness, you will discover that the sadness is not even sadness! Leave behind the story of sadness. When sadness appears, fully experience it. Do not act it out. Do not discharge it. Do not repress it. Do not deny it. Take none of those usual actions, and simply, without commentary, directly experience sadness.

Please, bring some sadness here and we will examine it. Can you imagine something that makes you sad?

I have some sadness.

Good. Just let it grow for a minute.

I'm good at it. I've been worshipping it.

Yes, I understand. Now we want to see what it is that you have so faithfully worshipped. While you are sitting here, stop all of the story line about sadness, and tell me, where is it? Do you feel it somewhere?

I have trouble finding it without the story.

Yes! But maybe it is hidden somewhere in the subconscious, where the story is not even verbalized. It has been told so long that maybe it is embedded on a cellular level or experienced as some weight. Are you aware of that?

Yes.

Now, with your consciousness devoid of commentary, go into the core of sadness. Don't try to get rid of sadness. Just experience what exists at the core.

It makes me laugh.

It makes you laugh! Now isn't that interesting? Are you sure?

It makes me laugh.

Good. This is the proper use of sadness. Do you understand now?

I know it, but I don't understand it.

I am pointing you toward direct experience. Most people think that if they are feeling an emotion, they are directly experiencing it. Usually, feeling sadness is actually hovering around the drama of sadness, the story of sadness. Without any mental action taken to deny, discharge, or indulge, plunge directly, totally, into the core of sadness or *anything,* and tell me what is revealed.

Direct experience is great good news. It is the promise of all the Buddhas. It is the promise of Christ. It is the promise of everyone who has ever directly experienced emotional phenomena. At the core of every supposed emotion or event or physical manifestation is . . . well, you experience it and tell me, what is at the core? I tell you all the time.

❖

I want to understand the difference between the emotional pain that is and the pain that is unnecessary.

Whatever the pain, be willing to experience it directly, completely, absolutely, holding nothing back. Now, in this experience, speak from this.

It is the fear of a small child being hurt again.

That child is gone. Don't believe that there is some little child walking around in your chest. The inner-child image can be useful at a certain stage, but remember, it is only an image. It is all in the mind. Obviously, it is important to release any denial of painful, childhood experiences, but if you just substitute that denial with a belief in the reality of a little child imprisoned inside you, then you continue to wander in illusion and attempt to protect what is nonexistent. Release her. Let her be free. True release comes from the willingness to experience pain completely, absolutely, right now.

You are not a little child. You are not even a woman or a man. Drop that story, too. Be as you are, not knowing or imagining what that is.

The mental tendency is to get into some story about a feeling. First a memory arises, and then either a recoiling from that memory or a kind of sentimental wallowing in that memory, right?

Yes.

All of that is not necessary.

I've been seeing the obsession so strongly lately.

Wonderful. Seeing obsessive suffering means you are ready. Obsessive thinking is an avoidance of the direct experience of what you fear. If you are still avoiding hurt from some earlier time in this lifestream, face that hurt now.

I am right here with you. All the angelic beings of all the realms are always with you whenever you have a sincere desire to stop and discover the truth of what *really* is. All helpers known and unknown are right here with you because they are all your own self, recognizing itself.

Now, without the story, directly experience the core of hurt.

How many times have I been through this? How many people know this about me, "The Sufferer"?

"You, The Sufferer" is the story. That story is either being wallowed in or rejected. Let go of that story you believe to be real. Drop the "sufferer," drop the "me," and tell me what is there, *really* .

I see having hoped and suffered, risen and fallen, a million times.

You haven't dropped the story yet. I am not speaking about rising and falling, inflation and deflation. I am speaking of directly experiencing this particular so-called entity, "The Hurt One." Where is this "sufferer"? What is it? When you face it, without the story about it, can you find it?

It feels like a shell, like an armoring.

From the core of this feeling, tell me what is the *reality* of the shell, of the armor.

In order to experience anything directly, you must stop thinking about it. Otherwise, it continues as an indirect experience, which is only supported by thought, commentary, evaluation, speculation, etc.

What I know is that I feel hurt. It's gripping, like a holding on.

Experience the hurt. Go deeper into the center of it. Not to get rid of the hurt. There is no need to get rid of it. There is no need to overcome it. There is no need even to be finished with it. Simply investigate, what *is* it?

Well, it has been—

We are not speaking about "has been." We are speaking about right now. Be willing to be that hurt so that the hurt is total, and there is no hope of ever escaping the hurt.

I feel the shame of so many people having wanted to see me better, finally.

This is a sidetrack. This is a sentimental story.

It's connected to the center.

This story is a strategy to avoid the center. Surrender to direct experience. Let yourself be finally, absolutely, totally hurt.

Great traditions have arisen in different times all over the planet. In the West, one of these is the psychological tradition. It has many uses, and it has many abuses. Psychology can take you, as all traditions can take you, to the edge. From there, you must leave it behind, unless you want to continually loop through images and thoughts about the past. Pay your respects to the psychological tradition. It has served you well. Now, just for an instant, leave it behind.

I feel the hurt as some denial.

Denial takes many forms, and in your particular story it has taken the form of "Poor Me." There may be horrible experiences around that story. I am not denying your experiences of suffering. I am saying that if you will meet the hurt rather than continue telling the story about it, you will find the most unbelievable, unimagined revelation alive in the core of hurt. This revelation is also present in the core of fear and all other modes of suffering. It is in the core of everything.

There's great feeling in the hurt. There's—

Stop. This is a mental trap again, entitled "Great Feeling and the Great Love Affair with Great Feeling." You may think that feeling is very deep, but the vastness revealed through direct experience is inconceivable. It is revealed in the willingness to not get caught up in an old familiar relationship with feeling. I am not saying to deny feeling. There is nothing wrong with feeling. Just don't set up another story around it.

The dilemma is in the identification of yourself as a feeling person, as a hurt person, as a wounded child. You are not that, and the only way you can recognize fully and completely that you are not that, is to be that, to not resist or run from the hurt—to not run from the fear that this wounded child will always be there, will always be wounded, and to not wallow in the story of the wounded child. Turn and see, *what* is this wound, *where* is it—*who* is wounded?

I have someone who says to me all the time, "You could let go of it in one instant."

You *can* let it go in an instant. You don't need to think another thought about it. That is the truth. There is no more discussion needed. How many times have you replayed it? How many times have you squeezed it and milked it?

But that letting go in an instant seems other than going into it.

It is the same. All you are letting go of is the story, and when you let go of the story, you discover the true nature of this wound. You discover directly, firsthand, the true nature not only of this wound but of all phenomena.

When I go into the hurt and the fear, I really feel they come from not knowing who I am.

Now you have come up with a theory about hurt and fear. I am not interested in theories at this moment. You must leave all theories behind about why this hurt is or what this hurt is. Just experience hurt itself. Discover what exists in the core of it.

There! In that instant, you were realizing it. Then there was some reincarnation of the story around it. I know what is discovered is unbelievable. I appreciate that. What I am speaking of cannot be believed. It is not in any belief system. It is not mapped. Speak from that recognition.

In my experience, I would call it an openness or acceptance of pain.

When you accept and open to pain, what is pain? What is revealed to be at the core?

Oneness.

When you accept or meet oneness, what is there?

Nothingness.

And when you meet nothingness? Don't even make a story of nothingness.

I'm not contacting the pain now.

This *I* itself that is not contacting the pain, *what* is that, *where* is that—*who* is that?

I don't know.

Well, find it. Where is this *I*? You made the statement "I am not contacting the pain." Just roll that statement back: pain . . . not . . . contacting . . . am . . . I.

What is the experience of this instant when there is no speculation, no theory, no explanation, and no conclusion?

Happiness.

Yes! Discovered in an instant. Discovered not by reaching for happiness or running from unhappiness.

There is joy!

Yes, naturally! Now directly experience happiness. Go deeper. To "go deeper" really means to not follow any story, any commentary.

The great secret discovered when you directly experience the so-called negative emotions—which may seem endless, limitless—is that not only are they not limitless, they are not even really there. What a discovery! Then of course bliss arises, and there may be fear to experience bliss because you want it to really be there. When you directly experience bliss, which does not mean holding on to it and does not mean rejecting it, you discover the bliss that is limitlessness. It does not go away. This is your true nature. The rest is false nature, imitation of nature, perceived nature.

Direct experience is a penetration *through* what has been imitated, believed, or perceived, to what is true. This is the good news of awakening.

⬦

When I think of raising my hand, fear arises. In the last satsang, it was just really immense. I went to the fear and stayed with it, and it just hovered there. It didn't go away, and I don't think I really know what's beneath it, what's at the core of it.

That's right. You have yet to directly experience it. You are hovering around it. Even if you say "I am with it," there is still "me" and "my fear." "I see it. I feel it. I sense it." Fear is then experienced as an object. What I am suggesting is that you leave this *I* behind, and then there is only this *thing* called fear. See what it really is when there is no one who has it.

This is effortless. I am not saying to push yourself into it. I am not talking about getting rid of fear. I am not interested in your getting rid of fear. Attempting to get rid of is a very old strategy, and it doesn't work. I am talking about realizing the truth of what fear is, sadness is, despair is, or what any *thing* is.

There is no need to get rid of anything. Once you recognize the truth of everything, what is there to get rid of?

◈

I don't want to feel this numbness that I feel, this lifelessness.

In your resistance to numbness, isn't numbness perpetuated? This is where you have to be wise now. Feel numb and lifeless whether you want to or not. Not wanting to feel it hasn't worked. Making war on what we don't like hasn't worked, has it? Attacking it, trying to drive it away hasn't worked. Surely there is enough wisdom to see that.

I feel on the one hand I invite it, and on the other hand I don't. I know that the point is to really feel it, but I'm so afraid of it.

Be the fear. Move out of intellectual understanding. Move out of the intellectual speculation of what the outcome will be. Be willing to just be here, and if resistance is here, it too is welcome. This is the natural course of wisdom.

Trust that which keeps you from bolting, running away, leaving. It is bigger than the resistance, and it has no problem with the resistance. Someone told you that you shouldn't be resistant. Someone told you that it is bad to be resistant. Forget that. Resistance has a right to be. Let it have a right to be, and then see. See how happy resistance is to be liberated.

I think there's a lot of juice in resistance.

Find the resistance. You cannot find it by thinking about it. You have thought about it, analyzed it, speculated on it, and made many conclusions. Finally experience it firsthand. You have tried resisting it, running from it, denying it, and numbing out around it. Don't try anything, and see what is there.

That is all I am ever saying in satsang. Don't try anything, and see what doesn't need trying to be. See what already is.

❖

Ever since the first time I saw you on video, I've been hopelessly lost. I feel like I've come to the end of my rope.

Wonderful! When you are at the end of the rope, you have to throw the rope away. Then you know for certain that the rope was a figment of your imagination.

I don't know how to throw the rope away.

Simply stop holding on. If you are really, hopelessly lost, then instantly you are found. It is only when you can give up the last shred of hope of being found that you can recognize, *I am here.*

Who is lost?

No one. I mean, there is only . . . I can't say it.

Well, you just did. There is no lost *I.* This presupposed lost *I* is false.

You feel lost, and you have thoughts of being lost, or conclusions of being "at the end of your rope," but when you check, when you turn toward the *I* who is lost, you can find no one lost.

Yes, it's true. But more and more I experience being lost, and I just feel ever more desperate.

Find *who* is feeling desperate. The feeling of desperation continues only because you assume that you are, in fact, something that the feeling is hooked on to. You don't like the feeling. It doesn't feel good. There are experiences of hurt, suffering, and being lost.

The experience of separation can be a terrible experience. But in any moment, you can check *who* is lost. Find the *I* that you imagine to be lost, and shout out the truth.

Well, I can say the truth, but it doesn't—

Then speak the truth. You spend so much time saying the lie. We are so totally conditioned and supported in saying the lie. At least once, say the truth.

I am free . . . but it feels like—

Find the *I* who is free. Then you will be done with both "lost" and "free." Then you will recognize that feelings and states come and go in the truth of *I* that cannot be found in any place or absent from any place. If you cling to "I am free," then every time the feeling "I am lost" appears, you will fall into self-doubt.

"I am free" is good medicine for "I am lost." Now let them both be finished. Then you can just say, "I AM."

It just sounds too much like an affirmation: "I am free, I am free, I am free."

Yes. That is exactly what I just said. You are free.

You have lived in denial saying, "I am lost. I am lost. I am lost." Then a beautiful affirmation arises: "I am free. I am free." Oh, what a feeling! Now bring them together. *Who* is lost? *Who* is free? Can you find the one who is lost? Can you find the one who is free?

There is only . . . (silence)

Yes, it's very good that you cannot even attempt to put that into a word.

Direct self-inquiry is the gift of Ramana. It cuts through all denial and all affirmation.

If you cry out, "I am not enlightened," Ramana asks, "*Who* is not enlightened?" If you cry out, "I am enlightened," Ramana asks, "*Who* is enlightened?" There, you will find no *thing* at all, free of both bondage and enlightenment, free of whatever feeling arises. Free of whatever thought passes through. Free. It is a freedom that has nothing to do with bondage. Only relative freedom has to do with bondage. Absolute freedom is untouched by relative freedom or relative bondage, and you are that.

❖

The past two weeks have been a real whirlwind of emotions. I've been totally confused. Everything has just hit me in the face, and it's ridiculous. Sometimes I'm crying. Sometimes I'm laughing. Everything just seems so intense in the moment.

In this moment?

It's beautiful in this moment.

Good. Let's not forget that, please. It is very easy to focus on the past—"I was crying. I was moaning. I was confused." I am not saying to blank out on the past. Obviously, you can learn from the past. Primarily, you learn that it passed. You learn that even in the midst of confusion, suffering, or tears, there was a presence that did not pass, and it is present now and every moment.

It's exactly the same presence, only confusion's still there.

Yes, the presence is the same. The presence is continual. This is the truth, and the continuance of presence must be realized. Presence is permanent. Experiences of joy or experiences of unhappiness are overlaid on that presence. Experiences of confusion or experiences of clarity are overlaid on pure presence. Presence is not an experience. It is bigger than the mind. It is bigger than the emotions. It is bigger than the circumstances. Presence is always present. About this, there can be no confusion.

Let confusion come to partake of this presence. Let the confusion of aeons come into this presence. Welcome confusion to satsang. Once you recognize that presence is here and that it's continual, this is the announcement: "Satsang is being given here." This announcement goes out on the airwaves, and it attracts confusion, fear, and doubt.

It's a big magnet.

Yes. When you recognize that you are presence, confusion, fear, and doubt are set free.

What satsang points to is the perpetual presence of truth. Whenever satsang reveals itself, it opens the door to what must be liberated. It is not you that must be liberated. You are already inherently liberated. It is only the ideas you have imposed on yourself that must be set free.

I still feel that I'd like to get rid of my fear.

Fear does not need to be gotten rid of, just simply investigated.

The experience of fear is the experience of some kind of force, isn't it? Usually, there are all kinds of strategies to deal with this force, to either be strong in the face of fear or try to run from it. But no strategy works because fear is still believed to be some entity, some power. Eventually, a moment arises when you say, "Okay, I am not moving. Come in, fear. Who are you? What are you?"

In this moment, as you sit here, are you aware of fear?

At this moment, I am in control of fear.

Then invite some.

I can if I see a tiger right here or something.

A tiger in the room elicits an instinctual body fear, and this is appropriate. I am not saying to get rid of instinctive fear. If a bus is swerving down the road toward you and there is a sense of fear, then yes, listen to that. There is nothing wrong with that. When fear is appropriate, it is your servant. I am speaking of psychological fears that are inappropriate—recurring inner nightmares, recurring mental torment. Fear that runs your life is inappropriate.

Inappropriate fear is a psychic force that is given great power by the mind in the attempt to run from it or to overcome it. There comes a certain point in the dark night where finally you must know what the reality of this fear is that seems to have you by the throat. When the nightmare is directly examined, the tiger is discovered to have no substance. It is just the workings of the mind.

There's great strength in fear.

Yes, you experience enormous strength in fear. I am not making light of the strength of illusion. Start with the first intimation of fear, when it is just a small ghost. Fear only accumulates strength as you put your mental powers into avoiding it, struggling with it, and fearing it.

The beginning is always the easiest moment. Ask yourself, *What is this really? Who is fearing what?* This kind of questioning is itself the opening. Questioning fear demonstrates a willingness to not run from it.

I know fear seems to have enormous power, but this is only the power that you have given it. Fear is nothing without that power. In the direct experience of fear, its power is finished.

It is the same with any suffering, whether despair, anger, or any of the other so-called negative emotions that entangle the mind. Meet any emotion at its beginning. Neither express it nor indulge it. Simply meet it in stillness.

You may feel like you are being shaken and torn apart, but in the willingness to remain still, you see that it is only the defenses of the mind that get shaken. You will recognize that in the core of fear is limitless, joyful intelligence. It is not usually recognized in the periphery because there is so much mind activity, but when you sink right into the core, true freedom is revealed.

Your realization through small fears will encourage you to meet bigger fears. Eventually, you will face the final fear. The fear that it is possible to not exist—the fear of death. Fear of death is based on the belief that you are limited to your body. You know very well that it is possible for the body to not exist. Death of the body moves closer and closer every moment. When you are willing to face the fear of nonexistence, you discover what existence is. You discover *who* existence is. You discover true self. Then fear, suffering, and even death are your allies.

Hinduism depicts Shiva with a cobra around his neck. In this image the most dreaded fear is portrayed as the ally. May your fear be revealed as your ally, your call to what is both forever beyond fear and forever the truth at the core of fear.

✧

When I feel that I'm not in control, I get panic-stricken.

I am not counseling you to overcome panic. It doesn't need to be overcome. I am directing you to discover what is in the core of the panic. I am directing you right into the center of what you are fearing. In order to experience the core, simply stop all definition and evaluation.

Where are you experiencing this panic? Where is it located?

In the body.

Is it radiating? Where is the source of it?

I feel rigid.

Like frozen? Like your body is frozen rigid?

Yes.

Psychological fear is habitually avoided. It is possible to face it fully and completely with your mind open. If you attempt to face fear, dragging along all your concepts of what you think it might mean, then there is no possibility of a true meeting. Continue to open your mind. Open your mind in the center of that rigidity, that frozenness, that panic, and tell me what is discovered.

First I felt this frozenness, and then nothing. But it's an alive nothing. I feel free.

Excellent! Experience this nothingness without any name for it. Fall into the center of that. If there is any struggle, let it go. If there is any story line, put the story aside. Relax into this that you call nothing. See if it has any boundaries. See if you can make a separation between who you are and nothingness. If you are successful in making some separation between who you are and nothingness, see if the separation exists in reality or only in the imagination.

❖

I've had an experience like you were just talking about. I was in my bedroom one night, feeling uncomfortable. Something was wrong, and I'd spent a lifetime running away from what was uncomfortable. At a certain point I just saw it to be nothing, and then it was wonderful. After that I almost wished these bad feelings would come again.

Bad feelings and good feelings are all potential vehicles for sublime discovery. A secret is discovered in that instant of ceasing all activity to suppress, cover, deny, run away from, overcome, follow, or indulge. All activity of the mind ceases in the instant of direct experience.

This secret cannot be taught. It can only be discovered. There is no way to put it into words. All words fall short. What a surprise is discovered in the willingness, just once, to stop all mental activity and *be*. Whether in comfort or discomfort, the same discovery is made—in fear, boredom, frozenness, despair, bliss, joy, any experience. The whole play of perceptions and emotions, whether uncomfortable or not, becomes a play that serves to deepen revelation. Nothing has to be overcome, just simply met.

This is self-inquiry, and self-inquiry is endless. Limitless consciousness is present in all thoughts, forms, emotions, or experiences. Truth is present in everything, in all phenomena. That realization does not change. It only deepens in its changelessness. Experiences change. States change. Let them change. If you attempt to cling to a particular state, you will overlook what is present regardless of state.

Not wanting to experience something, or wanting to keep a particular experience, creates the illusion of bondage. Until you are willing to experience anything, you will experience bondage, because there will always be some mental activity around the desire to escape or the desire to indulge. If you are willing to experience anything, you discover that the experience of bondage is in fact illusion. The glue that holds this illusion together is the mental activity of escape or indulgence.

❖

Direct experience is so simple that it is easily overlooked. In the course of any lifestream, there have been many opportunities to face fear. There have been many times of repressing it, acting it out, or being haunted by it. Any activity that feeds the belief that fear is a real entity, that it will swallow you, destroy you, drive you mad, or annihilate you, is only a story about fear.

I am telling you a profound yet simple truth. If you stop all mental running away from or running toward, if you will be absolutely still, then direct experience *is*. In direct experience, you discover the emptiness of all phenomena. This emptiness is full, impersonal consciousness, and it is bliss. Mental activity is "thinking," what Papaji calls "chewing on bones from the graveyard." Stop chewing on these old bones, searching for some nectar. Put these bones aside.

Fear may arise again. If it arises again, there is an even deeper opportunity. There may appear to be layer upon layer of negative emotion. Directly experiencing layer upon layer reveals illusions mentally carried forth since the beginning of time. Illusion discovered to be illusion reveals true self.

In the instant of stopping and experiencing the emptiness in all phenomena for what it is, you discover the core of everything to be the eternal truth of who you are.

This is the greatest news. You are everywhere, in everything, waiting to be found, calling to be found. Let yourself be found.

LIBERATING ANGER

Gangaji, I have heard certain spiritual traditions say that anger is something that disturbs the mind and is a defilement. I don't understand this.

When I see something that, in my eyes, isn't right, anger comes out spontaneously. In that moment, I feel I have to say something, and I feel fine about that.

Anger is spoken about as a defilement or an obstruction because of the bondage experienced through the mental relationship with anger. Anger as an obsessive pattern of mind is an entanglement. Anger that must be either obsessively expressed or obsessively denied is mind-generated and mind-perpetuated, and yes, this is an obstruction.

Natural anger can be a great cyclone that washes clean, such as the anger a mother feels when she sees something harmful happening to her child. Natural anger can be a great purifying force not separate from compassion.

What must be examined is your relationship with anger. Is there some pattern of fearing it or using it to avoid feeling hurt, sad, or despairing? Anger, like any so-called negative emotion, must be met. This meeting naturally dissolves the protective relationship, and then you will see you needn't act as a slave to anger.

Many religious teachings are given as codes of conduct. Hearing that anger is an obstruction gets interpreted as an instruction to suppress it. Habitual suppression only turns anger into numbness or rigidity. The goal of true spirituality is freedom. In freedom there is power, softness, and welcoming, so that even the demon anger is liberated. When anger is liberated, it serves the truth. When it is bound by personal identification, it serves the ego.

Look into the deepest meaning of any teaching. Teachings are first given to allow people to gather in the same enclosed space. A certain level of socialization is required; otherwise, there is just wildness of expression, and horrible problems are created. There is no error in this. It is not a mistake to take on certain conditioning that allows us to put our animal instincts aside so that we can come together and hear the news of this precious treasure.

As you leave your shoes outside the door, you leave your normal mode of expression outside the door so that perhaps you can receive what is being offered. If you stop with this level of understanding, then leaving shoes outside the door becomes a practice, and you are always leaving your shoes somewhere, or always repressing some emotion as if that is where the truth lies. This kind of conditioning is only a means; so don't get stuck in the means. There is the possibility of hearing what is deeper than either repression or expression.

Considerations about anger are particularly tricky because anger does not facilitate harmony in groups or family gatherings. There can be no harmony if everybody is always expressing their anger. Always repressing anger does not work either. It makes society work better as a machine, and it allows people to gather, but the gathering is sterile and bound by a law of repression. It is possible to meet anger directly and discover what is at the core of anger. In this meeting, you can recognize true harmony, which is the core of your true nature, deeper than your human animal nature.

I do not mean to meet anger in analysis, although that may be appropriate at a certain stage. I am speaking about simply meeting anger—not denying it, not expressing it, but simply meeting it. In a true meeting, you discover what all teachings have promised. You discover that there is nothing separate from God. There is nothing excluded from the Absolute. Your physical body is not excluded from that. Your mindstream is not excluded from that. Your emotional body is not excluded from that. With this realization, you can begin to hear God speak itself in all forms.

Meet whatever anger is inside you now. Then your life is in service to that which is revealed in that meeting. Your whole life is realized to be an expression of self meeting itself everywhere. Then whatever mood or weather pattern appears, it is quite miraculously and mysteriously in service to truth.

❖

The other night when I came to satsang, I was experiencing a lot of rage. I hadn't been acting it out, but I still got caught in the idea that I had to do something about it, so it became more and more of a congestion.

When you experienced the rage and the congestion and the sense that you had to do something with it, was there a shift?

The shift was in sitting here and being reminded that I am not the rage or the issues. Previously I had gotten to the point where I felt that I had to resolve the rage before I could be free of it. Being here in satsang, I was able to have the rage and experience freedom at the same time.

You didn't have to repress it, and you didn't have to act it out. You did not have to do anything with it.

Exactly.

Because you realized it was not the determinant of who you are.

Yes. What I was realizing today is that the emotional being also needs tending, just like we have to clean the house and tend our body.

How, did you discover, can you best tend the emotional body?

By not identifying with it.

Excellent. This is emotional liberation. You are already free. Now you are speaking of liberating ideas and concepts, whether they are in the physical body, the emotional body, or the mental body. You directly discovered that by not touching any story about the rage, you were freed of the impulse to do something with it. Then naturally, as you say, rage is free to move, free to finish, free to resolve itself. It does not need picking at and dissecting.

By realizing who you are, everything is tended. The world is tended. I do not mean tended so that you can drift into complacency where you once again ignore or deny emotions. Realization is in the present. It is not something in the past. If you relegate it to the past and then rage arises, the same pattern will reincarnate.

In every moment, you have the absolute freedom to discover yourself as freedom. In that discovery, everything is tended. Then the mind is a conduit for revelation. Insights around rage, hurt, and fear will arise naturally.

What did you mean when you spoke about "not touching" any story?

I mean to not grasp for a story line that justifies the emotion or reject the emotion with a story line that condemns it. Without grasping or rejecting, there is no work for the ego. When rage arose in you, there was a tendency to want to do something with it, even if that meant to just sit on it or endure it. If you are willing for rage to arise, and you neither do anything to drive it away nor act it out, you neither repress it nor express it, then you see in an instant what is deeper. Either you will see a deeper emotion or you will see into the depth of being.

The mind is really tricky.

Expose the trickery of the mind. The mind can be very subtle. The challenge is in being attentive to this very subtle tendency to move into mental activity. For instance, if the emotion arising had been bliss, the tendency might have been to try to keep it. Attempting to keep bliss doesn't work of course. If you simply let bliss be, with no story line attached to it, the great good news is that bliss dissolves into deeper bliss, which finally is beyond definition.

This is the good news about both negative and positive emotions. The negative emotions are limited. Their lifetime is based on past mental relationships. Whether they are your mother's, your society's, or your own, all past patterns of relating to negative emotions cause present and future patterns to arise. The true emotions of bliss and joy are causeless and limitless.

This is extraordinary news! If you are willing to neither grasp nor reject bliss, and you are willing to neither grasp nor reject rage, you will discover the limitlessness joy of your true nature. When the history is dropped, the emotion is finished, and you are headed in the direction of the experience of the truth of your being.

Dropping the story exposes the trickery. It is a trick we have played on ourselves for a long, long time. Be willing to finish the trick.

Can I go a step further?

Oh yes, please.

I have the tendency to make an effort to be present.

In the moment of being aware of effort, relax. Following thoughts of rejecting or grasping only perpetuates the investment in effort, and you know these thoughts very well. They are not fresh, original thoughts. They are not insights and revelations. They are old, worn-out thoughts. You know them by the sense in your body. You know them by the contraction or the sanctimoniousness that follows these thoughts. You know the story line very well, so don't touch it. If you do not touch it, these thoughts cannot continue. It is so simple.

It's very challenging.

Simplicity is only challenging because we are conditioned to effort, work, do, and achieve. Regarding the spiritual search, what we are working at achieving is to arrive where we already are! You have experienced this simplicity. It is always present in its limitless vastness. It is already here in the joy of itself, in the peace of itself, in the perfection of itself.

The exposure of the trickery is simply the exposure of an apparent veil caused by following thoughts like *I have to do something with rage.*

Yes, because before I know it, I'm in the game again.

Now you know how to play the game, so play it well. Play it deeply. Play it ruthlessly, honestly, effortlessly. Real playing is vigilance. When it is effortless, it plays itself.

Let the challenges come! They are exhilarating! You will be thrown to the mat, and thrown to the mat, and thrown to the mat. Pretty soon you will cease taking the emotion personally. You will stop the mind activity.

I am not speaking of withdrawal from life, or going into a dissociated state, or stopping the play. *Play fully.* To play fully, stop your personal identification. Stop imagining that you are a particular player. You are, in totality, the player, the played, and the play itself.

To be vigilant means to give up my process of thought and counter-thought. What a challenge. Effortless being is the simplest, yet the deepest, challenge of a lifetime. I am ready. Thank you.

◈

I have found that anger is a covering for despair. Are you saying that I should just feel the despair?

Yes, stop running from it. Dive into the core of it. You know you have not surrendered when despair lasts in duration. You may spend a night in despair, or a day in despair, but the moment the struggle against despair stops, where is despair? It is the struggle with despair or the acting out of despair that gives despair its life. Your imagination is what keeps the struggle going.

Mental wards are filled with people who are struggling against emotions, either suppressing emotions or dramatizing emotions. The psychotic experience is of fragmentation, which is very different from dissolution. In psychosis, the ego is experienced as being fragmented into multiple parts. I am not recommending fragmentation! I am speaking about the possibility of the dissolution of the false *I*. Ego means false *I*.

At the gate of despair, despair appears endless, and all neurotic impulses arise to avoid being consumed by it. The psychotic impulse is to act out despair in some way such as suicide.

Is despair limitless?

The discovery is that the despair is, at most, limited. If you dive into the core of despair, you discover no despair at all. What is limitless is peace, silence, joy. If you dive into peace, it doesn't dissolve. Isn't that amazing? Peace does not dissolve. Your idea of who you are dissolves, and you are revealed as peace. You are silence, you are joy, and you are fathomless, endless, limitlessness.

It is no good just to hear me say it, though. This is something you must directly experience for yourself.

❖

I can meet the sadness about the anger, especially sitting here with you, but in meeting anger itself, I feel like a mouse meeting a tiger.

Yes, and the impulse arises to take some action to defend the mouse or to run into your little hole and hide.

Do not hide from anger. Neither take a stance with anger, either by expressing it or by discharging it. Then the true nature of anger has an opportunity to be revealed.

I do not have anything against anger. I am not saying you should live your life never expressing anger, never shouting. What kind of life is that? Anger can be quite beautiful, unless it is the guard dog that keeps you from experiencing patterns of hurt and fear or the basic vulnerability of being human.

Usually anger is presupposed to be a force that will devour you. Be willing to be immovable. Be willing to be devoured by this fire. Willingness to be devoured means that you are not ignoring it, or using it for some egocentric purpose, or trying to get rid of it.

I let the anger happen when it happens, but I still don't get it. I remember you said, "Stop, just stop." Well, if I try to do that, it gets much worse.

If you have you been sitting on a storehouse of anger, it's good that you are seeing it more deeply than an easily justifiable response.

It feels like I am going to physically explode. You were speaking the other day of the possibility of some certain personality traits being in our genes, in our DNA. That's just what it feels like. My father got angry in exactly the same way.

I am not speaking about *getting* angry. I am not speaking about something needing to be *done* with anger. I am speaking about *directly experiencing* anger. Direct experience is not about *getting* angry. Getting angry indicates that you still have some story about the anger, either that it should be there or that it should not be there. If you think that anger should not be there, you expend energy trying to get rid of it. If you think that you need to justify anger, you expend energy trying to express it.

I am speaking about being devoured by stillness, a stillness that can penetrate the core of any anger attack. In this moment of stillness, in the eye of the emotional hurricane, you put an end to the anger karma for yourself, your father, and all that has been passed on to you, accumulated, and believed to be real.

Surrender. Be crucified on the cross of anger. To be crucified, you cannot move. You are tied up, so you cannot lash out at anyone, not even yourself. You are in a very awkward position, so you cannot go to sleep or ignore the anger. You cannot pretend that it is not happening. You can make no movement to "deal" with the idea that anger is so big it will explode you.

Some people fear the anger itself. For others, it may be fear of insanity or going berserk. Ironically, out of following the fear that one might go berserk, one usually expresses anger in either covertly or overtly insane ways. People who are in psychotic wards either are desperately attempting to not go berserk or are caught in the grip of what gets called "expression."

At a certain point you say, as the Buddha said, "I will not be moved. If I explode, so be it. If this is the end of my form through some kind of spontaneous combustion, so be it. If all the negative forces of my whole lineage come in and tear me apart, so be it."

In immovability, you will see the truth of anger, and you will be able to give up the old destructive game. Getting off the wheel of samsara means to give up the game. Giving up the game is possible by being willing to meet whatever arises without moving.

In the midst of anger, I have no awareness of eternal, unmoving truth. Although I feel it while sitting here with you, that quiet doesn't seem to be available for me when I'm angry.

Then you are not in the center of the anger. You are attending to the periphery by maintaining some story about the anger. In the maintenance of the story, all you can relate to is the story. The story is held together by mental activity. Drop the story. It takes some degree of effort to continue the story. Give up being right. Give up being wrong. Give up being the victim. Give up being the aggressor. Give up everything your parents did to you, your lover did to you, and the world did to you. Give up everything you did to your parents, you did to your lover, and you did to the world. Give it all up. Give up the world.

This is not a usual moment! Nor is it normal. What is normal is to be in a kind of functioning neurosis, sometimes controlling the anger, sometimes repressing the anger, sometimes discharging the anger, sometimes expressing the anger.

I am not saying that these mental activities are wrong. There is a time and place for them all. I am saying that, by imagining these strategies to be the limit of what is available, a treasure remains undiscovered. The only way possible to penetrate to the core of anger is to leave behind every idea about anger. To penetrate to the core of any phenomenon, you must give up every idea about that phenomenon and the one who is penetrating.

To penetrate the ocean, to penetrate the sunset, to penetrate what is called love, to penetrate anything, you have to release your world of concepts. Before penetration, there is a story about an experience or about a phenomenon. In this case, anger. Anger can have enormous charge to it, along with an enormous investment in the story that holds the charge together. Maybe it is a genetic story. Maybe it doesn't even have words to it.

With anger comes the impulse to move. Maybe it's a powerful, physical instinct, but what is deeper and more powerful than any instinct? This is what must be discovered for any lasting happiness.

What must be cut is the identification that the anger is more powerful than that which it arises in. You are that in which all phenomena arise. When you discover you are that, phenomena are just phenomena, and you realize that whatever their display, they are limited in duration and power.

Discover what has always been. Before that discovery, your attention is fixated on your personal life, its personal anger, and its personal joys. There is no need to settle for that. A vast sky of being is inviting you to meet it. In order to enter, turn your attention away from this one little wisp of cloud called "me and my anger." In order to shift your attention away from that, penetrate through it to the source. Penetrate to the beginning, not to the initial event of anger but to the source of all events, all display, all emotions.

If you've played in the waves at the ocean, you know that the secret is to dive right through them. At first, you may try running from them, because you imagine they have the power to keep you out of the depths of the ocean. Then one day you see someone who has made it into the depths, and you ask, "How did you get there?"

"Through the wave!"

"But I can't! It will destroy me!"

"Just dive right through and see."

Be willing to be swallowed by the ocean of being. Face the fear of destruction. Of course the bigger the wave, the deeper you must dive. The more you dive, the deeper you can dive, and the less power the waves have in your life. In this willingness, the egocentric activity of mind has no power. A life truly lived is not fixated on preservation. In fact, the prayer is that everything that *can* be destroyed be revealed as destroyed. When everything is destroyed, what is beyond destruction is self-apparent.

I am not saying willingness is usual or known or easy to do. It is beyond easy or difficult. It is impossible to do. Willingness is the absolute ease present when you do not "do." Our training is to do something, and that is where your trouble is. You want to figure out how to do it. If you can figure out how to do it, then when it comes up and bothers you again, you know how to get rid of it.

This is no good! You have to first discover what *it* is. When you discover that the wave is, in fact, never separate from the ocean, why do you need to get rid of it? When you no longer have to get rid of anger, it is not as you have previously experienced it. It is not as you have believed it to be, and you are not as you have known yourself to be.

Already, I can see you sense the relief. Realization cannot be done. If you *really* hear this, then you will stop trying to do anything to be realized. What a relief! Realization is not about learning some task. Tasks can be learned and done. Lessons can be learned, languages can be learned, skills can be learned. Freedom is not a skill to be learned. You cannot learn who you are. You cannot do who you are. You cannot practice who you are. It is impossible. You can only be who you are.

I still want to ask you and Papaji and Ramana for help with the anger.

Help surrounds you. You do not even need to ask anymore. Just check and see if it is there. You have asked deeply, truly, with your whole heart, and help has been promised. Now check. Rather than asking for more help, receive the help that is waiting for you.

I feel luckier than the person who has everything this world could offer, because I have what the world doesn't offer!

This is the secret of recognizing what is already given. In this instant, where is all the suffering? You will see that this very anger you were afraid of revealed that help. Then anger, despair, insanity, whatever the demon may be, reveals the limitless help that you have asked for and that is eternally given. How could it not be so? You are only asking yourself. When you check, you are overcome with gratitude. What luck!

Of course, anger may be attracted to that luck. Luck is a bright light shining in the midst of a dark forest. All kinds of creatures may come to see what is going on. Do you know that the rhinoceros charges fires in the forest? Let the rhinoceros come in. Then perhaps the rhinoceros will discover what is at the core of its charging. What a discovery! Then the rhinoceros is liberated, anger is liberated, and so much more.

I can speak about these things, but I cannot speak about what is more. The capacity has not been formed in the brain to speak about that. It is the truth of who you are.

The anger I feel is like an erupting volcano.

Don't take it personally.

Okay! (laughing) Say more.

To not take it personally means to unmovingly discover what is at the core. Then you will discover what is deeper than the anger. Then the anger will just be an energy, a voltage around the core.

I feel like that energy drives me. Sometimes I don't know what to do with it.

Yes, a volcano is large, and a volcanic eruption can cause much destruction.

Don't do anything to repress the anger, and don't do anything to let it come. Then this fiery energy is an ally, a wind–horse, a gift. It is the gift of the lightening bolt when you realize what is absolutely untouched, unmoved, and undisturbed. It reveals the truth of what is indestructible.

As long as anger is being either repressed or acted out, indestructibleness is being overlooked. That indestructibleness is your true self.

Do you follow this?

Yes, but it's still hard to let it in.

What will be lost if you let it in?

Safety.

Yes! That's right. Very accurate answer. Somehow anger has been used for protection, hasn't it?

Yes, maybe.

Well, you said safety would be lost, so if you let this in, then you don't have the anger as a controlling force.

In this moment, why not just experience a total lack of safety?

Okay.

Really? Are you sure you're not holding on to some possibility of safety? I am speaking of a *total* lack of safety.

It's actually exhilarating to stand up here and speak to you with no protection.

That's right. You are speaking of vulnerability. Vulnerability is actually exhilarating, isn't it? That which is most feared, when experienced, is actually quite wonderful.

As long as you are falsely identified as the body, you will fight vulnerability. The body must be protected, fed, clothed, and sheltered, or it will be destroyed. As you know, the body will eventually be destroyed anyway, so there is no real safety for the body.

In the moment that you are truly willing to experience no safety anywhere, identification is cut, and you recognize what *is* indestructible. Not the body—the body is obviously destructible. What animates the body, what the body exists in, is life itself, and life itself is indestructible. Not the particular life form, but the life that gives the life form its life. Life is awareness, intelligence, love. This is who you are. In your willingness to experience vulnerability, lack of safety, and the fear that is under the impulse to erupt, there is the potential to realize yourself as that indestructibility. Then your fiery nature will be a servant to that. Then you will roar, and the roar of awakening is a roar of welcome.

States and Experiences

mnipresent being, revealed in the most extraor-
dinary events and the most ordinary events, is
the sublime realization of truth. A most sublime
state often follows the revelation of eternal presence. To be true to that
revelation—whether you have experienced it in a split second, an hour,
a week, a year, or thirty years—is to honor and serve it all the days of
your life.

⟡

I know that my state of consciousness, in this moment, is perfect, is God,
but I've also experienced states that seemed more like God.

So what? A mountain can seem more perfect than a cockroach. That is
the nature of seeming. That is the nature of comparison. In truth, they
are the same perfection. If you were to really receive that which seems
more like God—some mountain of power—and receive it all the way,
you would recognize that here too, in this ordinary state, is the same
God. Then there would no longer be any suffering based on comparison of states.

As awesome and beautiful as special states are, they are still states. Of course, they are wonderful, but to honor these special states, to honor the mountain, to honor God, go *all the way.* You will see that all the way is stateless and present in *all ways.* Then how can you suffer over wanting to feel some other particular, special state? Do you understand that the desire for a particular state is a trap of the mind?

If you attempt to hold some special state together, to find it again or recreate it in the future, you begin to deny what is simply here in all ways, and the cycle of suffering is perpetuated.

Does effort to bring a special state back work?

Well, no, it hasn't.

In your attempt to try to recreate some special state, you are basing what you want on what you had in the past. In this attempt, you overlook what is present now. This that you have now is not in the past, nor in the future, nor even in the present. It is timeless. What is timeless is God, true self, perfection. Anything not here in *all ways* simply appears to be here and then quickly disappear from here.

There are many teachers who can work magic to evoke certain states. That is very useful if the magical state points to what is stateless. If it does not, then it is just another magic trip. Being hooked into following magic does not reveal fulfillment. You know that with the highest highs come the lowest lows. That is the nature of manifestation. I am not saying don't let the highest highs come. Let them come. The highest highs, the lowest lows, let them come. What remains through the highs and through the lows? This is essential. What is untouched by both the lowest low and the highest high? The highest high reflects eternal, stateless truth, which is also present in the lowest low! Recognize that peace and truth can be revealed in any state.

Just for one split second, be who you are. If you are in love with that, then let it overflow. Stop trying to hide it, control it, contain it, fix it, do it, or recreate it. Just let it overflow.

Does this bring satisfaction?

I guess so. I guess I'm there now. This must be it.

Not if it is just a guess. That is the mind's trickery. Doubtless conviction is the natural result of realization. Not a guess, not a hope, not a thought.

This moment is "it." But realizing it is very different from guessing, hoping, thinking, or even experiencing it.

Realizing it is different from experiencing it?

Yes, yes, yes! Experience comes and goes; realization does not move.

The beings that I have the most respect for speak as if the ego sense of being a separate "I" completely disappears.

Yes, and that realization is recognized to be the eternal purity that is before, during, and after all states.

In timelessness, there is no experience and no experiencer. There is just pure consciousness, free of any illusion of name and form. From that, an unforeseeable state of bliss and ecstasy occurs where one can experience, *I am one with everything, I am perfection, I am God, I am self.*

This that is permanent is revealed *in* realization, and *is* the realization. It is exactly the same in *individual* and in *all*. It does not move. Perfection is present whether you always realize yourself to be one with perfection or whether you experience yourself as separate from perfection. Only your mind moves in this perfection. Perfection itself does not move.

In that highest state you refer to, there is no possibility of thinking yourself separate. Now, if a "lower" state comes and you think yourself separate again, find out what has changed and what has not changed. That is all. It is that simple.

Do you think God only wears glowing robes? Do you think God is clothed at all? God is only clothed by your mind.

❖

Some months ago, after being exposed to this understanding and to your teachings, I experienced a settling in. I physiologically settled down and got quiet. It came by itself. I did nothing for it.

When you stop doing, you naturally rest.

It is very important to understand this. You are absolutely correct in that it was nothing that you did, but you must also see the other side of that.

I don't think I see the other side.

What were you doing that kept you from this "experience of settling"?

Wondering what the experience was about. I was looking for it again, desiring it.

This is all mental doing. Do you see? When there is penetration by truth, doing stops and revelation is apparent.

It seemed to start with a glimpse of what reality really is, and it seemed to be a little shimmering, transparent something or other out of the corner of my eye. Then the sinking in happened. Then good experiences came and went on their own, and with them came the understanding that this is all grace; there is nothing I can do for this.

Yes, this is accurate. Mysteriously, the embrace of grace has chosen you. Out of all the people who perhaps worked harder, did better things, gave more, sacrificed more, somehow, as you say, you are graced with this divine welcoming.

You can spend time resisting grace, denying grace, and feeling unworthy of grace, or you can simply give your life totally to grace, to be enfolded in this embrace.

For months, this went on, and it felt completely natural. Yet I still felt like myself having these experiences rather than "nothing" having these experiences, and I wonder about that.

What do you mean when you say "myself" who was, and is, having these experiences?

It felt as if it was the personality.

Can a personality have experiences? Is there any inherent animation of personality?

No. Without the spirit, it's nothing.

When you dissect personality, it is primarily physical, emotional, and mental gestures.

And habits.

Can habits experience anything?

You are at the crux of the dilemma. You identify yourself as personality until you actually see that personality is nothing but habits. When you look at habits more closely, you see that they are nothing but gestures.

What is a gesture? Who owns a gesture? Personality, habit, and gesture are all inert. It's as if you are saying what a wonderful day your dress had yesterday.

You said you still felt like yourself. I am saying that who you are is not a *thing*. You are not a personality, even though you wear a personality. Perhaps you wear it so tightly that you have overlooked that whenever you drop it, you remain whole and full, while it lies lifeless on the floor. The mistake is objectifying yourself and assigning that objectification to a body, a personality, or an emotional state. You are the *awareness* of all states, bodies, and personalities, all everything, and all nothing. Awareness is not a *thing*.

That was my next question. One time during this delightful period of my life, I woke up at night for no apparent reason and decided, while I'm awake, why not inquire, *Who am I?* Unlike the other times I had inquired, this time I immediately experienced who I was. What I saw was a complete emptiness, a complete nothingness.

Who saw this?

(laughing) That's a good question.

That laughter is a good answer.
 Who saw this? (laughing)

Is that it!!!? I can see that it's not a thing!

Yes! Very good. You are not a thing. Are you nothing?

Nothing and not nothing!

Yes! This is very important, because often when an experience of nothingness occurs, that experience gets filed away in memory, and nothingness then becomes a somethingness called nothingness.

Then I had a sledding accident and hit my tailbone very hard. It seemed as if instantly a switch was flipped. Everything I had known, the silence that was everywhere, that was me, the cosmic truth that I seem to intuit now, just stopped.

So you were pulled back into physical incarnation.
 My teacher picked me up and tossed me across the sea, back into my past life. He said, "Now, from there, tell me, who are you?"
 At first I thought, *Oh, how I long to go back to the bliss of being at the feet of my beloved Master.*
 And he said, "Don't come back here. You discovered it here; now discover it there."
 Do you think that who you are is limited to some experience of bliss? Do you think that who you are disappears when the impulses of the nervous system shift from cosmic consciousness to mundane consciousness?

What has remained? What has been constant throughout all shifts? Now, *you* tell *me,* who are you?

Something has remained, yet it just seems less available.

Really? Where are you looking for it?

That's my confusion.

Well, I suspect you are looking for it in imagery, in memory, or in some desire for sensual or intellectual stimulation.

Look to the looker and tell me, what happens to the concept of availability?

Right here, now, availability is irrelevant.

That's right. It does not make any sense. Who is left to measure? Who measures in the first place, and by what indicator?

I see that measurement is only in the mind.

Yes, you were making a boundary between more and less. You believed the boundary between the experience of more and the experience of less to be real. What is the reality of that boundary?

From the experience of being in a body, of being a person who has glimpsed the limitless, no-thingness of who you truly are, now, from this experience, tell me, what is excluded from cosmic consciousness? What is excluded from the truth of who you are?

Nothing. All is included.

I am happy that you had this whack to the base of your spine. Otherwise, you might have been preaching transcendentalism. The experience and the realization of transcendentalism is exquisite and crucial, yet the circle must be completed.

I remember Papaji said to me, "So now, speak to me from the unspeakable place. Speak to me!"

I said, "Papaji, it is impossible to speak from that place."

Then I would drift into an experience of deep bliss, and he would again say, "Now! Now! Now! Come! Speak! Right now!"

Again I said, "Papaji, I can't speak from that place."

Finally he said, "Then come back and speak."

Now, from coming back, tell me, where were you, and where can you go from here?

There is only here.

Yes. Now see only here.

❖

"Here" has different flavors at different times?

Here has no flavor whatsoever, yet different flavors pass through.

Clear light, when refracted, reveals a rainbow, yet as clear light, there are no colors. If you get attached to the rainbow, you overlook the realization of clear light—clear of color, clear of name, clear of form. If you realize clear light, then when name and form appear, they are more proof of clear light. Name and form are not obstacles to pure awareness. Name and form are refractions of pure awareness.

We have spent lifetimes clinging to some idea of name and form, and then, in a very lucky lifetime, there is penetration by this unspeakable, mysterious, divine grace that reveals in an instant the vast emptiness of your true nature.

Why is there clinging?

Since you have spent so much time clinging, you must like to cling. Now you also have the opportunity to experience release.

You like experiencing yourself in all ways. I am not saying clinging is wrong. However, if you believe it to be necessary for the revelation of who you are, you are simply mistaken. Life does not need to cling to life to be life.

You hide because you like to be found. You experience separation because you love the experience of reunion. You experience being lost in the woods so that you can experience the relief of finding your way home. All of this occurs *here* where you always already are.

There is nothing wrong with experience. This is the play of God, the play of perfection. If you are ready to be found, be still. If you are not ready, continue your experience of being lost and suffering. When you are ready, you will know it. You will raise your hand and say, "I have a passion for truth even greater than the inclination to wander away. I have a love of truth that is greater than any other infatuations."

You will see that truth is here waiting for you, whatever flavors, experiences, or states are passing through.

✧

Recently, I had an experience of sitting on the beach, and I felt myself go far out. At that point, I really knew there was no individual "me." It was an amazing experience of pure intelligence. Then there was a moment when I remembered my name and came back into my known self.

Yes?

Yet in that experience, I did not have the feeling of love I have felt at other times, in other experiences. Part of me was surprised, thinking, "I am experiencing universal intelligence, but I am not experiencing love, so I had better get back in my body."

You are speaking of a moment out of time where self recognizes itself as pure, vast intelligence. The fear that love was missing comes from a past mistake. The mistake is some prior definition of love believed to be the *reality* of love.

The body is the conduit for the sensual experience of love as love is defined. You are speaking of having experienced phenomena through the sensory nervous system and then having concluded that certain sensations prove or disprove love. Usually the conclusion is that love has warmth or tingling or any number of sensations—some pleasant, some unpleasant—as its components. No particular sensations therefore means no love.

What follows is a fear that if we experience pure consciousness or nothingness, then we might lose our experience of love or compassion.

There is a point where the concept of love, as it has been defined, is lost. A point when there is only pure intelligence.

If you accept pure intelligence, with no holding back for some idea of love, you will see that love is revealed in more subtle ways than any one feeling or group of sensations can claim.

Once one has had such an experience, once one has had a glimpse of who one really is, then how does that experience become the permanent reality of your life?

Until one has had some glimpse, all talk of perfection, truth, or God is an abstract, theoretical hope or belief. Once there has been a glimpse, then we can speak of choice, of what is to be honored and surrendered to in the face of all seeming proof to the contrary. After this glimpse, there is really free choice, regardless of the tidal wave of conditioned existence that may arise or the aeons of practiced denial that may come to attack.

Your question is how to make this sublime experience a permanent reality. Honor, serve, and surrender to that which is revealed.

Regardless of what you are feeling, regardless of circumstance, state of mind, or mental evaluation—surrender to that.

This surrender, once again, is Ramana's transmission of *stillness*. In stillness, what can be glimpsed is the permanent reality of your being.

This sacred choice takes enormous, twenty-four-hour-a-day, effortless resolve. Effortless resolve is the secret, because if resolve requires effort, it is something that must be maintained and practiced. Whenever an inkling of some propensity to identify oneself as the sufferer arises, this resolve must be present. It must be present night and day, sleeping, waking, eating, moving, being happy, being sad, feeling high, and feeling low. Resolve is the effortless attention to what is effortlessly present at every instant.

❖

A few mornings ago, I meditated on "Who am I?" I am going to try describe this, even though I know it is not accurate. What I experienced, and the reason it's not accurate, is that there was no "I." The "I" disappeared.

This is accurate!

It was consciousness aware of consciousness as consciousness.

Oh, this is beautiful!

And it was so blissful.

Yes, it is blissful.

I felt like I was exploding.

Don't even say *was*. Don't put realization in the past tense. It *is*. The explosion is the byproduct of the realization of consciousness conscious of itself. Not as some separate *I*, but as itself in its totality. Yes, bliss is the nature of that discovery. Expansion is the nature of that discovery.

Originality is the nature of that discovery. That which has never been thought is the nature of that discovery.

Now the experience has left me, and it makes me wonder if there was any realization at all.

There is a slight but essential misunderstanding here.

The bliss of that explosion, as wonderful as it is, is still an experience, and all experience is limited. Before that experience occurred, it wasn't. Experience occurs, and experience goes.

True recognition reveals what simply *is*. The explosion you experienced was a byproduct of that recognition. You turned your attention away from the source of the explosion, and you began to cling to the byproduct as the indication that now you are someplace, now you are enlightened, now you are fulfilled.

In the opening that follows this divine explosion, anything that has been suppressed is likely to arise. If there is no clinging to the bliss of the experience, there will be no more need for any particular experience. Finally, you will recognize that all experiences are revealed in that.

What I am pointing to is deeper than any particular state or experience. Realization does not contradict human experience. This human wave occurs in consciousness, as consciousness, in the form of wave of consciousness. Conscious recognizing itself does not require the flattening of the wave. Wave appears as wave as long as it appears as wave. As long as there is experiencing, there is also human experience.

There will be, and are, sublime, unforeseeable experiences of ecstasy, peace, and clarity, but these are still not "it." The it is the discovery, fresh in every moment, *I am this! I am this that is speaking. I am this that is listening. I am this that is spoken. I am beyond all that is spoken and heard and yet present in all that is spoken and heard.*

◈

How is it that I can feel happy so much of the time and still not be satisfied?

You are paying attention to the *experience* of happiness rather than the *awareness* of the experience. Bliss and happiness are states. As states, they are still illusion, and ultimately you are never satisfied with illusion.

I realize that it takes trust to stop identifying myself with the illusion and defer to a higher self, which is something I may not always be able to sustain the awareness of.

You are still speaking of some object or some particular state. You say, "I want to sustain the awareness of ecstasy," or "I want to sustain the awareness of clarity," or "I want to sustain the awareness of higher self." These are all states. They are beautiful states, but they are only states, and as states, they come and they go. The awareness of these states needs no sustaining. Awareness is self-sustaining.

Most of the great spiritual traditions speak of establishment and sustaining. Really what is being pointed to is what is already, firmly, wholly established as that, already self-sustained, already self-evident. If you begin the effort of trying to sustain something, then once again, a split in the mind occurs, and you think, *I must sustain this because this is who I really am.* If this is who you really are, then this *is* who you really are, *period.* You are not separate from who you are with the need or the option to either sustain yourself or lose yourself.

The challenge is to trust this totally, because the entrancement is that you are not that. You believe you are some image of yourself, some physical representation, or some sensation, and with this belief comes fear. With fear, mental scurrying and searching begin for what is perceived to be lost. In some moment of grace, trust is revealed. Relax into that trust, and let it be done.

There may be some very intense moments. There may be experiences of shaking and terror and suffering. These moments pass. What is left is clarity itself. If you search for clarity and wisdom, you overlook that the searcher itself is part of the illusion. The idea of a lower self and a higher self is the illusion. There is only the essential self, one's true nature, sometimes dressed in rags, sometimes dressed in royal robes. Throw your rags away. Because you have worn these rags for aeons, you have infused them with an illusory reality.

Recognize that your old rags are nothing. They are concepts disintegrating as we speak. Your body is disintegrating as we speak. Your world is disintegrating as we speak. What remains?

What is the power that gives life to everything? Rags, robes, bodies, worlds? Discover this. This that has given power to "higher self" is self, period. It is who you are.

When your rags are long gone, when your body is long gone, self remains. Discover this even while wearing your body, and you will discover great happiness, peace, joy, and beyond.

Don't wear old rags *or* royal robes. Be naked in the splendor of the truth of who you are.

❖

I've made the feeling of bliss a prerequisite for freedom, and now it feels like a burden.

Be willing to give up all burdens, including feelings of bliss. Clinging to bliss is where many people get hooked. You can see that if you attempt to cling to feelings of bliss, and then there is no bliss, there is great and unnecessary suffering. If you are willing to release everything, you will realize the bliss behind the bliss that does not need to be blissful to be, the dance behind the dancing that does not need movement for its dance, the music behind the music, the core.

❖

What about the experience of physical pain?

If you identify yourself as the experience of pain, and then attempt to reject the pain, there is unnecessary suffering.

Regardless of whatever experience there is, whether it is of pain, of joy, or no sensory experience at all, pure awareness is always present. Awareness is not bound by any name or experience. Your true name is that namelessness. Claim it. It belongs to you.

And when there is awareness of pleasure?

Pleasure is a sensory experience. It comes and it goes. If you chase pleasure, you end up with unnecessary suffering.

Pain is a sensory experience. It comes and it goes. If you reject pain, you end up with unnecessary suffering.

Drop everything, including and most essentially the image or the thought of the one who is chasing the pleasure and the one who is running from the pain.

Rather than focusing on the experience of pleasure or the experience of pain, find the experiencer and see if *that* is limited. See if pain and pleasure, as well as all other states, begin and end there. See if that has any needs, any aversions, any boundaries.

You have assumed you are a thing, a somebody, but this is a false assumption. When you actually return to *I*, what is pleasure and pain in that?

Don't move from true *I*. Stay right there, and speak from that.

I can't find who *I* is.

But when you look, who is found?

Nothing.

Is this nothing a dead, blank nothing, or is this nothing limitlessness itself?

I think so.

You think so? You must know so. This is why you are here. It is time to stop thinking about it! You seek confidence in who you are, do you not? You want conviction, not some idea that I is limitless, but the direct experience of limitlessness.

You say, "I can't find anything there," and this is the truth. Now, tell me, what *is* there? Is awareness there?

Yes.

You can find no *thing*, just awareness? Excellent! Remain in the awareness of awareness—not awareness as some *thing* or some *body*, just pure awareness. In your willingness to experience awareness even more deeply, everything you have been searching for in some *thing* is revealed. Awareness is the source of all revelation.

This that is glimpsed in that instant is the invitation. Come *home*. Return to what has *always been*.

Return to the simplicity of *I* itself. Not simplicity that is limited or conceptual, but the immeasurable simplicity of *I*. Then revelations happen naturally, without any searching, calibrating, or measuring. This is the promise.

❖

Recently I was having an experience of ecstasy, and it occurred to me that this also was a form of the mind's resistance to going deeper. But when I vowed to just be, the excitement wasn't there.

The body is quite refreshed from ecstasy. At a cellular level, a vibrational cleansing and a healing occur. You do not have to push ecstasy aside. It will pass when it passes.

The ecstasy you have experienced is beautiful, and yes, it can reveal something even deeper. If you have any idea that any state, even ecstasy, is the limit, then that state is the problem.

Neither do you have to push pain aside. It will pass when it passes. Then pain and ecstasy are not seen as different.

Pain too can be very cleansing. It may feel like the body cannot contain the pain, and yet every cell can be cleansed by relaxing into it.

✥

I've had several glimpses, like a lightening bolt and a state of total relaxation and connection to everything. They felt almost biological. But as soon as there was an awareness of a "me," I was my old self again and the experience left.

As soon as there was the thought *"I" experienced this,* or *Now "I" have got something,* the state of relaxation left. This is the clue that you are defining some *thing* as *I.* The moment the I-thought arises, there is some kind of tension, some limitation, an image, a sensation, or a definition of "me." If there is identification with that definition, then there is something to be defended. Something has been lost that must be regained. Then, as you say, the "old you" is back. Following the I-thought outward toward definition always has this result. In this case, the definition is, "I who am connected to everything," and then, "I who have lost that connection."

If the I-thought arises and you turn your mind to see *I* rather than attending to the definitions that follow *I*, you will see that it is simply a thought arising, nonexistent in reality. The habit of following or rejecting or denying this I-thought is once again revealed to be just activity of the mind. Do you follow this?

Yes.

Good. Because I am speaking to that which saw through the I-thought, which relaxed attention on the I-thought and actually saw that the *I* you have defined yourself as is illusion.

There is no need to mourn the loss of any experience, even the loss of the lightening-bolt experience. In mourning that apparent loss, there is clinging to the idea of the experiencer as some real entity separate from consciousness.

If I would ask anything, it would be, is there a way to always experience that let-go?

You ask for a way, but every way is some attempt or some strategy to either reject something or cling to something. Simply let go all strategies—all attempts to hold, and all attempts to keep away. However, letting go is not the correct terminology because this, too, implies an activity. The secret is even more subtle than letting go. The secret is to discover, in fact, *who* is holding on. It is that simple.

I understand that it may not seem simple, because we are conditioned to fixate on chasing, searching, and clinging, or pushing aside, ignoring, and denying. You know that none of these really give you what you want. The more you try to chase, search, or cling to a phenomenon, the more it escapes you. The more you try to reject, deny, or ignore a phenomenon, the more it has a hold on you.

I called it biological because it seemed to just happen to me. I didn't do it.

Calling it biological limits the phenomenon to somehow being initiated biologically. Definitely, biological events follow self-recognition. The lightening bolt, the energy, the sensations follow, but this that I am pointing to is before biology, includes biology, and is after biology.

Permanence is who you are. The relative identifications of yourself as a something that glimpses truth and a something that loses the glimpse both occur within the absolute truth of who you are. For an instant, the ocean can recognize itself within the form of a wave.

The ramifications are endless. The manifestations are endless. The byproducts are endless. But the basic, absolute truth is simple beyond imagination. That is how it's a secret.

❖

So, no matter what the experience, pleasurable or unpleasurable, do I just allow it to come and allow it to go?

Even "allow" is too much effort. It comes. It goes. Allowing is closer than resisting, but to *really* allow is to let go of both resisting and allowing.

You are that which sees. See. The experience is deeper, newer, and fresher every moment. The moment you cling to any experience as reality, you are attempting to resist. With the attempt to resist, you experience yourself as back in the cycle of reaching for something you think should be happening or rejecting something you think should not be happening.

There is great beauty and depth of experience in being willing to experience bliss, joy, and happiness. Also, great beauty and depth of experience are available in directly experiencing pain, grief, and despair.

Many people turn from grief and pain, but many also turn from bliss and joy. There is fear of pain and grief, and there is fear of bliss and joy. With any fear, there is the impulse to contract.

Have the willingness to simply be. All experience follows beingness. When this simple fact is recognized, the depth of experience is unimaginable. In the willingness to experience the perfection of pain, and in the willingness to experience the perfection of joy, there is such depth of understanding that, finally, you cannot find a boundary between pain and joy. You cannot say *this* is more joyful than *that*, because in the willingness to fully experience whatever arises, you find what is immeasurable.

THE HEART OF RELATIONSHIP

'm facing what feels like a lot of temptation as far as emotional involvement in a relationship. This temptation seems to disappear for
long periods of time, and then all of a sudden it's everywhere.

What do you mean by emotional involvement?

Well, attraction . . . when attraction happens in a natural way, when it
doesn't feel sought after, and there's some kind of resonance.

Any problem with this kind of resonance?

No, not initially.

The problem is not the attraction, or the resonance, or falling in love,
or even involvement in relationship. The problem is what your mind
does with all of that. How can you not be attracted? There is no need
to resist beauty.

There are times when I see the same beauty on every face around me. At
other times, I have a tendency to think that this attraction can be used as
some sort of vehicle, maybe as a vehicle for personal pleasure.

It is important to see the activity of the mind. What you're becoming
aware of are habitual mental strategies. Vigilance is the willingness to see

everything that arises, however unattractive, including how the mind takes what is beautiful and fresh and twists it into something old and rotten. Be willing to feel the pain that results from the twisting. Experience it unsentimentally.

Don't follow the tendency to take the beauty, chasteness, and pureness that are freely offered and twist them into something that can be used. If you use them, they will be used up. Be quiet, and let the twisting burn up.

Karma can never burn if you are unwilling to see these mental habits. It can be quite shocking to see the workings of the mind. It is very easy to point the finger at what is read or seen in the news about what "others" are doing. It is easy to see the destructiveness of others who act and react in negative ways. Vigilance is not to react to the thoughts by either repressing them into the subconscious or following them as reality. Karma cannot survive the willingness to directly experience whatever arises.

Vigilance must be present twenty-four hours a day. Vigilance is not hard and rigid. It is not some kind of carefulness. Vigilance is not separate from awareness. See what arises in your life moment to moment. Then experience what is behind the arisings.

The fear arises when the mind shifts and becomes focused or attached to another physical form.

What is it you are really attracted to in physical form, however beautiful it appears?

If you tell the truth, you see that the real beauty is not the form. Form may be beautiful, and different forms are beautiful in different ways, but what is it you really love? What is it that you are really attracted to?

Is it true self?

True self shines out from every form, without which no form has any animation or even existence. Recognize true self as that which you love, and then there is no distraction from your full attention on that. Enjoy the infinite forms that self takes.

Obviously, there will be some forms you are more attracted to than others. Look deeper to the source of attraction, and you will see. Even as a particular form changes, as all form does, and even if it disappears, which eventually all form does, you will not be distraught. You will not feel yourself to be lost because your attention will not have wavered from true self, the true changeless beauty.

Many people have tried getting away from attractions by going into caves, going into monasteries, going onto mountaintops, or just going under the covers. Attraction is present in everyday life as the play of all form—as man and woman, man and man, woman and woman, old and young, old and old, moth and light, bee and flower. All of nature is a dance of self-attraction. See the truth, and temptations to follow habits of clutching or denying will burn in that truth.

In certain disciplines, effort is made to deny sensory experience. Other belief systems practice glorifying the senses as if they will fulfill the ultimate desire. Both ways are dead ends. Renounce the indulgence of following the senses as master, and renounce denying the arising of sensual experience.

Neither follow nor deny. This is the secret. We have all tried both paths—earnestly denying and earnestly indulging. Both the tension of denying sensory impulses and the dissipation of following these impulses cause unnecessary suffering. The challenge is to be still, not to repress, and not to follow. Then any meeting is satsang, and satsang is meeting in truth. The past is always welcome to come to satsang.

If you are afraid of something, you tend to turn your attention away from it. Face the feared temptation of attraction to form. See what is at the root of it. If, at the root, you find desire for acquisition or control, experience the futility and suffering of that desire. Experience lack of control, experience loss, experience not getting what you want. In direct, unflinching experience, you will see clearly that what you truly love and desire is true self. Self is always shining from the core of your being.

I actually see that quite a bit. I also see the latent tendencies of mind that come up around the fear of growing old alone.

Lie down and experience growing old alone, suffering and penniless. Don't waste another moment. Lie down and experience this fear.

Growing old is the death of the hope of eternal youthfulness. Face your death. Think of all the time wasted in young bodies on the hope of never growing old.

Experience that fear. Then the rest of the life of your body—whether it be one hour, one day, thirty years, or one hundred years—is lived freely.

Whatever latent tendency haunts you also serves you. It serves as it reveals the fear of something unexperienced. The invitation is to directly experience what has been rejected. In direct experience, false identification is burned.

❖

When I am on my own, I experience a lot of the peace that is spoken of in satsang quite easily, and then when I am in an intimate relationship, suddenly there is a lot more drama, a lot more story, a lot more difficulty staying with what I experience as truth.

You say that peace is obvious when you are alone, then there is "being with something." This "being with something" is subject/object relationship.

Relationship with objects is the ground of drama. In drama, the object is presupposed to be separate from you, the subject. Naming the object "man" begins the characterization of object. Next, in your mind, the categories arise: "me" or "not me," "him" or "not him," "intimate" or "not intimate," "enough" or "not enough." This is only the basic sketch. The familiar drama that arises from usual relationships gets quite operatic: Who is winning, the subject or the object? How to get more from the object? How to milk it? How to squeeze it? How to have the object not disappear? How to have the object disappear? And on and on.

Subject/object relationship is eternal frustration, because what you truly desire is not the object. What is truly desired is that which gives life to all objects—limitless self. The object itself is simply an object of perception. Since perception is limited, it can only perceive limitation.

Recognize this play as divine tragic comedy. Your frustration at attempting to objectify truth can be seen as the ultimate comedy. You will have some good laughs. In a good laugh, where is man and where is woman? In an instant of true laughter, objectless beauty is revealed.

I do not mean that now you must see everything that looks like a man as "not man." First see yourself and then tell me, when this that you truly are is recognized, is it man or woman? Is it human or plant or rock or tree or animal? Is it limited by any definition that arises in it?

The belief in "me" and "other" reflects deep conditioning. In moments when no apparent other is around, you have been graced to recognize expansive peace. Now it is important that the appearance of other arises. Now you have the opportunity to discover the true depth of grace first recognized in no appearance of other.

If grace is limited to no appearance of other, it is a conditional grace. Be true to revealed grace by seeing if appearance of other *really* clouds anything. Be vigilant. Experience how conceptual clouds only appear to cover pure and perfect peace. See from the core of being and you see peacefully through all clouds.

It is time to come down from your mountaintop and recognize satsang in the marketplace, on the street, and in the bedroom, as well as beyond space and time. Otherwise, this that you have experienced while seemingly alone is limited.

When you discover what is boundless, you discover what is beyond the experience of either other or no-other. This is realization. Regardless of experience, true realization cannot be moved.

❖

Although someone can physically leave me, their consciousness can't because their consciousness and my consciousness are the same, right?

If this is committed to memory so that it will help you in moments of experiencing being left, it should be titled "Relying on Philosophy in Moments of Need."

What you are saying is true, but so what? If it has not truly been realized, it is only something you want to be true, or you hope to be true, or maybe you even try to make true with an affirmation such as *I am not separate; maybe they can leave me in form, but their consciousness is the same as mine.*

You can get comfort from affirmation, but I am not speaking of comfort. Realize who you are by forgetting all relationships. Awaken to your true nature. When experiencing hurt or loss, meet hurt and loss fully, completely, and discover that in the core of hurt, there you are, unhurt. In the core of loss, there you are, found. The meeting must be total. Otherwise, it is just an exercise. I am not giving you exercises. I am taking your exercises away.

Truth must be realized firsthand. Secondhand information may be all right for a bridge, but finally, you are not satisfied with just standing on the bridge and reciting what you have heard about the other side. Finally, you must know for yourself. Obviously, enormous resolve and surrender are required. Enormous resolve is required because past conditioning denies or distorts true desire. Even spiritual conditioning delays your crossing with tales of what is on the other side.

Direct experience, direct meeting, is a radical ending to the search— no excuses accepted, nothing excluded.

With my lover, I tend to open up and then pull back.

So stop.

I've stopped a lot of it.

Stop all of it. Can you find any good reason to continue?

No.

Good, then stop it. What could be simpler?

I stop and then I sort of pick it up again.

Rather that pick it up, go deeper into stopping, deeper into opening. Open beyond the body, beyond the emotions. True intimacy is beyond the sense of *me* and *my lover.*

The open mind reveals the eternally open core. The core does not close. The core does not go back and forth. The projecting and veiling power of the mind creates experiences of opening and closing. These experiences do not affect the pure, unchanging awareness that is your true self.

Open unsentimentally, ruthlessly, and courageously. With openness, there is no discussion of why you can't open or what is blocking opening. Be finished with the discussion. You don't have to look back. If the impulse to close arises, let that impulse be the signal for no discussion, just openness. You may feel the discomfort and pain of past closings. Opening is also opening to all past closings.

Experience the pain directly, and be finished. End the karmic drama of opening and closing. Whether you stay with your lover or leave your lover, stay open. Opening is not about staying or leaving. Appropriate action follows true opening.

If closing gives you a sense of power, offer this closing power to openness. The thought may arise, *Well, what if I want to close?* Give up the possibility of closing, and then even the impulse to close is the vehicle for deeper opening. The open mind reflects the limitless openness of the core of being.

◈

What I notice is that I'll feel in love, and then it feels too overwhelming.

Yes, fear of love is the same as fear of death. In surrendering to love, a death occurs. It is the death of objectification. Let yourself get caught by love, and there is no going back.

Is that the reason why even love is painful?

True love pain is divine pain. It is the pain of completion. This exquisite pain is the explosion of the consummation of God and soul.

◈

Please talk about making the decision to end a relationship with someone you love.

If you haven't ended the relationship, then you aren't clear about ending it.

What is it you really want? If you want truth more than the relationship, then clarity naturally reveals itself.

When truth is primary, it is obvious whether the relationship is to be continued or ended. If you place the relationship above truth, then there will never be clarity. When the relationship is primary, you are asking that relationship to give you something it has no capacity to give.

Stop everything. That in which the relationship occurs is far larger than the relationship. It is that which you love in relationship and in everything else you love. It is that which is bigger than any object, anywhere. It is that which is the source of all clarity.

There are deeply painful experiences, and there are deeply joyful experiences. Truth is bigger than all experiences. You are truth itself. Be true to yourself, then all is clear. If there is something abusive, sick, or distorted in a relationship, it cannot remain hidden in the light of truth.

⟡

When I'm with someone in relationship, I seem to perceive certain things going on with them, yet I'm never really sure if it's a projection within my own mind or something that's actually coming from them.

Ultimately, it doesn't matter because it is all coming from the same source. Return to source. Your own return to silence is the purification for all mind activity.

But I'm not sure which is which.

It doesn't matter which is which. Just be quiet and everything is released. Whether something originated in your mind or in their mind, ultimately it is the same mind, the same source. Return to open mind. Recognize that the presence revealed in open mind is continuous. Your recognition changes the vibration of the whole world and invites the whole world to openness. In that invitation, if anything is left unburned, it is revealed. Be vigilant to what is unburned, and burning continues.

You experience the suffering of the world as "other." Regardless of experience, it is all still your own self.

If you are willing to return to silent presence rather than become involved in the story of who is to blame, then suffering is liberated. Clarity of action naturally follows this instant of liberation.

First discover continuous presence within yourself. That which is always present must be discovered. This is essential. When continuous presence is discovered here, where you are, your whole life is a vehicle for discovery of that everywhere.

⟡

My understanding is that a true meeting can only occur right in the present. At the moment, there seem to be some difficulties between my girlfriend and me and she's asking to work through things. Working through things for her seems to mean going right into the past. I see that only in a fresh meeting every moment can things really be released and resolved.

Be careful not to use the concept of truth as a philosophical weapon. If the past is facing you, do not deny that past. The mastery is in not denying it, not repressing it, and not following it. Then past is realized to be nonexistent. If past is experienced as existing, and then is covered with the philosophical concept that it doesn't exist or is really not important, then the philosophical concept is being used as a strategy to either deny or control. The freshness of directly experiencing that the past essentially does not exist is not revealed through conceptual knowing.

As long as there is a sense of past and the willingness to face it fully, then past is discovered to be nonexistent. Not believed to be nonexistent, hoped to be nonexistent, thought to be nonexistent, but *discovered* to be nonexistent.

Often what follows having momentarily experienced the past as nonexistent, or having heard someone say the past is nonexistent, is the formulation of nonexistence into a concept. What follows conceptualization is a very subtle—or not so subtle—denial of what is arising. As long as anything seems to exist, face it and discover eternal truth to be all that truly exists. When you are willing to fully meet everything as it appears, you discover eternity itself at the core of all past, present, or future.

If working it out means some kind of endless analysis of who said or did what and for what reason, finally, working it out is useless. Endless analysis is useful only to finally prove its uselessness. What a great relief in that.

As long as your bodymind appears, there is some semblance of the past appearing. When hunger arises and you have the desire to eat, this desire comes from remembrance of satiation of hunger through eating.

You have recognized, since you first identified yourself as form, from protoplasm to human being, that satisfying hunger continues the organism. There is no problem with continuing the organism unless you mistake yourself as limited to that organism. This is an ancient mistake. Perhaps the original sin.

If you identify yourself as your body, you experience desire as actual need for survival of self. Of course, your body must be fed to survive, but you are not your body. You survive all bodies. You are not limited to the past, you are not limited to the present, and you are not limited to the future.

Drop all identification with limitation and see what remains. Then, if experiences of limitation reappear, they are realized to be only the great play of consciousness. In that instant, you have discovered the secret that releases identification as either the victim or the aggressor. This is such a hair-thin edge, and that is the exquisiteness of it.

It has been said that the body can be discarded immediately upon awakening. If this happens, fine. If it doesn't happen, then participate in the exquisite play of consciousness. There may be difficult moments, difficult relationships, and difficult experiences. In the core of the worst difficulty, the worst horror, the worst suffering, in the absolute core of all, truth is discovered, discovering itself.

✧

I've requested that my husband of twenty-four years somehow meet me in this spiritual journey. What I want of him is like a resonant field that comes from the heart. His brilliant intellect is so often not in the heart.

The problem might be with the word "heart." Often the word "heart" refers to an emotional center. When I use the word "heart," I am speaking of the core of being, the actual presence of beingness, the life of beingness revealed when everything else is peeled away. Everything arises from that core. True heart is the core of being.

The journey to the core is not about past knowledge. The Buddha is not about the past. Christ is not about the past. What is beyond past, present, and future? What is more present than present?

Be who you are. This is what my teacher's teacher said. To be who you are, you must first discover who you are. So the essential question is "Who am I?" You know who you have been *told* you are. You know who you have *believed* yourself to be, and all of that is changeable.

To be who you *are* means to be real, finally. Reality is unchangeable. To be real means to be unmovable in that which is unchangeable. Then your husband does not have to meet you in some place that only you have experienced. He may never speak of a resonant field. He may never speak of the heart. Discover your own self in him, rediscovered in a different formulation.

By being myself?

Yes, by being true to who you are. If you are totally true to who you are, you already recognize that he is your own self. What great, infinite amazement in that.

Of course, you want to invite him, your own self, to full potential. Your being true to the truth is the most attractive invitation.

The other revelation I had is this feeling of immense love.

Yes, this is true love. The emotions that emanate from realizing true love are true emotions, not sentimental emotions revolving around an imaginary *you* and *your needs*. True love has never been measured. Immense, boundless love is true love.

❖

In five weeks' time, I'm going to get married. I've never considered myself the marrying type. I've enjoyed the freedom of going wherever I fancied. It's bringing up a lot of discomfort.

The play of marriage is a divine play, a symbol and a celebration of the truth of what already is.

Many people have the idea that true freedom is freedom of the body, of doing only what is desired. You have experienced that relative freedom, and you have recognized that following personal desire is limited, that true freedom is something more. There is a more profound freedom than following desires. To think that you are free because you get to do what you want is a childish idea of freedom. True freedom has nothing to do with any desire.

The commitment to marriage is a kind of death, isn't it? It is the death of one's ideas of *me* and *my freedom*.

I celebrate true marriage. When you recognize that who you are is unlimited in the first place, then the limits of marriage are paradoxical expressions of that freedom and beauty. True marriage is a reflection of the inseparable connection with all of life. Be faithful to that embrace regardless of discomfort, regardless of the pull of desire.

Many marriages are merely institutions of servitude and property arrangement. True marriage is a celebration of freedom. True marriage is a support of one another in devotion to truth. It is the marriage of oneself with oneself.

✧

Is it a problem if my wife doesn't share with me the same yearning for truth?

Your partner will catch it from you, or the marriage will be finished. It is that simple.

When I met my husband, and before we were married, all I wanted was a husband. I thought that getting married would be total fulfillment.

I caught the yearning for truth from him. His whole life revolved around truth. How lucky that destiny brought me to a man who loved truth more than he loved me. He served truth more than he served me.

He was married to truth before he was married to me. For our marriage to be, I also had to meet truth. Once truth is met, one cannot help but fall in love.

Let your marriage be in service to that. Then, regardless of the problems, the discomforts, and the trials, it will be a true marriage. If marriage is in service to each other's ego, it is the usual, false marriage.

Serve truth, which is never separate from love.

LONGING FOR THE BELOVED

Longing for the true Beloved is not content with even the last moment's realization. The Beloved's embrace must be always fresh, always alive, always new.

Whenever longing arises, it may trigger habitual responses of attempting to satisfy the longing with some object, some experience, or something other than itself. These responses are latent tendencies of mind. These tendencies reflect the way we have been taught to deal with longing.

Divine longing is for deeper realization of the fullness of self. It is very useful. Don't put it aside. Don't move into mental agitation around it. It exposes even the slightest misidentification of you as separate from the Beloved.

This longing is a great gift. It is God's gift. It is the longing of the soul, and it will continue until, without a shadow of a doubt, you are submerged in the Beloved.

Sometimes I confuse longing with a sense of doubt.

Doubt comes from mental activity. Longing is deeper than mental activity. Rather than diving into longing and directly experiencing it, there is often an impulse to move into mental relationship with it: *What does this mean? Does it mean I'm bad? Does it mean I haven't got it? Does it mean that I'll never get it?*

The longing is a call, a reminder that attention has been turned toward some object.

Longing is your great ally. It is your guardian angel crying, "Return. Return." Don't shunt it aside. Don't try to fill it with ideas, expectations, conversation, or doubt. Fall directly into it. It is a waiting vehicle.

Do you mean to open fully to it?

Yes, open fully.

There is often misunderstanding around the arising of longing. To correct the misunderstanding, stop trying to feed it in the hope that it will go away. Thank goodness attempts to get rid of true longing don't work. True longing is a persistent lover. It won't go away with some trifle. It won't go away with some ordinary experience. True longing goes away only in the consummation of itself.

Opening is possible only if you stop all thoughts about it. Put all thoughts aside and allow yourself to *be longing*. Make no separation between you and the longing. When met directly, longing reveals that which is longed for.

Are the "I" who longs and the longing the same thing? Are they both just a sensate experience?

I longs for itself. Longing is recognized *through* the sensate experience, but the source of longing is deeper than senses. Fall in through the senses. Pass the senses on your way to the source.

If you understand the language of longing, you know a secret language. It cannot be translated. Sufis have attempted to translate it. Hindus have attempted to translate it. Christian mystics have attempted to translate it. Now you must translate it, yes?

It's in the yes! (laughing)

Yes! And it is in the laughter.

Don't hold back anything. Even if you don't hear anything else I say, hear this: *Longing is your own soul's call.* You are in satsang, so I assume you are here because longing has called you.

Listen.

Give the longing the totality of your being.

✦

When we find out who we are, will the yearning and longing cease?

Find out and then tell me. Put others' opinions aside. No one else's opinion will satisfy you. I could share with you my experience, but so what? It is more valuable if I can point you to the direct experience for yourself. Then you will speak from your own experience—not from some belief or some hope, but from your own direct experience.

Are you ready to discover for yourself the truth of your yearning?

Yes.

Then turn directly into it. Be absolutely aware of it. Stop the distraction of wondering what might be or what might have been. Give everything to pure longing. In this moment, give every sensation, every thought, and every emotion to longing. Throw everything you have onto this fire.

There is a beautiful story of a Zen master who, upon returning home from market, saw all his neighbors running toward his house with buckets of water.

"What's happening?" he said.

"Your house is on fire," they replied.

They were running to throw buckets of water on his house and pulling his belongings out of the house to safety. He immediately started throwing his belongings back into the burning house. He began to light torches to add to the fire.

Throwing everything onto the fire is required in the call of the Beloved.

If some concept of what will satisfy your longing starts to slip out, or some friendly neighbor starts to pull something out, take it back and throw it all in the fire. Let the fire get huge, and if your neighbors are wise, they will bring torches over to their own houses.

When a fire is worked up to a certain frenzy, it spreads. Let the fire of longing rage. Throw all concepts of yourself into it. Let everything be burned. Then you will know directly what this longing is. In that knowledge, you will know what cannot be burned. You will know your true self.

This is a holy fire. It is an ecstatic fire. It is only painful if you put your foot in and pull it out, put your foot back in and pull it out. Jump into the fire!

Don't waste a moment. Don't consider this any longer. Jump!

❖

Is the yearning greed?

Greed for more objects is a distortion of true yearning. Greed for more sensate experience has to do with the body, with feeding the senses to avoid the call of this deeper yearning. The deepest yearning is the desire for that which is truth.

Recognize that misplaced greed has led only to suffering, and any object, any sensual pleasure, or any attainment still has not satisfied the yearning. This recognition is maturity.

The usual habit of relating to yearning is to turn to mind activity. You may hide in fantasies of being back with your first lover, or entertain fantasies of more, new lovers. You may imagine that being back in your mother's womb or returning to the Garden of Eden would put an end to your yearning. All this fantasizing and entertaining hope for cessation of longing are attempts to escape the call.

The fulfillment of the call of longing is not found back in your mother's womb. It is not found back anywhere. Don't look back. It is not found forward either. Don't look ahead. Give yourself to the yearning itself, now. This giving reveals the Beloved.

Your yearning is for the true romance. True romance can never be satisfied by mere infatuation or biochemical response. True romance is the love of the soul for God. It is the call of the soul for God. It is God's call to the soul. Satsang points the soul back to the source that it yearns for.

Before yearning first arises, there is a numbness of spirit. Somehow, within the course of evolution, the desire arises for that which is unknown. The habitual impulse is to fill the space of the unknown with what has been known. This impulse fixates on desire for the lover, the mother, the father, or some object promising fulfillment. Forget yearning for something and *be* yearning. Discover that you are what you have yearned for.

By "you," I don't mean any image of you, any sensation of you, any memory of you, or any conception of you. I mean you as you really are. Not as you imagine, feel, sense, or believe yourself to be. You as you really are is the unknown you yearn for.

Are you ready? Have you tried greed? Have you tried lust?

You have tried everything, but have you tried no-thing?

Be no-thing. Do you think you know what being no-thing means? Any assumption about the meaning of "nothing" is based on the false assumption that you are a something.

You have believed yourself to be a something, and you have worked hard to better that something and maintain that something in the false hope of finding fulfillment.

Your longing is a powerful, stark reminder of your failure.

Face your failure. Face the longing you have worked so hard to ignore or feed with proof of somethingness.

When you truly face longing and surrender to its call, no-thingness reveals itself.

No-thingness is not a dead abyss of space. True no-thingness is the endless radiant face of your own self.

❖

It feels like this longing is a deep wound inside me. That no matter how good my life is, this painful longing doesn't change. I've looked at it psychologically, and I've wondered if maybe I just can't be happy.

Circumstances can be perfect relative to past desires, but you will not be truly happy until you discover the truth of who you are.

It is good that this perceived wound, this longing, will not let you rest. It will not let you settle for some idea of happiness.

Do you know the story of the princess and the pea? No matter how many mattresses were placed under this very sensitive princess, she could still feel the grit of a pea.

Finally, all the mattresses must be shoved aside to discover what is calling attention to itself. Follow the call to the core.

Plunge into the call, and discover what is the grit that will not let you rest.

It makes me feel restless.

Yes, it is a restlessness. Without this restlessness, you might have been content to live the lifestyle that was preprogrammed for you. You might have been content with your success or your compromise, but in fact you are not content. This is divine discontent. Restlessness or discontent holds within itself, within its core, the truth of fulfillment.

You have seen that circumstances have nothing to do with real, lasting happiness. Luckily, accumulation of more good things has not covered the restlessness, the pea. Now dive directly into the restlessness, and see what is really there.

The story of Buddha is a story of restlessness, unresolved by circumstance, wealth, honor, or fame. Buddha was a prince. He had everything, and yet there was something that pulled him from the palace to face suffering and discontentment. He was pulled to discover what is at the core of suffering. He was not pulled to find a more convenient isolation or protection from suffering. He was pulled to face suffering directly.

Usual mental activity is an attempt to insulate oneself from suffering. With insulation, there is still subtle discontentment. Discontentment is the tip of the longing. Find where the longing originates. Follow it inwardly, rather than following the usual useless attempts to satisfy it outwardly.

◈

Does longing exist without the mind?

No, but it arises out of that aspect of the mind that is calling and pulling mind back to its source.

It feels like loneliness.

If loneliness is met fully and completely, then loneliness reveals fulfillment. This is a great secret. Divine yearning will only be satisfied when it is met fully and completely. A great mouth of loneliness may be perceived. If you fall into that mouth, all the way into the core, that which you long for eats you.

I am not suggesting that you dramatize or wallow in loneliness. To fall into the core of loneliness, you must leave all postures of loneliness behind.

The whole world is searching for release from the experience of separation. The worldly search is in reaching for more to acquire and accumulate. Finally, through grace, your search has pointed you back into the loneliness itself, back into the experience of loneliness, back into what the whole world is attempting to escape, back into what you assume to be the beast.

The truth is that you *are* absolutely alone, and this recognition reveals profound satisfaction and fulfillment. In directly meeting what is most feared, most dreaded, you realize your true home.

❖

Shyness has been a lifelong struggle for me. An overwhelming shyness coupled with a longing to be recognized.

I love shyness. There is real beauty in shyness. We don't have enough shyness in the world. We have all been overly trained in assertion and aggression.

In many cultures, your shyness would be called modesty, but in our culture, shyness is viewed as something to be overcome.

Most appropriately, there is trembling shyness in the face of divinity, which cannot be captured by the mind or grasped by the intellect.

Everywhere I look, I see the cry for self-recognition, and however assertive the personality may be, I have never yet seen a lack of trembling shyness in the face of that recognition.

Put your personality aside. Whether it is a "good" personality or a "bad" personality, whether the personality is pleasant or unpleasant, put it aside and see what naturally and inherently shines.

❖

I remember forcing myself to be a cheerleader in high school, performing horrendous feats before crowds of people in order to satisfy this longing for recognition. Still, the emptiness remained.

Without true self-recognition, performing for crowds is never enough. We are trained in our society to believe that if we please enough people, we will be pleased. Still, in pleasing others, the hunger for self-recognition remains. Almost everyone hungers to be really seen, to be really known. No matter how much the world recognizes you, you are still dissatisfied until you recognize your true self.

How many roads have we all traveled to get recognition?

Celebrities often speak of longing by declaring that fame is never enough. Ten thousand people come to the performance, and still it is not enough. Finally, you recognize that true yearning is never satisfied by external references. Then you are prepared to really ask yourself, to finally ask yourself, *What is this longing? Who is longing?*

✧

I can become consumed with loneliness, and as I dive deeper and deeper into this loneliness, I realize that this, too, is a story. My tears turn into tears of joy coupled with uncontrollable laughter.

Yes . . . oh yes!

Papaji on right, Gangaji center, walking in Lucknow, India, 1991.

Papaji and Gangaji at a
wedding ceremony in
Lucknow, India, 1992.

ABOVE: Gangaji seated with Papaji in Hardwar, 1990. The garland of flowers placed around Gangaji's neck by Papaji acknowledged that she had received Papaji's teaching.

CENTER: Gangaji with Papaji and her husband, Eli Jaxon-Bear.

BELOW: Papaji in satsang with students in Lucknow, 1992.

COURTESY OF DAN BAUMBACH

COURTESY OF ELI JAXON-BEAR

COURTESY OF GANGAJI FOUNDATION

ABOVE LEFT: Gangaji walking with letters, date unknown.

ABOVE RIGHT: Papaji asked Gangaji to hold meetings at several of India's most sacred sites. Here, Gangaji holds satsang in Sarnath where the Buddha offered his first discourse after awakening, 1992.

BELOW LEFT: Byron Bay, Australia, 1996.

ABOVE LEFT: In a boat on the Ganges, Gangaji holds satsang in the holy city of Banaras (also known as Varanasi), 1992.

ABOVE RIGHT: Gangaji small-group meeting, San Francisco Bay Area.

BELOW: Gangaji at Bodh Gaya holding satsang under the Bodhi Tree, 1991.

ABOVE: Gangaji holds a meeting with inmates at Englewood, a Federal prison in Colorado, 1994.

CENTER: Gangaji and Kenneth Johnson in Ashland, Oregon, 2006, nine years after his release from Englewood Prison. A former participant in Gangaji's Prison Program, Kenneth is the founder of This Sacred Space, a nonprofit organization dedicated to serving men and women in prison.

BELOW LEFT: Gangaji arrives for a meeting.

BELOW RIGHT: Gangaji holding Papaji's photo during a retreat in the Yosemite Valley, May 2006.

Satsang with Gangaji in Byron Bay, Australia, 1999.

Gangaji in a small meeting, San Francisco Bay Area.

SEX AND THE TRUE
MEANING OF TANTRA

sn't the goal of *Tantra* to merge with another so that you know without a doubt you are one?

Merging is an exquisite experience that reflects truth, and yes, it is the
teaching of true Tantra. But sexual activity is not needed for the recognition of non-separation between yourself and everything. The real
meaning of Tantra is the recognition that true *I* is uninterrupted, pure,
pristine, untouched consciousness and cannot, in truth, be interrupted
by any perception, illusion, or appearance of other.

The problem with the concept of merging is that it presupposes
there was, in reality, some separation to begin with. Merging, as sublime
as it is, is already one step into the story of separation.

Sex can be beautiful. Touching can be beautiful. But when fulfillment is associated with some cause-and-effect concept of sex or
touching, suffering is created. Then the physicality of sex is an obscu-
ration to truth.

Deep longing for intimacy must be realized. Don't miss the opportunity to experience this longing directly, with no action taken to satiate
it. Then the longing can speak. Love can speak to itself.

True intimacy is endless. It has nothing to do even with human beings. It is an intimacy with the whole universe. This is the real meaning of Tantra, the true meaning of Tantra. It is an embrace of the universe with itself in all its horror and all its beauty—in love with that, intimate with that. This is self-love.

❖

I have been confirming my sexuality at a deep level. I am trying to just let it be there and not act it out. You make it sound so easy, but for me it's so intense.

Yes, it can be very intense.

I've been trying to contain it, and there is warfare going on inside me.

The point where it becomes quite easy is when you are actually, directly experiencing it. Yet the approach to that direct experience can seem very difficult because of the deep conditioning to do something with this enormous sexual force.

I have been seeing how much sexual desire is wrapped in my mind, and how much the thoughts whip it up.

You're referring to fantasy. Some people, after realizing how much the mind is entangled in sex, are no longer interested in sex because they are no longer interested in feeding the mind. This is not true for everyone, of course.

Right! I've experienced that here in satsang. I can watch sexual thoughts come, and I can just dissolve them into that spaciousness. I can laugh at them and say, "No, I won't go for that."

I read somewhere that one of the qualities Papaji liked about you was your chasteness. For me, this is a first glimpse of what chasteness might be.

Chasteness is a state of mind. It means to be open and unsoiled. It is not that sexuality is necessarily unchaste. Although some sexuality is very soiled and distorted, sexuality can also be pure and pristine.

I want to correct one thing you said, though, about dissolving sexual thoughts into spaciousness. You don't need to dissolve them. If sexual thoughts are not fed, they dissolve effortlessly.

Obviously, an enormous mind-play spins around the dance of sexuality. Sex is where most people experience some kind of bliss, release, silence, or peace. In linking bliss, silence, and peace with the sexual act, a regeneration of struggle, tension, acquisition, and loss also occurs. Many people will say that sex is as good as it gets, and they are quite willing to perpetuate the sensual chase.

In the moment of sexual release, a bodily explosion occurs that cannot be contained, a revelation of nobody, no-thing, a vast peace. This is the end of the searching and the tension. The truth of what always *is*, is revealed. The problem arises when sexual intimacy is named as the source of this revelation. Sexual intimacy is not necessary for the discovery of the deepest intimacy, the discovery of peace with no cause.

If you are actually more interested in pristine, pure, immaculate peace than in what has been imagined will give you that peace, then as sexuality arises and dissolves, it points you toward that peace.

Sexual repression is another example of distortion in the hope of liberation. If repression worked, the group in India called the *Nagas*, who cut off their genitals so that they will not have to experience the sexual force, would all be enlightened, but they aren't. They are eunuchs.

I am not an advocate for repression. However, in our Western culture in particular, we have worshipped sexual power. We have worshipped it, followed it, fed it, bowed to it, and ultimately been enslaved to this sexual tyrant. If you follow sexuality with thought and energy and devotion, you are following a limited god. When limited gods are worshipped, the devotees suffer.

The peace that is revealed in the moment after orgasm—where there is no you, no other, just vast limitless space—is already the truth of who you are. It is always and *already* present. You can immediately surrender to that vastness with no need of the sexual dance. Then you will not assume that somebody or some act is needed for fulfillment or bliss. All that is needed is to recognize who you already are. Experience that directly, and sexuality takes its rightful place as follower, not leader.

See through the sexual game, and you will recognize the source that sexual energy arises from and dissolves into. Then sexuality is in its rightful place. Then it is possible to be pure, to be chaste. Then it is possible for sex to not cause suffering.

Peace is not about acquiring other sexual experiences or other sexual partners. Peace is about realizing that you are already at peace. You are already fulfilled if you will but recognize the truth. Whether or not you ever have sex again, discover the truth of your nature and you are fulfilled.

People get very afraid of the thought of never having sex again. Liberating this thought cuts the bondage of the belief that without sex your life would be dead or meaningless. If you are bound to sex to provide your life with meaning, then life can be quite meaningless. Discover true meaning in what has no need of anything for its meaning, what has no need of name or form, no need of unnamed or unformed.

The revelation of not needing anything is the truth of your being. You have the potential to realize this for yourself, not just from hearing it said, but from directly discovering it within yourself. Then the tendencies of repressing or indulging no longer have the power to cause re-identification with suffering. They are only powerful prior to direct experience.

Repression is not freedom, but neither is what gets called expression. What gets called expression is usually some kind of childish acting out as a means to acquire pleasure. The treasure is revealed in neither repressing nor acting out. In nonaction, there is no work for the mind. In either repressing or acting out, there are the thoughts *I am doing this, I am getting this, I am keeping this, I am avoiding this, I am ignoring this.* With no mental movement toward or against, there is no work for the I-thought.

Give the mind no work, and see what remains. See for yourself. Investigate. Experiment. What have you got to lose? You can always go back to worshipping the god of sex. Our culture certainly supports it. Turn on the television, open a magazine, walk down the street, look at men's, women's, and even children's fashions, and you see that sex is worshipped. You can always restimulate the sexual chakra if that is where your interest is. Just as an experiment, why not see what is deeper than that. See what has always been chaste, has always been pure, what cannot be defiled.

❖

I spend a lot of my energy in the area of lust and the preoccupation with lust. I am also a gay man, and I have a lot of trouble with my sexuality and feeling good about myself.

Don't even identify yourself as a man, much less a gay man. When a man recognizes he is not a man, this recognition is liberation.

In identification as a male body with particular hormones coursing through it, and with the onslaught of our cultural conditioning and stimulation, the usual course of action is to either hate or be devoted to that identification.

This holds true for any gender or any form of sexuality. Identification is the distraction. Come back to the beginning, before you were told, and before you believed, *I am a man.* When you roll back all your thought processes to before you even identified yourself as a person, what distraction do you find there?

There is no distraction.

Yes! And this is present every moment. Everything that follows is what you and your ancestors before you believed, read, or have been told. It gets factored into the DNA, and identification becomes the preprogrammed, usual course of action.

You are pure, undifferentiated consciousness. All name and form and sub-name and sub-form are secondary and ultimately irrelevant to that pure consciousness. If you identify with the secondary and irrelevant, there must be some suffering, because it is false identification. When you identify with the source of everything, there is no distraction with the false. The source is present every moment because it is unborn and therefore not subject to death.

Source has been named eternity or God or truth. Whatever names your culture has tried to put on it, eternal truth is untouched by any name. It is before name. You are that which is before name. Recognize yourself as who you are, and see that no seductive identification can give you that. Self-recognition of source is joy beyond belief. This recognition makes pleasure, sexual or otherwise, pale in comparison. There is nothing wrong with pleasure, but it simply does not touch the joy of realizing the source.

Now, with your attention on the fullness of source, before any distraction, see if anything is lacking here, if anything is needed.

Nothing is needed.

This revelation stops the momentum of all past desires. It is the sweetest irony. When you are willing to die to all distractions of desire, fulfillment is revealed.

Continue to discover what is before the first identification.

❖

I have been accused of sinning because of my sexual actions. What is sin? Does it exist?

Sin means mistake, dire mistake. The original sin is the mistake that you are separate from God. All sins come from the original sin. In the play of the mind, there is horrible sinning. There is perpetuation of harm and suffering. In following the perception of separation as reality, fear, grasping, greed, and lust arise. When these are thwarted, hatred and rage arise. Sex often plays a major role in this familiar tragedy.

My sin was fornication.

If it causes suffering for yourself or others, then yes, it is a sin; it is a mistake.

Sometimes people take freedom to mean free license for the physical body. While there can be an experience of relative freedom for the body in terms of physical circumstance, there is no possibility of absolute freedom for the physical body. Stop searching for everlasting freedom with the body. The forces of nature imprison the physical body. There is no way out. The emotional body is imprisoned in feelings of "me, me, me." The mental body is imprisoned in thoughts of "Why? Why? Why?" True freedom is not about freedom of body, mind, or emotion. It is about recognizing what is beyond and untouched by body, mind, and emotion.

If you are no longer identified with the body needing its freedoms, or the emotions needing their freedoms, or the mind needing its freedoms, then you realize absolute, everlasting freedom.

✧✧✧

Recently, I have been trying to discover all the ways in which I get pulled away from what I really want. I have a woman's body, and she wants sex, she wants love, she wants chocolate, or whatever distraction. Observing all of this has brought an immediate recognition of how all things just come and go, all kinds of sensual pleasures, and so I have turned it all back in, asking, "What do I really want?" I want to feel bliss, love, joy, and a remembering that this is already here. It's really beautiful because then there are still all the joys of sensual life but without the disappointment of being pulled away.

I would just make one caution. When you say "the joys of sensual life," you designate sensual pleasure as the cause for joy. Causeless joy is within you, whether there is sensual stimulation or not. As long as you have any misunderstanding that joy is outside you in some object, then there is identification with body and sensuality and the outward activity of the mind. When you recognize that joy is within, untouched by anything, then you also realize that true joy has no need of sensual pleasure, and the mind ceases its outward activity.

All objects begin and end, and in that, there is usually some disappointment because they can't be maintained.

The disappointment arises when they are given the title "That's Where My Joy Is," because this is a lie.

When I follow peace and bliss and feel calm within, suddenly a vibration starts in my whole being, and it is as if I'm walking around in an orgasmic experience that doesn't end.

You recognize that what you want is here already. You recognize the futility in these habits of reaching for "it" out there in some object or some different activity. This recognition is maturity.

In certain lifetimes, sensual passions are very strong. Genetically, culturally, there may be very strong identification with passions. It is wonderful in a lifetime when this strength of passion is turned to passion for truth. Then there can be an ever-deepening realization of truth.

In the recognition of true passion, sexual neurosis is obliterated by sacred gratitude.

❖

I'm finding that sex just doesn't do it anymore. It doesn't take me to that peaceful place where I'm feeling satisfied and happy. In fact, nothing's doing it anymore.

Excellent. Now you don't even have hope.

Sleep also doesn't do it anymore.

As you say, nothing does it.

Isn't there something that does it? I would pay any price for this.

Will you really pay any price? Because this is what it finally leads to. What price is willing to be paid?

Are you willing to give up your search for it?

My search has led me this far.

Sex led you so far. Sleep led you so far. Whatever else you had thought "did it" for you led you so far.

So where do I go from here?

What if you stop? What if you don't reach for another experience? What if you are actually still? Not still so that you will get something—stillness to get something is not stillness. Really stop. Give up hope.

I am not asking that you pick up hopelessness in place of hope. Hopelessness is just the other side of hope. Give it all up. Are you willing to pay that price? I know your stories of what has brought you here so far, but now you are here, and here is too subtle for any vehicle that brought you here. You cannot drive any vehicle into here, however well it has served you. It is too gross.

You must be willing to pay everything. Give up your defeats. Give up your victories. Give up your worthlessness. Give up your arrogance. Give up your non-importance. Give up your importance. Give up what you know, and give up what you don't know. This is the price required.

How?

By not picking any of it up, and if you pick any of it up, drop it immediately. Recognize that what you are giving up is only the poison of
false identification.

That brings up a lot of fear inside.

Now that the protective barrier has been crushed, fear is revealed.
   Where is the fear? Where do you perceive it?

Right now, physically, I perceive it here in my gut.

From the core of the fear in your gut, see the reality of this fear. Not
honoring where you imagine it to be, not honoring its boundary, not
honoring its story—give up that honoring. Go into the core of this and
see what it really is.
   What do you find?

The fear of letting go of everything that I am.

Now you are honoring some story about this fear. Drop that. You have
given that up, remember? Don't take it back. Speak from the core of
fear itself. Not some story about fear, not an evaluation of fear, not a
definition of fear. Drop deeper than your commentary about fear. This
commentary pays obeisance to fear as a god. It keeps fear imagined to
be real. It keeps fear experienced as reality.

In other words, don't intellectualize it so much?

That's right. Do not intellectualize it at all. In this moment, at least,
simply relax. Then you have the capacity to experience this that you
have defined, this that you have analyzed, and this that you have been
haunted by. I am asking you for one second to stop all mental activity, to
be absolutely still. In that stillness, you are at the core of what was previously defined as fear. Since you perceive it somewhere in your belly, put
your consciousness into the center of that, into the core of that.

I feel more fear, then the fear starts to go away.

Yes. Then feel even more fear. There must be a willingness to feel what has never been felt. I am not talking about the willingness to dramatize what has never been felt, or intellectualize what has never been felt, but to directly experience what has never been felt, to be willing to experience that more and more.

If I relax and feel what I'm feeling, it's not so bad.

Not so bad is a good beginning. Now relax even more. Relax completely. Let go of everything. You need do nothing. Discover what is already here, what has always been here in the heart of the fear.

I feel at peace.

Yes. There is peace. You cannot *do* peace. Nothing can do that for you. Peace just *is*.

❖

I have been observing that so much of sexual energy is in the mind. Once one relaxes into being, sex does not seem so important. I find this worrying, and maybe it's just a fear of leaving the past behind.

You fear leaving your identification as a sexual being. Our whole society says that if you leave sex behind, you are nothing, and life is less rich. When you realize that you are already nothing, then yes, sex doesn't seem so important!

If one acts from a place of no-mind, does sex also happen, or does sex need to be dropped before enlightenment?

Sexual desires arise. Sexual desires cease. If sexual desires arise again, sexual desires cease again. What is the big deal? It is really, inherently, not such a big deal. It has been made a big deal by our society and by our fears that if sex goes, it means the end of joy.

It's not a question of dropping sex before enlightenment. That would be similar to the idea of dropping hunger or some other natural phenomenon before enlightenment. What must be dropped is false identification. Drop your identification as a sexual being. Return to original being. Then sex as phenomenon is no problem.

Can one be Zorba the Buddha, living totally in the world, enjoying all the pleasures and delights as an enlightened being, or do you perceive this as impossibility?

If you model yourself after anybody, there is big trouble. If you emulate a model, you then have an idea or an image of what enlightenment looks or acts like.

You can model the freedom and the surrender of both Zorba and Buddha, and you can then see how that manifests in this phenomenon you have named yourself. But if you look at the Buddha and think that enlightenment must mean no sex, or if you look at Zorba and think that freedom must mean a certain amount of sex, then you are missing the mark. These models cause the comparisons that feed further mind activity.

What if you do not look anywhere, for any model, and simply be as you are?

Beingness is primary. Sex is secondary. Recognize yourself as this that is primary, and let secondary be secondary. If you are not focused on sex as "should be" or "shouldn't be," you will see whether sex is appropriate, or if it is ever appropriate again. Then it is simply clear.

❖

It was a real shock when I once heard you say, "Imagine never having sex again." I could imagine dying in this instant rather than never having sex again.

Then for you this is dying. Do you see?

If you imagine that your sex is more important than your very life, then you are bound by sexual fixation. I am suggesting that you imagine the opposite polarity. Imagine your worst fear. If imagining that you will never have sex again is worse than death for you, then you have inadvertently stumbled onto the key for your freedom. Now I suggest that you imagine you will never again participate in the sexual act. Imagine yourself paralyzed, castrated, the sexual act impossible for you.

Imagine that you can never again do what you want to do. See how you have identified your body and your experiences as the source of fulfillment. When the body is identified as the source of fulfillment, then aging, hormonal changes, or whatever debilitating shifts of the body can cause great suffering.

Imagine and experience death—physically, mentally, emotionally, and sexually. Imagine your worst fear. Let it come so that you can meet it, so that you can finally realize you are truly and completely fulfilled by the very nature of beingness. You are fulfillment itself. Consciously recognize yourself as this fulfillment.

For some people, sexual desire falls away after realization. For others, sexual desire may arise, but there is no desire to act on it ever again. For still others, sexual desire arises, and there is acting on it.

You cannot formulate the face of an enlightened being. There is no face. It is in the formulation of enlightenment, fulfillment, or even satisfaction that worrying and suffering arise.

See if there is some knot of identification tying the pleasure of sex together with fulfillment. True fulfillment is more profound than any pleasure.

Please don't misunderstand me. I am not against sex. I am just simply not *for* it.

At a time in my life, I too worshipped sex. I understand this phenomenon of our subculture, this offshoot of the 1960s and 1970s, and the reaction to our parents' generation's repression of sex and denial of sexual joy.

I too pursued sex. I experienced great, deep pleasure, ecstasy, and merging, and I identified myself as the seeker of that. But through that identification, I also began to recognize, *Wait a minute. However many times I experience merging, however many times I play the whole sexual dance, there is something missing here in my search for truth and fulfillment.*

In the same way, I searched for myself in being identified as a mother. I searched for myself in being identified as a healer. Each time I had to see that there was something missing. Yes, there were great pleasures in all of those, certainly there was a sense of satisfaction, but there was still yearning that I couldn't quite satisfy through any activity I knew.

That is when I said, "I want to be free. Whatever it takes, I will give it. Give up my job? . . . Okay, job gone. Give up my identification as healer? . . . Healer gone. Give up my identification as mother? . . . Gone. Give up my identification as sexual being? . . . Gone. Give up my identification as this body? . . . Gone."

What is revealed is what cannot be given up—the absolute truth of who you are. The truth that has been here all along, through the experience of being a baby, then a teenager, then an adult, as sexual being, parent, teacher, healer, even a person at all. By giving up all identification *whatsoever,* true fulfillment, waiting for your discovery all along, is realized, and it is a satisfaction beyond sexual satisfaction, as joyous as that may be. It is the satisfaction of needing nothing, of overflowing fulfillment in itself.

Parents and Children

've believed my child to be the one obstacle between freedom and myself. It feels like I can't be free and be responsible at the same time.

This is the great fear of a parent. Isn't it a joke? We have considered freedom to be freedom of the body, and we imagine freedom of the body as the following of the desires of the body. Yet we know that following personal desires is very often narcissistic indulgence. As you know, bondage to personal desires causes enormous suffering.

What is inherently free is who you are. Who you are does not *become* free. It *is* free. In recognizing this, there is naturally the ability to respond. Before that, responsibility is a concept of duty or of something to be shouldered. It may be tempered with love and care, but it is also something to be borne. Therefore, your child becomes an objectification, a separation between you and that which you really are. This is a deadly joke. You are this very child! Recognize this and you are not searching around for personal freedom. Then nothing can be an intrusion.

Your child crying or exhibiting infantile behavior may not be pleasant. I am not advising you to foolishly smile and say, "How precious." But you can recognize that behavior has nothing to do with the inherent freedom of that child. In your clear recognition, it is much easier to be a responsible parent.

Right action is not usually preconceived action. It is fresh and clear. It is stabilized in the confidence of knowing the difference between what a child must be taught and confirming for them the inherently shining truth of their being. Your child will be very happy to receive this transmission.

The duty of the parent is to first transmit truth, and then to transmit skills of survival and the accumulated lore of a particular culture. Then the child's body will not be experienced as a burden to you or to themselves. Nothing will have to be forced to prove "I am."

Obviously, children need directing. They need some conditioning. But when you point to that which is untouched by conditioning, then certain skills like how to use a fork, to look both ways to cross a street, to be in a public place, to be a doctor, lawyer, teacher, or parent, are all recognized as secondary to who they are in the depth of being. This pointing is what a true parent gives to children.

Conditioning can be very useful, but if the conditioning teaches that you are the conditioned, it is a gross mistake, and it results in unnecessary suffering.

Recognize freedom in mother and child, father and child, friend and friend, lover and lover, husband and wife, student and teacher. All these relationships of oneself are to be recognized as refractions of truth. Then there can be useful discipline and teaching and conditioning.

The childish idea of freedom as an expectation of every desire being met comes from the mentality of a two-year-old. This is not freedom; it is suffering. It is imagining that fulfilling your personal desires will give you freedom. Spiritual maturity is seeing the result of the trap of expecting objects of desire ever to provide what is truly wanted.

❖

What is true mothering?

You and your child will teach each other what it is to be a mother and a child. A direct line of communication takes place in the most unexpected, spontaneous, and mysterious ways, whether it involves vaccinations or school crossings or the transmission of love, beauty, and trust. You have nothing to ask me about that. Ask the inner wisdom that abides in your heart and in the heart of the child. It is the same source. If an external authority is needed, let your heart guide you to it.

When I'm with her, everything that you talk about is so present. I guess I just hope for her that she doesn't have to pretend that she's not that.

Don't burden her with your hopes.

You are saying that when you are with her, it is satsang. What is the real boundary between you and her?

I know there is no real boundary.

When you recognize it is impossible to not be with her, truth will be transmitted. She will not grow up taking the appearance of separation to be reality.

Isn't this shred of distrust ridiculous in the face of your experience of satsang with your daughter? If you feed distrust, it will lead you into speculations of what might happen to her or might not happen to her, and then you will be dismayed to discover that your time with her is strained and awkward. Don't feed and then transmit distrust.

Parenting is a great role in the mysterious play of one self. Let it be that. You cannot control it. Don't confuse yourself as the role you play. Then you are not burdened by motherhood, and she is not burdened as "your" child. Play the role fully and completely *as a role*. Trust yourself.

❖

I have a four-year-old son, and I feel he looks to me for boundaries and for understanding who he is. I don't want to mess him up the way that I've been messed up.

Maybe you are not messed up.

Maybe not, but I feel like I am.

Yes, I understand you feel like that, but that is probably because your mother felt that she wasn't going to mess you up the way her mother messed her up. Then "messed up" is the message that gets transmitted.

Then could you give me some advice?

Yes. Relax. As you naturally teach your child what is appropriate behavior and inappropriate behavior, don't add on to the teaching that he is the behavior, that he is "bad" or he is "good." Then perhaps this child will pick up the truth that behavior is simply behavior, and certain behavior is appropriate in certain situations, but he is truly consciousness itself.

Before he has any possibility of picking that up from you, you have to realize it yourself. Begin by stopping this story, "I've been messed up."

❖

You've said how important it is to accept children for who they are, in the same way that we ourselves want to be accepted for who we are. My children are coming into adolescence. There is tremendous anger and a pushing of boundaries. They are doing normal teenager stuff, but I don't want to see them do something that might cause serious trouble. It brings up all kinds of questions in me about how to accept them and yet also be a responsible parent.

Responsibility is not found in a formula. It is free and comes from the willingness and the courage to respond appropriately. The appropriate response is unknown beforehand. It cannot be rehearsed.

Most people are still stuck in an adolescent frame of mind. You must discover if there is some of your own unresolved adolescent experience manifesting by wanting things your way. Adolescence is like a larger version of the two-year-old, only now it is about more power and more dangerous toys. It is further complicated by the torrent of hormones and all their emotional and physiological imperatives.

I don't want to make light of this. The truth is, many adolescents do get killed or kill themselves. It is a turbulent time. It is obviously one of the big shifts in life.

Adolescents push parents, and in that push, whatever is unresolved can be seen. If you are willing to actually experience the fear and terror and anger that may be evoked in this relationship, if you are willing to experience these emotions without indulging them and without blaming your children or letting them walk all over you, then there arises an appropriate natural response. It may not always look appropriate, since *natural* often does not conform to *normal*.

True responsibility is intuitive wisdom and the courage to be true to that.

Will that letting-go process aid the child in moving through difficult times more rapidly?

Some things cannot be known. You cannot know what it is a child has to resolve in this life. You can only be there as the truest kind of support. True support does not rule with an unloving, iron hand. It doesn't ignore the child. It doesn't say, "Oh honey, sure, whatever you want." It is true to the moment, ruthlessly true.

It is also important to be willing to make a mistake, and to be willing to see when a mistake has been made so that it can be corrected. If there is no willingness to make a mistake, there is no possibility of spontaneity and appropriate action.

But I find that when I'm on my own path, away from my child, I'm able to feel peaceful.

Your child is on your path! Doesn't he show up on your own path?

But it brings up anger and fear and despair.

Yes, of course it does. What can be harder than being a parent or a child? Those are the two most demanding roles to play because they *do* evoke anger, fear, and despair.

When you are willing to stop practicing your own neurosis, the transmission of neurosis is finished, and the finishing is retroactive. It permeates every cell of your ancestry in both directions. Even your child's potential unborn child is affected by your awakening. The acceptance, the willingness to see everyone as they truly are, spreads like a wildfire. It is the truth, and it penetrates all the disguises and lies. All anyone wants is to be truly seen as they are. That is all your child wants, and that is all you want.

Seeing doesn't mean you have to like his terms. True seeing is to still see him through all the difficulties. When you are seen, then you can see, and seeing gives birth to true responsibility. Not from some textbook, not even from what worked the last time, but freely responding. Isn't this what you want in your life? Don't you want people to respond to you freely, and don't you want to respond to people and events freely?

Yes . . . it is what I want for myself and for him.

You cannot wait for anybody else to see you. First be still and recognize your own completeness. Then you are able to see everyone clearly.

Of course, if you are concerned that your child have a good position in the world, that everyone accept him, or that he lead a safe, predictable life, then you are simply supporting him as a robot.

I just don't want him to kill himself.

Yes, certainly, but the hard truth is, he may kill himself. Before he kills himself, if he does, you can be with him fully, completely, so that his life will not have been a waste. If he lives to be a hundred and five and he has not experienced being seen and therefore is unable to see, his life will have been a waste.

His life is not separate from your life. He is not an interruption of your life. Parenting is a catalyst that breaks up any crystallized ideas of complacency or comfort or knowing what things will look like. The parent/child drama is a beautiful plan, divinely ordained. It is not meant to be comfortable all the time, even though, of course, many times it is deeply joyous. If played fully and truthfully, it is humbling and heart-opening.

❖

I'm about to become a grandmother again, and my son is suffering a lot. He wasn't nursed, and I feel this may be why he has a lot of problems.

Don't believe this story about why he suffers. Plenty of people *were* nursed, and they are still miserable. I hear from many who weren't nursed yet still received what they needed most from their mothers. Often what is given with the mother's milk is not nourishing anyway. True nourishment comes from the open heart, not the milk. Most mothers are children still looking for true nourishment when they have their own children.

Let your story about why he is suffering be finished. It is the past. The sooner you can drop it, the sooner the possibility that he can also drop it.

I used to firmly believe a particular story I had about my daughter. I had been neurotic and afraid, and I hadn't known how to be with my daughter. Her behavior reflected that, and we had a difficult time for some time. I finally recognized that the entanglement going on with this person I called my daughter was wrapped in guilt. In coming to face the guilt, by some grace, I was able to let the whole story go.

In the joy of release, I took my daughter out for dinner, and I said, "I want to ask your forgiveness for all the stupidity that I perpetuated as a mother. I simply want to ask your forgiveness."

She looked at me strangely and said, "You have asked me that about a hundred times. It's over! I forgave you a long time ago."

It was true, yet I hadn't been able to see her forgiveness and openness. I was too caught in my own story of guilt. In my story, she was an extension of my guilt, some proof of my failing. The moment that story was cut, I could see her. I could see this being for who she is and not just as some projection of mine. Not as "my" daughter, not as "my" object, but as who she is. Then we could be together truly.

Guilt is a saboteur, and there comes a time to say no to guilt. I don't mean to cover it. There may be apologies that have to be made, but let guilt be finished. When the guilt is finished, you can directly experience the pain that is under the guilt—the suffering, loneliness, fear, and sadness. In being willing to experience emotions under the guilt, you are willing to get to the basis of the relationship.

I don't know what your relationship is with your son, but you can refuse the relationship with guilt. Guilt is a nasty and abusive relationship. It is a denial of the love that is there and has always been there.

Maybe you don't even like your son. This happens sometimes. But the love present is always present because it is really self-love. The moment you objectify him as "my" son, the truth is overlooked. Then you begin to believe that your object should look a certain way, act a certain way, or react a certain way. If the object does not look or act the way you want it to, you may try to force it. If it won't be forced, you will probably blame yourself or your child. All this unnecessary suffering overlooks the truth at the basis of the relationship. Love is the basis, and true love is free of objectification.

✧

When you mention guilt, I feel like that is what keeps me in relationship with both my children and my parents. It must take courage to let it go.

Do you have this kind of courage, even if it means losing the relationship? When it is a distorted relationship, keeping the relationship doesn't necessarily serve truth. You actually serve your children more by severing a distorted tie. Then there is the possibility of coming together as being to being, not victim to victimizer. This means being willing to lose everything.

Freedom means being willing to lose everything, all suffering, judgments, ideas, concepts, expectations, images, experiences, and identifications. Guilt cannot exist without all those components.

Is facing guilt the same as with the other emotions?

Guilt is not an emotion.

Does it cover up the other feelings?

That's right. Guilt overlays emotions with images and stories and violence, either internal violence or external violence.

Guilt is perpetuated, self-inflicted violence. Put an end to the violence. You cannot meet any emotion in violence, and guilt is violence. You can only meet in openness. In openness, there is no guilt. Peace is in the openness.

Are you saying guilt is a justification for continued violence?

Yes. I am saying to stop this horrible game of torture. Guilt is a learned torture. It is the same with doubt. Guilt and doubt are not pure emotions. They are both used to deflect attention from what is feared to be experienced.

❖

My mother is much more than my mother. She knows the truth as much as anyone else, and she's so simple.

And who would have expected it there!

Yes! We were both so surprised about that freedom.

What good fortune that this discovery happened while she is still alive.
When a mother discovers it in her child, and a child discovers it in a
parent, then it is seen everywhere.

Maybe the vastness of self can be seen and experienced more easily
in the ocean. Maybe it's not so obvious in the little spider scurrying up
the wall. However, once you have clearly seen truth, then it is seen everywhere. In the tiniest little ant, there you are. It is not by some mistake
that this spider appeared in your path. It is not by some mistake that you
find yourself in the middle of the ocean. Make good use of everything
for deeper investigation into truth.

Thank you!

Allowing yourself to be seen is the thanks. You are seen, and then you
see. Let yourself be seen, and let yourself see. Then you will see through
apparent differences. Whether mother, daughter, father, son, cousin, uncle,
spider, or ocean—see through the differences to what is eternally the
same. Then your response is natural. It doesn't need to be rehearsed.

❖

My nine-year-old son has no interest in the academics that he's being
pushed into, and yet our culture so strongly supports that. I know there
is no real rulebook for parenting, but I would love to hear you speak
about that.

Do you know how upset Ramana's mother was when he ran away from
home?

Yes, that's right!

She came and pleaded with him and begged him to come back home, and he wouldn't even speak to her. His brother also came and said, "You aren't being responsible. You have a family. You have a culture. Our father's dead, and you are responsible for your part in the family. What are you doing sitting here like a beggar?"

Isn't there a way to do both?

Maybe, but it's not for you to say. See what you want for your son, finally and above everything, so that when you are long gone, this is what he will have.

I want to be of the truest support to his development.

In the final say, the best that you can give him is the encouragement to be true to the depth of his being, and the sooner, the better.

The reason people flock to gurus is because they did not have spiritual parenting. I call Papaji "Papaji" because he refuses to let me be untrue to truth.

Of course, there are differences in styles, personality, and destiny, but of primary and universal importance is to be true to the truth of who you are and the truth of who he is.

Ramana wasn't an outstanding student. He liked sports more than anything else. He was versed in religion, but he wasn't a religious pundit, and this is all to our benefit. Had he been immersed in religion, maybe he would have believed that religious education led to his awakening. Instead, out of the blue, as a sixteen-year-old boy, by some mysterious, causeless intervention, Ramana was able to directly experience his fear of death, with no one apparently guiding him. That innocent, immediate, causeless awakening is the promise to all of us here and to all of those who are touched by all of us. This awakening spreads infinitely.

The challenge is to be true. Being true to the truth of your being is the transmission of truth to your children and to everyone you meet.

We have the example of great teachers, artists, and scientists, but the world as a whole, the "normal" world, does not support being true to awakening.

This is the challenge. It is the challenge of a lifetime.

Give your life to that. Give your role of "mother" to that. Give your son's life to that, your husband's life to that, and then see.

Yes, it is a radical surrender, and it does not exclude conditioning and training of our children, but conditioning and training are secondary to the primary, essential transmission.

I understand. I get it that it's living the truth.

Yes, living the truth!

✧

How much do I talk about the truth with my nine-year-old child?

Don't restrain yourself. As it comes up, be willing to speak the truth. If you fall prey to the temptation to preach, be still immediately. Let truth speak through you rather than you speak through truth. Speaking is more than sounds made through the vocal chords. Speaking is the emanation of your life. Speak silently, and you will speak truly. Live truly, and you will respond fully and appropriately.

If you live satsang, you speak the language of the heart, a language of truth. It speaks to you from a nine-year-old as easily as from any other age, because it is alive at any age.

FACING THE FEAR OF DEATH

I n our culture, the way that death and fear of death are usually seen and experienced is a clear indication of deep misalignment with truth. Because of our conditioning, physical death is seen as the problem. In actuality, facing the death of personal identity is an immense opportunity to directly encounter eternal, undying presence.

There is a strong, conditioned belief that you are a psychological entity located in a body. In truth, there is no real psychological entity except as an image or a thought coupled with physical sensation.

When fear of death is directly investigated, it is discovered that only form is born and dies. Consciousness is free of formation, free of birth, free of death.

❖

I have the experience of a continuing dread of death that just hangs around me like a cloud.

If you invite this cloud called death closer, you can experience it directly. In this extraordinary experience, what dies and what remains is discovered.

How do I discover that?

By being still. By neither repressing nor following any thought that arises. By not moving the mind in any direction. By ceasing all attempts to escape. Then where is this thing called death?

It's squirming in me right now.

Find it. Go into it with your consciousness. What do you discover?

A sensation.

Meet the sensation directly. What is at the core of this sensation?

It feels like sadness.

Meet the core of the sadness. Be aware if your meeting is deflected by a mental discussion about the sadness.

It just feels like a deep, old grief.

Without qualifying, evaluating, or measuring, continue into the core. Directly experience that which is at the center.

What are you experiencing?

It's like a long thing. A sensation of a pole that sits in a cemetery.

An image is the result of separation between you and the sensation. With any image, there must be someone sensing and something sensed. I am speaking of being right inside the sensation. Leave the boundaries separating you and it behind. Release all imagery and dive into the core of the sensation.

I find myself going into it, then bouncing off and pulling back.

You are describing a mental image, another strategy of mind to avoid direct experience. When the image of bouncing starts, continue to re-lax. Drop into the core of the grief that you have dreaded and avoided. Other images or names might arise, but for now, rather than speculating about the grief, analyzing it, or overcoming it, discover what is present at the core.

In an open meeting, the nature of all phenomena, subtle or gross, is discovered directly. Any phenomenon can be met directly, whether it is the emotion of sadness, the thought of *me*, or death itself.

This is a great discovery. I am simply saying to put everything aside and discover the underlying nature of everything.

The usual strategy is mental movement away from direct experience and toward techniques of overcoming, escaping, changing, denying, repressing, acting out, or discharging. This habit of mind is ego. If this habit is recognized and set free, then where is ego? When you are not preoccupied and distracted by thoughts of escaping or clinging, seeing is clear. Seeing clearly is the inherent nature of consciousness.

Egoic habits of mind have been passed from generation to generation for millions of years. Strategies of escape or defense nourish the momentum of conditioned existence. In the willingness to experience what has not been experienced, the core of all internal and external phenomena is revealed, and the momentum of conditioning is stopped.

Expose and release the lie of ego. All our lives are conditioned toward complexity, yet release is absolutely simple.

Every emotion, sensation, or energy faced purely and simply reveals eternal life.

❖

I'm troubled because the doctors say I must work with them or I'll die.

Are you ready to die?

I don't think that would be as bad as mucking around with doctors.

I have nothing against medical procedures or medicine. What I am for is you facing your death. Not just because someone has now spoken to you of the possibility of death, but because every body will die at some point.

Until death has been faced, there can be no lasting clarity. Countless hours are spent ignoring, fearing, chasing, wallowing in, or running from this thing we call death. Every decision and every choice is based on some kind of mental relationship with death. When the mind is kept busy running from, worrying about, thinking about, or denying thoughts about death, what is eternal is overlooked. Surrender the relationship with your mind, and have a meeting with death.

Let me stress that surrender has nothing to do with either tending the body or not tending it. Once death has been met, the decision to care for the body is not muddied with needs and hopes and expectations.

When Ramana was a sixteen-year-old boy, he experienced a fear of death. Rather than run to his mother or to the doctors, he lay down on the floor and faced death fully—not just intellectually—but fully and completely. He allowed himself to experience directly what it is that actually dies. From a true meeting, great awakening occurs. In finally facing death fully and completely, there is recognition of eternal life, life that is not born and therefore not subject to death.

Most people spend their lives ignoring the reality of the death of the body, and then they are quite surprised when it is their body's turn. Ninety-year-old people are still surprised. It is part of the education of our culture to pretend that death is something separate from life. In our culture, death usually takes place in the back room. Bring the specter of death into the front room. Welcome death to satsang.

What a gift the prognosis of death can be. What an attention-getter! What a way to draw attention to what does not die. The most feared event is announced. That announcement is your invitation to direct experience.

❖

When I met you the very first time, I was so touched by what you said. Afterwards, at home, I felt like everything was breaking and burning.

Wonderful.

Yes, but it's scary.

Yes, it is not casual. It is not trivial. The whole mental house of cards is shaken.

Then I tried to accept it, to meet it, and it was very difficult because it's so scary.

Now you can stop trying anything. Let it be scary.

The fear arises that I cannot manage my life.

Yes, I know this fear. You fear that you will not be able to manage your life or even survive. Those fears are all the fear *of* something—the fear of death, the fear of homelessness, the fear of irresponsibility. Fear *of* goes on and on. Approach fear itself. As long as you stay with fear *of* something, you are hovering on the perimeter. Discover, in truth, what fear is.

   Are you aware of this fear now?

Yes.

Leaving all speculations behind, report to me from the core of it.

It's difficult.

In the core of fear, where is difficulty? Where, even, is fear?

Something that I learned.

Well, that's true, but I want your report to be deeper than an analysis. In the midst of this something that you have learned to call fear, what is found?

It is a fear of not existing.

Yes! The primary fear is the possibility of nonexistence.

Let yourself fall effortlessly into and *be* the fear of nonexistence. Any mental effort is another tactic to try to escape nonexistence. Let go of all struggling to not be touched by that fear, and meet nonexistence.

The fear is huge!

I appreciate that it is a colossal fear. In your willingness to meet this colossus directly, truth is discovered.

Notice if you are telling yourself a story, or even just aimlessly talking to yourself. If so, stop. Allow the mind to be open.

Now I feel a lot of body sensations.

Let them be. They mean nothing. Let sensations, energy, phenomena of all kind, be.

See how easy it is?

Now where is fear?

Nowhere!

Yes. Now you know the truth of ease, and the truth of difficulty. Difficulty arises when you try to escape the experience of something. Ease is present when you are willing to stop and meet whatever has been haunting you.

When you finally, completely, face fear itself, it is nowhere to be found. Fear can never survive a total meeting with conscious awareness.

❖

The closer I come to being in labor, to giving birth, the more I fear death.

The fear of death is deep in the psyche. When it rises to the surface, there is usually the impulse to either overcome it or get away from it. Open to the fear of death today, right now. Don't continue the habitual tendency to contract the mind. Right now is the time. For this opening, all the stories about death must end.

It doesn't seem scary if I open to it.

That's right. That's the truth.

Certainly death is an extremely powerful event, as is birth. Whatever appears to be born dies. Whatever appears disappears. Whether it is flesh, idea, thought, emotion, or state.

What is not born cannot die. Death is not the end of life. Death is not the polar opposite of life. Birth and death are opposites. Life is the constant. Life is the presence that both birth and death appear in.

Be willing to die before the flesh dies. Give up the struggle against the fear of death. When you face the fear of death, you discover it to be a nonexistent guardian of the gates of realization. You do not need to overcome what is nonexistent.

Usually fear is transmitted through the womb, as well as anguish, desire, hope, failure, and success. When you are willing to meet the fear of death, the realization of what is true is transmitted from being to being. You will transmit an extraordinary secret of life through the womb.

I've been going through a lot of loss lately. Today I thought I was going to lose my life. A lot of fear came up, and I'm wondering how to address that fear.

Invite the fear back. Right now, as you sit here, invite it to show its face in the light of satsang.

I can't seem to get it to come.

Yes, this is the secret. Fear is powerful only when you are trying to escape it. Turn to fear and say, "Yes, come now. I am ready." You will see how fearful fear is. It is not to be found.

Through past generations your ancestors have run from fear. Finally down the line, one of you awakens and says, "Okay, fear, I'm ready to meet you. Where are you?" Direct experience goes against the momentum of conditioned existence.

Look for fear and tell me, what is present? Call it in even more strongly. If fear of death shows up at satsang, it is ready to be liberated. If it is not ready to be liberated, it runs as far from you as it can.

Welcome all to satsang. This meeting called satsang is not different from the simple willingness to be. Just be.

Now you know the secret of fear, because you have spent so much time running from it, and more importantly, because you have stopped to face it. Now fear is a useful vehicle to discover the divine secret.

Keep the invitation open. The minute you begin to close your mind, some fear from back in time may appear to chase you. Open the door and where can it be found?

❖

My son just wrote me, and he is in a very dangerous place. I fear for his life, and I really don't know how to face that fear.

Your fear is not about your child's death; it is about your own death. Until the nature of your own death is recognized, you will project your fear onto others.

Every *body* is in a dangerous situation at every moment. The body is a walking time bomb. At any moment it could cease to be. Your body and your children's bodies will one day cease to exist. To become involved in your children's death before you meet your own is a distraction that serves only the continuance of fear.

I understand the pull on you, but facing your own death is all you can do. And, in fact, it is enough. If your child has stirred up this fear of death, very good. Bow to him. Stirring up what hasn't been faced is one of the great gifts of children.

It is impossible to know how long a child will live. If you are distracted by the thought of that, you overlook the opportunity to meet what has been stirred up. Stop using your thoughts to delay meeting any emotion that appears from this stirring. Take five seconds to turn and face what you have run from.

Your children will be much happier if you face your own death. They will receive a transmission from you of the willingness to meet death fully. Then, when you speak to them about anything, you will speak from that realization.

He also worries about death.

He learned to worry from you. The same way he learned his name or his first word. The fear of death is contagious. You must stop the contagion. Facing death is the medicine to cure the disease. If the disease is exposed to the medicine, the disease cannot survive.

But he can be stabbed. He can be beat up.

Yes, of course. Always. The difference that meeting death makes is in the quality and experience of life. Are you wandering around looking for the potential stabbing, imagining the potential stabbing, while fantasizing the loneliness? This is the way most people spend their lives, isn't it?

He says he hears gunfire in his neighborhood, and it's not his imagination.

Death is in every neighborhood. Do you think death is located only in particular neighborhoods just because it is obvious there? Death is in every house.

I am not speaking of the outer circumstances of his life. I am speaking of the inner circumstances of your life. Your life right now. Your own death.

You have learned the horror of death. You have seen pictures of it, and you have read books about it. You have thought about it, and now you are imagining your child in that horror. This is a nightmare. Wake up in this nightmare.

You cannot control death. You can move to the biggest house with the biggest security fence, and still you cannot control death. You need only read the newspapers to see that this is so. Violence is the byproduct of a fearful, violent society. There is no help for a society running from fear.

Running from fear leads to isolation and separation. The desperate attempt to control the enormous fear of death fosters more fear, more isolation, and more violence.

It must begin with you. The whole world is waiting for you.

I am serious. I am speaking to everyone. It is no good to wait for someone else to awaken so that all will then be taken care of. It is you the world is waiting for. Not just for your children, but for all children, all neighborhoods everywhere. It is up to you. *You* must awaken and discover directly what has never been born and therefore cannot die. This is a child's real heritage. Anything else is just passing on further conditioning based on fear.

❖

I have a question about the mind and the body. I often have this tiredness that affects my everyday life, and I am wondering about the power of the mind to heal.

The power of mind is enormous and can be used to support either sickness or health. I suggest you accept only the true healing, the true refuge. All the rest is playing with feelings of personal power.

Many people seek personal power because they think it promises security. Then one day the body dies. I suggest you discover what is beyond healing the body.

Take care of your body; even love your body. Feed it properly, exercise it properly, and give it proper rest. If it is sick, give it medicine, but don't think that the body is who you are. If you think the body is who you are, it will never satisfy you. This misidentification and the dissatisfaction that follows are the larger sickness.

Generally, when I speak about illness, I am addressing psychological illness. I define psychological illness as the notion that you are separate from the source of fulfillment or that you need something else to make you happy. This sickness is epidemic.

If you believe *I am sick,* then there is suffering and the attempt to escape suffering. Stop all attempts to escape, and ask yourself *who* is sick.

Be willing to discover the truth behind your sense of lack of fulfillment. Be willing to receive the revelation of what is always whole—your own self.

One of the clarifying experiences of an aging body is the recognition that death of the form really happens. It is not abstract. The body does return to dust.

Some bodies will have more sickness than other bodies. Some plants grow stronger than others do. This is simply the nature of form. If you cease seeking fulfillment through the body, there is no problem. There may be physical discomfort, but discomfort does not mean anything about the source of fulfillment. The truth is that who you truly and always are is already complete.

First face the psychological lie that you are incomplete, that you are not good enough. Face this directly, rather than trying to get complete, or to become enlightened, or to be worth something. Face incompleteness directly, and discover immediately what is true.

Rather than continually trying to outrun some physical or psychological sickness, face whatever it is that you imagine separates you from fulfillment.

Extraordinarily good news is revealed at the core of every fear, as well as at the core of every other emotion. With exquisite irony, when you stop expecting the body and its condition to lead you to fulfillment, you can see clearly what your particular body actually needs and provide for it.

❖

I recently had the experience of being in an MRI machine. I could not move, and I had a panic attack. I thought I was going to die, and there was a loss of control that I couldn't let go into.

Most everyone has a great fear of losing control, but the truth is that each night before you drop into deep sleep, you have to lose all control. It is impossible to go into deep sleep without losing control. If you are still attempting to control anything, either you won't sleep or your sleep will be very light and filled with dreams.

As you give up control, the definition of who you are is released. With the death of definition, all thoughts of what you can and cannot do naturally die. Since there is no thought of you, there are no thoughts of what can or cannot be borne, what can or cannot be done. Thoughts of what should have been or might have been are all finished, in simply giving up the illusion of control.

I understand the great fear that if you give up control, you might become like a vegetable or a madman or something horrible. But you are like a madman in your attempt to keep control over what cannot be controlled.

Life cannot be controlled.

At a certain stage of maturity, you recognize you have no control over life. However you may try, you will never be able to control the true teacher, which is life itself. When you recognize life as the uncontrollable teacher, the concept of control is humbled. In this humbling, life then has the possibility of living its own fulfillment through a life form.

I am not suggesting you give up control to somebody in particular. I am saying to surrender your idea of who you are and all definitions of who you are. These ideas are all just some futile attempt to control life.

❖

If this body, this form, is illusion and not the true self, it almost seems like a cosmic joke. Why aren't we just the source?

You are the source. Limitlessness has no problem with form. Why limit true self to either form or formlessness? Do you think we should be limited to no jokes? Do you think God is not playful?

Well, I guess I don't mind a joke unless it's played on me!

The best joke is the one played on oneself. That joke destroys any idea of self-importance.

If you were two or three or even ten years old, maybe I would not speak to you like this, but now you are long past your time of maturity, so get the joke. Enjoy the joke. The joke itself destroys the knot of identification. Self-righteousness and self-importance are ego-righteousness and ego-importance. Recognizing the joke is the medicine for the disease of egoic importance.

It is a beautiful joke, a joke with uncountable levels and permutations, tears and laughter, longing, beauty, and silence. It is a divine joke, not a paltry joke that can be read in a book. It is the most mysterious, far-reaching, never-ending joke. This is God's joke.

❖

It's as though my body is physically struggling with this. My heart is beating very, very fast. The fear grows, and I open to the fear. I realize it is the fear of losing this body.

The primal identification, the primal struggle, the primal fear, is that without your body, you do not exist. You believe that your body is where you exist and is the proof of your existence. The purpose of sat-sang is to meet this fear.

Relax and allow the fear to be. There may be great shaking. There may be energy released. There may be sweating. There may be tears. There may be the impulse to bolt, the impulse to cover your face. All of this is normal, given the deep conditioning of identification with the body.

Relax. The fear is a good sign. If people tell me they never have fear, I realize they probably have not touched this primal fear.

Self-inquiry is not intellectual inquiry. It is inquiry of the deepest order. It is the great good luck of this human incarnation that you possess the capacity to ask a question of such depth, to actually question death itself.

You are the source, untouched by birth or death. You are pure, bound-less, unborn consciousness, giving birth to all bodies and reclaiming all bodies in death. You have nothing to fear! Take a moment to die, and you can see clearly, obviously, what dies and what is eternal self. Then your body, for as long as it may exist, is no problem. Even though it may have its problems, it is no problem.

BEING IN THE WORLD

Someone once asked, "What is the difference between surrender to uncontrollable, unspeakable, unnameable 'thatness' and being crazy?"

The primary difference is in the words "me" and "my." Even speaking about "your" realization is the beginning of the fall into at least mild delusion and craziness. There is a tinge of craziness in claiming *anything* as "mine."

When you recognize that there is no "me," that there is only truth recognizing itself through perception of form, this is real sanity. Not what passes for sanity in the world, but true sanity, the bliss of being.

Yes, there can be a fear of being crazy with happiness in the world. Dare to be that happy! Then you will see that you are happy because you are nothing. You are no *thing* at all. You will laugh and laugh. When you laugh, the mind is stopped. In the instant of laughing, there is no thought. In any instant of no thought, your true face is revealed. Live in the world of false faces, knowing your true face.

❖

In that moment of both emptiness and fullness, I feel like nothing matters. If you are in that space, how can you get anything done in the world?

Why would you want to work?

The idea that nothing matters is very different from the experience that nothing matters. The experience that nothing matters is one of expansion. It is not a nihilistic dismissal of responsibility. If you relegate the experience to the *idea* of nothing mattering, you miss the mark. When the mind rests in the stillness of its source, the concepts *everything matters* and *nothing matters* both collapse.

There is no formula for the manifestation of realization. Ramana stayed at the foot of the holy mountain Arunachala all of his life. He lived a life in retreat from the world, and yet the whole world has been touched. How that was done, who can say? Looking for a particular formula or activity for the "enlightened life" is the attempt to imitate or model space itself. Living by imitation is living indirectly. You are space. Be as you are, and then see.

So the radiance comes out of just being anything?

For seekers in India, the life of a *sadhu*, a life of abstinence from the world, is considered a holy life. In other cultures, a life of total service is considered the correct life. Some truly holy lives will be celebrated by the world. Some will remain obscure and unknown by the world. A true life, a holy life, is a life lived in surrender to truth, however it looks.

Stop the practice of separating yourself from totality, and life is fully, unknowingly, mysteriously revealed. You will be quite surprised. Your life may not change at all, or it may change quite radically.

Satsang is being revealed in your lifestream, now. The ocean of truth is revealed in silence, speaking, eating, walking, sitting, action, and nonaction.

There is no particular face to enlightenment, no particular personality to enlightenment, and no particular action to enlightenment. Defining enlightenment does not make enlightenment. Any definition is somebody's version of enlightenment, and all versions are limited.

I have questions about living in the world and money. I don't have anything secured toward my future, and I guess there is some fear about that.

This fear has nothing to do with the future; it has only to do with the past. It has been passed on to you. Release the past from your mind, and it is truly and completely over. Every time a fear of survival arises, a thought or feeling of need, meet it as it is. As long as you are following fear-generated thought with instructions from the past, it may seem to have a kind of respectability. Respectable fear is called worry. It is a legacy passed on to you from your parents or culture, who received it from their parents or culture. It is a worthless gift from your ancestors.

Discard this worthless gift. Meet fear directly, clearly. In this direct meeting, you will discover there actually is no fear, and clarity naturally reveals itself.

Who can say whether you will have money next week, next year, or ever again? If you are willing to meet this fear, whether you have money or you don't have money, you realize you are free of the bondage of the past.

If you go back far enough in your ancestry, most likely there was the experience of imminent starvation. This is a huge fear, and it gets passed on from generation to generation. But look at the affluence of this lifetime. Look at the grace of this birth. If you waste this lifetime carrying around the old baggage from five generations ago, you will miss this exquisite window of opportunity to discover what is at the core of this and every fear.

Right now, you most likely have no real worry about your next meal or about shelter. Of course, you can fabricate many worries if you want a special meal or a better shelter, but I am speaking of the most elementary concerns. In your life at this very moment, there is no real need to worry.

What a rare lifetime! What a good birth. Use this opportunity. Don't throw it away. Meet life fully and completely. Discover who you are, *really* who you are.

All your circumstances support your awakening now. You find yourself in satsang. You find yourself where truth is being spoken directly to you, as you. What an opportunity. As you say, you recognize there is no real problem, and yet you still have this old fear. Drop all your mental baggage about fear, and meet it pure and simple. By baggage, I mean any concept concerning past, present, or future.

The fear of survival is a deep, animal fear, but the human animal is a rare incarnation. The human animal actually has the possibility of discovering its true identity as beingness itself. What a mystery. What a gift. I have heard it said that it is possible in other species. I don't know about that, but I know that it is possible in this species to awaken now.

There have definitely been times in the past when there was no food or shelter. There may come a time in the future when food and shelter are not so certain. At those moments of preoccupation with survival of the organism, the question of who you are is usually overlooked.

Now here you are without those concerns. Will you overlook this essential question from habitual concerns of survival, or will you now discover the truth?

✧

All my life, I've noticed how I constantly go out and come back, go out and come back. I have those moments of real peace and bliss inside myself, but then I go out again.

Where is out, and where is in?

I'm not sure, but it feels out, and it feels in.

Well, let's find out. Let's be sure where *out* and *in* really are, because these are important concepts. Find the boundary between the experience of being *out* and the experience of being *in*.

I can't put my finger on it.

That's a good beginning. When you first started talking, you were very certain you go *out* and then you go *in*. First you discovered peace, centeredness, and ease within, and then you discovered the inclination of out-in-out-in. This is very important. You discovered retreat. Then you made a separation between retreat and the rest of the time. This separation is only a mental conclusion based on what you believe exists *in* and what you believe exists *out*. In truth, that which is discovered within is not confined to any location. Boundlessness is not limited by any boundary! Discover peace within, and then see it everywhere. See that, in reality, there is no in and out. All is in oneself.

How, then, do I be in the world?

This is the same as the previous question. Stop making the distinction between "me" and "the world." At a certain stage, the distinction of *out* and *in* is an important distinction to make. Now the important distinction is between what is permanent and what is impermanent, what is real and what is unreal. This is called "discriminating wisdom."

From what you were just saying, however, it appears that discrimination has now become institutionalized in your mind. Now you have religious warfare between the *ins* and the *outs*. This familiar, old game is going on only in the mind. The way to end the game is to expose it. Where, *in reality*, is the boundary between *in* and *out*? I understand feeling *in* and *out*, and experiencing *in* and *out*, but in reality, can any boundaries be found?

At this moment, it is obvious there is no real boundary.

Good. Now discover what is the real boundary between this moment and any other moment.

❖

Conceptually, I get it about letting go and just being. I also know that "trying" to be is not being.

You are still being, whether you are trying to be or not. *Trying* simply demonstrates that you haven't realized the effortless peace of being without trying, but you still *are*. You cannot say that you're not, can you? Even if you say you are not, you can only say this because you are!

But what's missing is the realization and the peace. There is still the mind chatter, this ongoing internal conversation.

Are you tired of this conversation?

Yes.

If you are tired to the degree where you have lost all faith in these gods called "the commentator," "the evaluator," "the tryer," then perhaps you will stop paying allegiance to these gods. When you stop the habitual allegiance, you will naturally and easily recognize these mind games as the tricks of false gods.

❖

One of my biggest fears about enlightenment is that others in the world will judge me.

They will. It is a given. They do right now anyway. Judging is the nature of mind activity, and you are surrounded by it.

Let yourself feel totally judged insane, deluded, absurd, and stupid. Whatever it is you imagine that will be so hard to bear, let it come now. You will see that it is nothing, simply judgment. Then what force can it have? Anyway, if they are judging you, they are thinking of you. When you awaken, if they are thinking of you, even if they are judging you, they will receive the transmission of awakening. Let them judge you. It is their way of loving you. Distorted maybe, but at least their attention is on the announcement of awakening.

Invite the judgment. If you directly experience this judgment, if there is any residue of clinging to some particular entity and its status or position in the herd, it will be revealed. Let it be revealed. As long as you have a fear of judgment, there is a sensed lack of freedom to be who you are.

First receive the judgment that you are goodness, purity, beauty, and freedom. Fall into that. Then invite the negative judgment. You are stupidity, delusion, and bondage. Now, finally, what is true?

Be finished with the prison of others' opinions. You can never acquire a big enough supply of others' opinions to prove that you are goodness, you are truth, you are beauty, if you have not realized it yourself.

There is a story about a man who tended to Ramana Maharshi while he was living on the mountain in a cave. At first, there were just the two of them, but eventually other people began to be attracted to Ramana.

After eleven or so years of silence, Ramana started speaking. More and more people began to gather around Ramana, and then his attendant began getting possessive, even ordering Ramana around. Finally, he even told Ramana, "This is my cave; this is my ashram." At that time Ramana left the cave. He went down the mountain to where his mother was buried, and a bigger ashram was born.

Eventually the attendant followed him and took over the management of the new ashram. Because he was possessive and generally obnoxious, he generated a lot of strife. Ramana invited his brother to come in and manage the ashram, and the obnoxious man was ousted.

The man was furious and vengeful. One of the things he did was to publish a book about all of Ramana's faults. Ramana asked for the book to be brought to him. In the preface to the book, the man had written, "This book would have been much longer, but I ran out of funds."

Ramana saw this and said, "Oh please, we must raise funds for this man." Then he read more of the book and said, "He doesn't know the half of it! We have to get more money, and then we will put this man out in front of the ashram, and he can give these books away to whomever comes."

This is the way to deal with judgment.

I am afraid that others will judge me if my path changes too radically in their eyes.

To be bound by concerns of what others will think if you are original, free, true, intoxicated with God, if you look strange to them or you don't keep within the bounds of what they say you should be doing and thinking, is a sad state of imprisonment.

Everyone can relate to this. It is brainwashing and conditioning, and it obstructs satisfaction. No matter how much approval you receive, there is never enough, because true happiness does not depend on the approval of others.

You may even be hated for awakening to the truth. Certainly, some people will hate you for it. It is a threat to their neat little lives. When I was first with Papaji, a friend got upset with me. She hated me. I was shocked! How could this be? She was my spiritual friend. I asked Papaji about it and he said, "It is just to be expected."

You will also be adored and loved. Believing either the hate or the adoration is a trap. Don't take either one personally. If you are adored, it has to do with the adoration arising in the heart of the being in front of you. If you are hated, it has to do with the deep threat perceived and feared within the mind of the being in front of you. This is none of your business. Be radically true to who you are, blissfully, unknowingly true to who you are, and all is taken care of.

Why not just go to a cave and sit?

The cave is within your heart. Go there and sit. Rest there for one second. You cannot rest if you are immediately thinking, *But if I go there, what might happen with my friends, my job, my work, my life?* These are the thoughts that keep you from what you want most.

❖

I live in the country, and being in nature day in and day out has become a path of mirroring, a way of experiencing life. When I'm quiet and just sitting, all of a sudden, I start opening to the nothingness. That is a very peaceful place, and I just watch without judgment, but as soon as it is time to stand up to do a physical action, it's gone.

What is the problem with that?

I have lost that feeling of peace.

What hasn't been lost? What is present before the feeling, during the feeling, and after the feeling?

Well, peace is.

Is the peace separate from the activity?

When I totally lose the peace is when a human being walks toward me. All the habits come up, conscious and unconscious, even though I'm just standing there, because a human being has walked into my field.

Yes, it is so hard for humans to recognize other humans as part of nature. You have identified yourself and others like you as separate from nature, as separate from the totality of being.

Particularly when my mind is going click-click, and contraction is happening. It's like a bomb's gone off.

Yes, it is not so subtle.

And this other person and I haven't even started talking yet!

But you have. You started talking long before any actual physical conversation. This human aspect of nature has triggered all your old superstitious thinking of what *human* is, what this human reminds you of, and what this human might be. This internal talk arises from concepts of *yourself* and *other* as somehow separate from the totality of experience.

Nature is teaching you, parenting you, and being intimate with you in the most impersonal way. Learn the lessons of nature. When these so-called others like you reappear, you will see only yourself in all your infinite form, just as you see infinite form within nature.

Nature is experienced as completely relational, totally present, but not personal. When a tree relates to you, it relates totally but impersonally. You could drop dead and the tree would not cry. This is the great teaching of nature.

I also lose my peace when I have to meet some time agenda. All of a sudden, I think, Oh my gosh, I have a three o'clock appointment and . . .

That's right. That is an example of taking it personally. The crux of suffering is taking everything personally. Finally, you have to discover who you are. This *I* who is late for an appointment, where is this *I*?

❖

How do I live with uncertainty?

Really live! Any certainty is only within the mind. When you live in peace with uncertainty, you are naturally confident. Recognize the unknown as the reality of living, and you won't be distracted by thoughts of grasping and trying to make permanent what is by its own nature impermanent. Every event, every experience, every *thing* is impermanent. This recognition is divine uncertainty, and it reveals divine security.

❖

If I become more of that which I am, can I help to heal the world?

This idea of you becoming more of what you are, or of the world becoming something different, is nonsense. You are what you are. Stop all these ideas and beliefs and thoughts, and discover what you are. This is primary.

Discover who you are. Don't *become* more of who you are. Becoming more of who you are is imaginary. Discover who you are now, and tell me if you can find any location, boundary, limit, or anything that can "become" that.

You have assumed there is something else needed, but this assumption is based on your past idea of what the world is, who you are, what you are becoming, what healing is, who can heal what, and even what enough is. Who is measuring that, and by whose standards?

There is something vast, unknown, and unseen, where measurements of enough are left behind. Here, there is no possibility of measuring and no measurer. There is no world separate from who you are. There is only wholeness itself. Nothing becomes whole. It is recognized to be already whole.

But the world doesn't seem whole.

I understand that the world doesn't seem whole. I am not speaking about seeming. Many things seem one way or the other, and this seeming changes back and forth. Something seems one way one day, and within hours it can seem the other way. A cloud goes in front of the sun, and it seems the sun has disappeared. In the night sky, you see stars. In the day sky, it seems the stars have disappeared. In the desert a great lake may seem to be just over there. Drink from that lake and you discover it is sand. Drinking sand is believing "seems."

Seeming is ultimately unreliable because it is based on sensory information. Seeming is the interpretation of the world through the senses and through the conclusions based on past interpretations. Has it been reliable?

The senses are fickle, having to do with moods, biochemistry, genetics, and environmental events. Sensory information is changeable, and if you rely on what is changeable in searching for wholeness, I am afraid you will be searching endlessly. If you can recognize what is already whole, then you have recognized a very deep secret that is always untouched by changes and seemingness.

Recognize what is permanently whole, permanently here, and then your lifetime is no longer spent spinning and searching in seemingness.

You know this from your life experience. One set of beliefs is pushed aside for a new set of beliefs, and now the world is seen through the eyes of the new beliefs. Then that set is pushed aside for another set. You read the paper and the world seems one way. You hear another opinion and it seems another way.

I agree with you. But are you saying that the world is fine the way it is?

I am not saying that the world is fine. I am pointing to what is eternally whole. Before that discovery, any conclusion about either the world's fineness or its rottenness is speculative.

You follow the senses as if they give you real, true, accurate information. Obviously they don't, do they? Isn't it all tempered? You feel good, you take a walk, and everything looks good. You feel bad, you take a walk, and everything looks bad. There is a way to see that sees through what looks good and what looks bad, a way to see *wholly*. But this discovery must come from direct experience, or it is an imposition. Without direct experience, it is just another belief of the latest dogma.

Don't wait for someone to tell you how the world is or what the world is. Only settle for firsthand discovery. Don't wait for some leader to herd you into a particular direction. Even if you believe it is the best direction, you must not settle for anything less than the direct experience of what exists deeper than the senses, deeper than thoughts, feelings, conclusions, and the way you have put it all together.

Of this, I cannot speak a word. I have yet to find a word that comes close. I can only point you in that direction.

❖

In daily life, I feel like I lose sight of the truth because I'm preoccupied from the minute I wake up to the minute I go to sleep at night.

You cannot *lose* truth. It is only possible to *imagine* yourself separate from it. This imagining creates suffering. Truth is always present.

I guess I really know that.

Don't even know it. That is the catch. Truth can be attended to, but not as an *it,* not as an object. Truth cannot be known, and when you stop trying to capture it with the mind, there it is. The world itself, filled with all its suffering, cannot exist without truth.

Truth is everywhere, in everything, and if you are paying attention to that, you see it everywhere, in everything. Truth doesn't live in a place. All places appear in truth. If all places appear in truth, then they are of truth.

When I say *attend* to truth, I am not instructing you to focus your mind on something. To focus is to bring attention to a point. Total attention is three hundred and sixty degrees.

It seems like there's really nothing to do.

Living truth has nothing to do with activity or inactivity. There is no thought of making anything happen or not making anything happen. Those thoughts come from fear. They arise from the fear of emptiness, the fear of nothing, or the fear of nothing happening.

There may arise the desire for a certain outcome. To live in truth is to surrender this desire and put that surrendered attention on the truth that always is.

Then how do things happen?

Quite naturally, just as they always do. What is removed is the struggle. Your natural state is ease of being.

Some people have an idea that enlightenment is some kind of zombie state. You often see a manifestation of this idea in spiritual groups where there's a kind of numbing out, a modeling of nothing happening, pretending as if there is nothing happening. Ease of being cannot be pretended or modeled.

❖

Could you tell me what you understand prayer to be and how it works? How can I use my focused intention to benefit others in the world and ease their suffering?

You are asking about true prayer, not the usual prayer of acquisition.

I'm talking about when I pray for my brothers and sisters or for the world.

Pray for truth. Pray that truth be known. Pray that all being awakens to its true nature. Then pray to be used by truth fully, completely, without any expectation or need of personal or material gain.

You asked how you could use your intention, but if you imagine that you use truth, then truth is imagined as some object, your object. If you pray to let truth use your body, mind, and emotions, to let truth actually have your life, to let it direct your life, then all those previous ideas and agendas drop away. All ideas of what you need to do to be happy are finished.

My intention is that the greatest good is done, but how do I use my intention so that this happens?

What is it you want? What is it you *really* want?

That we remember who we are.

Your whole prayer is right there. If you really want this, the prayer must be one hundred percent. If you take ten percent off to also want something else, and then another five percent for something else, then you have less than a full prayer.

Yes, make your whole life prayer. The details are not up to you, because who can say how life should look? Visualizing how it should look can only come from some past conclusion based on cultural or political conditioning.

With maturity, this particularizing of wants and desires based on past experience is recognized to be futile. Recognize that you don't know what truth should look like, or how truth should reveal itself. Only know that above everything, you want the truth, as you say, for your brothers and sisters, and for yourself.

Let truth write the scenario. Let truth live your life. Truth cannot be visualized, because any visualization is still limiting its manifestation.

Truth is not limited. It is not limited to affluence and comfort. It is not limited to poverty and discomfort. If you are attached to any state or circumstance, you are missing the boundless fulfillment of truth. If you are fixated on a particular image of what your life should be or what your brothers' and sisters' lives should be, there is that much energy taken away from the prayer for truth.

Isn't true love about the absence of separation?

True love is the absence of the belief in the illusion of separation. It is the recognition of the truth of who you are, regardless of appearance, feeling, circumstance, comfort, or discomfort. If this is your prayer, this is a very serious prayer. This prayer takes enormous resolve. It takes the willingness to surrender your personal suffering. To surrender your personal suffering, you must discover what is the root of personal suffering.

The root of all suffering is the belief, and the continual practice of the belief, that you are separate from pure, limitless consciousness. That you are a separate entity, and that you are located in a particular body.

I am not asking that you substitute another belief such as "I am God," or "I am limitless," or "I am boundless." These, too, are beliefs. You are bigger than any belief. You are beyond measure.

The strong belief in "me" and "my needs" is the root of all evil. It is a great mistake.

Your prayer must begin exactly where you are. You imagine yourself to be a particular body because you sense the body. It feels like you are this body, and it looks like you are this body. Find what is closer than the senses, closer than appearances, closer than feelings. Quite remarkably, that realizes itself even through this manifestation of appearance of body and separateness.

This is what I mean when I speak of prayer. Realized prayer is not asking for something. In realization, your entire life becomes a prayer of thanksgiving. Satsang is thanksgiving. Give thanks for this moment of revelation. Have your life be a life of thanksgiving that naturally springs from revelation. Then all of life is revealed to be a confirmation of that.

⟡

I have desires and hopes of accomplishing something in the world. I want to publish my book. When I sit quietly, a lot comes in. I write. I paint. Finally, it's like there has to be an end to quiet. I have to get up and do something with what I am painting and writing.

Who says so?

The part of me that wants to always be on the quest.

If you follow that part, you will always be on the quest. You will always be doing something or imagining you are doing something. You will always stay busy.

This is where I don't get it. There's a missing piece.

It is the piece you have yet to surrender.

The truth is, if you stop for one pure instant of self-recognition, those things may either get done more than you could imagine, or they may not get done. There is no guarantee one way or the other. Your particular life form may be more active than it has ever been, or it may be inactive. What you give up by being absolutely still is the choice of appearing to direct the outcome. A true book comes from stopping absolutely. If a true book is to come through your form, it comes through because it cannot be held back.

It comes through the not-doing?

In music, art, literature, science, and in a full life, there is that which cannot be withheld, cannot be constrained, that which has to be expressed. It uses your intellect, voice, limbs, or the techniques you have learned. It uses your life; so give your life totally to that. How it is to be used cannot be known. Perhaps you will have many books. If they are true books, they will come.

Are you saying that that place of stillness, of letting go, of surrendering, is so divine that all these things get done anyway?

That place is already here. It is so divine it is eternal. It is divine beyond any concept of divine. Surrender all your ideas to that, and let it do as it wishes, as it wills. Truth is far beyond individual will. Individual will is just a spark of that.

You will see your life used, but it may be used by your never moving from your room. Truth is unpredictable and uncontrollable. It is divinely uncontrollable, exquisitely uncontrollable, and undeniably uncontrollable.

Do we become like a vehicle, a conduit, or a vessel?

Recognize your true self. Stop fighting that you are that. Surrender your intellect to that, and then your intellect is used. I don't know if it will be in books. I don't know if you will ever speak or write again.

That is irrelevant. How you will be used is bigger than you or I can know. Let the future be as it is—blessedly unknowable. Speak and write if the speaking and writing must come, and be silent if no speaking and writing come.

Ramana sat in one place, and his just sitting continues to shake the whole world. Many people said that he shouldn't just sit there, that he should be out in the world doing social action like Gandhi. But something bigger than what people thought and what he had been taught directed his life. Ramana, in his mastery, only answered them in silence. From the outside, it appeared that he was doing nothing, that he was inactive. But look, this formal satsang, here, in this time, in this part of the world, is the result of his "inactivity."

If it is the nature of a particular form to be active, let it be active. If it is the nature of a particular form to be inactive, let it be inactive. Compassion is not about the activity or inactivity of the form.

You are that which is the source of both activity and inactivity. In your willingness to be that totally and fully, you cannot help but help. Not by any intention of helping, not by any agenda of helping, but through your true nature as love.

Do you follow this? It is very important. People have such ideas about activity and inactivity. Truth is deeper than any idea. Realize truth. Your hidden question is a question of trust. Trust that silence. Trust that pure love, just for an instant. Then at the very least, you stop contributing to suffering.

There is a command that is deeper and closer than can be known, and it is more vast than I am able to speak of. It is exquisite. It is alive, present, spontaneous, and out of your mind's control.

You ask if that is all there is to it. There is no end to it! No one has ever reported an end or an all to true self. In the instant of being absolutely still, an opening of the mind occurs—an opening into eternity.

❖

I find myself on this roller coaster of emotions, getting very angry, getting very sad. Does that mean that I will never reach the state of the *bodhisattva,* where I can help others in the world?

First of all, the bodhisattva state cannot be reached. It can only be recognized as your preconditioned nature. *Sattva* is a Sanskrit term meaning tranquil, peaceful. *Bodhi* means awakened consciousness, awakened heart and mind. This is your original nature. As long as you are identified with the roller coaster of emotions, you are overlooking what is already and always calm and peaceful, what is already awake. You are overlooking the truth of yourself by fixating your thoughts on your emotions.

The awareness in which the roller coaster is moving is already tranquil and awake, with no rejection of the roller coaster and no clinging to the roller coaster. Recognize this tranquility, and the roller coaster naturally comes to a halt. There is no juice for it to continue. The passions that were fueling the roller coaster are consumed in the one passion for truth, for freedom, for God.

Without being fed, no *body* can exist—not the physical body, the mental body, or the emotional body. In Indian society it is customary at a certain age for a seeker to become a *sadhu,* leading a life of physical renunciation as a way to discover the bliss that is beyond bodily needs.

To truly *nourish* the emotional body, stop feeding the mental body! Discover the natural harmony of emotions that is beyond mental tyranny. By not feeding thoughts, the emotions come to rest in the tranquility of awareness. When some past pattern of emotionality arises, if thoughts are not fed around it, the pattern can cease.

Papaji was asked by Ramana to leave the ashram and go rescue his relatives from Pakistan, and then to support them.

He said, "No, I don't want to go. That is all a dream. I just want to stay here with you, my Master, at your feet."

Ramana said, "Well, if it's all a dream, then what is the problem?"

So Papaji returned to the world, working hard as a mining engineer, supporting a hundred people, and holding satsangs in the evenings.

What a great gift this teaching is for all of us! There is no necessity to do anything with the body. Truth is much more subtle than that. Let the body be as it is. The body is not the problem. The identification with the body as yourself is the problem. You must discover what is present, clear, pure, and untouched, regardless of emotional state. This is already bodhisattva. If you are attracted to that, if you love that, if you have a respect for that, then give even more love and respect to that, and see how your body is used.

❖

Sitting here with you, it is so easy. Outside, it is very often difficult, and a lot is troubling me.

Where is this "outside"?

Not sitting with you.

Then you must have mistaken me for some phenomenon. Don't limit me to any person. Then you will see that the word "outside" makes no sense. The phrase "not sitting with you" makes no sense. This makes as much sense as saying "I am not present."

I'm playing my old play.

Stop playing your old play. Part of the old play is following the thought that it is easy sitting here and difficult outside. This very thought gives credibility to the possibility of "outside" and "difficult."

Don't give these thoughts credibility. That is the old play of the past. It may arise out of past momentum, but the moment it arises, don't continue to feed it power. In that moment, let the thought sink back into nothingness. Let it be liberated.

But it seems to be my experience in the world.

Your experience is what the old play is. When this old play arises, don't follow it, and there will be no experience of it. The experience is only perpetuated if you continue to feed it by following these thoughts. In the moment these thoughts arise, or when you discover that you have followed them, let them go. At that moment, ask yourself *Who am I*, really?

Sometimes I do this, and it is helpful, and sometimes it feels like an effort.

When you feel the effort, let the effort go, and don't ask yourself anything.

Sometimes it just falls away by itself.

In either case the old play is finished. Either it falls on its own as you let go of any efforting, or you can direct your mind inward. This old play cannot continue without some effort. Maybe you are so used to this effort that it actually seems easy. Don't believe it. Not believing it is the same as not touching it.

So it only belongs to the old belief system?

That's right. Past experience belongs to the old belief system. Now you are reclaiming your soul from this past relationship with a tyrant god (the old play) who has been drinking your soul's blood.

That's why I wanted to speak, because I really wish to have this in my daily life.

Yes, truth must be realized to be in your daily life. Don't settle for anything less. In every second that you are willing to inquire, you will discover *I* is always here. *I* is always present. *I* is vast, limitless, pure awareness. You are *I*.

WILLINGNESS TO
TELL THE TRUTH

People often ask me what it means to stand in the truth, to live the truth, to rest in the truth. For this realization, you first have to know what the truth is.

In this instance, I am not referring to the absolute truth of being. By now, you must have received some glimpse of that, or you wouldn't still be here. Since you *are* still here, you of course want more of that, and I can assure you there *is* always more of that. However, the tendency in spiritual groups is often to discount the relative truth for the absolute truth as a justification for doing whatever it is you want to do.

What does it mean to know the truth? What does it mean to tell the truth? These questions get very tricky, because to really know the truth, you must first be willing to expose the lies.

Often we are under the delusion that we lie to protect others. But if you are really willing to tell the truth, you will see that your lies are usually a form of self-protection.

To be willing to tell the truth is to risk losing everything. When you have actually made the choice to be committed to truth, truth is a ruthless master. That commitment will expose every aspect of hiding and all the justifications for that hiding, which are usually some form of protection.

As a human species, we are trained to lie. Lying is a major part of survival. But when you are finally committed to discovering the complete, non-dualistic truth in which absolute and relative are the same, there must be a ruthless examination of how and where you are lying.

For many people, telling the relative truth may be as simple as, "Oh, I see where I'm lying; the truth is, I actually don't like you." That's the truth, and for some, this is where it stops. But this is a superficial truth, so superficial that you can toss it aside immediately. Undeniably, under that superficiality is a deeper truth that has much more to do with you than with the person you don't like. If you are willing to tell the deeper truth, you will begin to see that there is actually something about that person's energy that feels threatening to you, that triggers something in you, that reminds you of something uncomfortable, and keeps you lying as a means of self-protection. This awareness throws you right back into what you have been trying to avoid, which may be any number of things—fear, worthlessness, unlovability, incompetence, fraudulence, etc. At this point, the willingness to tell the relative truth becomes a conduit for discovering the deepest truth.

Everyone feels worthless to some degree, except those who feel superior, and superiority is a worthless feeling, so you can count that as worthless too!

Worthlessness usually gets avoided by lying in any number of ways: making yourself look like you're worth something, acting like you're worth something—or dramatizing and seeking support in your worthlessness as yet another way to avoid actually *experiencing* worthlessness.

Feeling worthless is actually more superficial than *experiencing* worthless. Feeling worthless involves some kind of emotional, mental, or physiological dread and negativity. To actually experience worthlessness, attention must be dropped deeper than feeling. When all the lies that you have told yourself or others are uncovered, you are left with this raw, ugly, unlovable, worthless thing.

At this depth of worthlessness, the deeper truth can now be told. If you attempt to stop there—*I am this raw, worthless, unlovable thing*—it becomes intolerable, so, once again you lie to cover it.

You may learn to repeat certain affirmations, get a makeover, learn how to walk correctly, or get your colors done. All of this is fine. Yet until that essential worthlessness is met and experienced all the way, you cannot know the absolute truth of who you are.

You may have glimpses of absolute truth in moments of grace, moments in nature, or moments in meditation, but until you are willing to tell the truth all the way through any emotion, you will never know the truth that you *are* living presence. Truth will continue to exist as something you've learned you are, hope you are, or remember you are.

Those tactics may work for a while. They are a type of trance you can put yourself into, and trance can be useful at times. But when you are fully committed to realizing the *truth* of yourself, you must face who and what you secretly *think* you are. What must be faced even prior to that is how you have lied to yourself to cover what you think you are.

The other essential question I frequently ask people is, "What do you really want?" If you believe that what you really want is enlightenment or freedom, then you must be willing to tell the deeper truth about what you think enlightenment will give you. Will it give you respect? Lovability? Fame? Power? Relief from the suffering of the world? Eternal happiness? The truth can be shocking—*Oh my God, I want respect, fame, power, more than I want enlightenment?*

These are not pretty truths, but they are very necessary truths, and this is only the beginning. If you are willing to tell the truth about what all of those attainments might give you, then you can get to what is most likely even deeper, which is, *Everyone will love me. I will be cared for. People will finally see who I am and give me what I want.* If you are willing to tell the truth to that extent, you begin to actually get closer to what your core yearning really is.

Are you willing to tell the truth all the way down to the depths? Are you willing to be shocked by what it is that you really want? If you are willing to be laid bare by what your life is really about, where your attention is really hiding in the name of enlightenment, God, or peace, if you are willing to be humiliated and humbled by the mechanisms running you, then you have an opportunity to meet the primal fear. This kind of exposure may bring you to the edge of a deep abyss, a huge hole that you have been running all your life to avoid. This huge hole is the intimation that, really, you are worse than worthless—you are nothing at all.

And, yes, that's correct. *You* are nothing at all, and everything about you has been a lie. Your identity, whether it is based on your body, your intellect, your emotional depth, or your spiritual attainment, is a lie.

Usually, when someone gets down into the abyss of being nothing at all, attention flees back to the top, back into the lie, because the lie is more comfortable. The lie has more hope, more promise. But if you are sincere and your intention is really to know the truth, whatever that might be; if you want it that badly, even if it gives you nothing—not fame, recognition, happiness, release, or universal love—then you are willing to meet the truth of yourself.

The extraordinary report that everyone who has met that abyss brings back is that this abyss, this nothingness that you are, is *awake consciousness, unconditional freedom, supreme love*. Everything you have been searching for in defining yourself as a somebody who is worth something is already and always right here in the depth of your being under all the lies. What has been here all along is what has been fled from all along.

This is the full circle. It is a coming home to yourself. Not an arrival into some transcendent realm, but a return to what is and always has been here. Throughout time you have fled from this homecoming because of your definition of "nothing."

In our minds, "nothing" means not to exist, an absence of self. In our minds, when something becomes nothing, it is vaporized; it is no more. Not to exist means death. This is horrifying to the egoic mind, so we would rather exist as something worthless, as something that could perhaps one day develop into something of worth, than to exist as nothingness. The whole human mechanism is designed to be a some-body—somebody who can get food, who can get shelter, and who can pass the genes on. That is the nature of the animal. It's the nature of the species. It's the nature of form.

The challenge and the invitation I am offering is to drop through all the lies. But before you can drop through the lies, you have to be will-ing to see the lies, to allow your consciousness to drop through them, to feel the burn, pain, ache, delusion, and horror.

Even if there has never been the slightest recognition of yourself as radiant consciousness, as alive, awake intelligence, there is an echo somewhere in your being that knows it to be true. Even if you don't understand it, there has to be a resonance, a vibration calling from the depths of your being. It has always been here, and now is the time for it to recognize itself in you.

Many of you have been seeking for years and years. Many of you have been deeply involved in various spiritual practices. Really, all I can offer you at this time is concrete support for discovering how it is you've been lying. This is true self-inquiry. It is not about doing any-thing or practicing anything.

It is time to discover the deepest truth, to uncover the totality of yourself, and part of that is to unravel all the spiritual conditioning.

When there is a willingness to bear the truth of what you have *truly* been wanting from your searching, when there's a willingness to not suppress those desires or act them out but to actually inquire deeper, it is possible to move past the natural animal instincts until the truth of who you are is finally revealed. When all the definitions and stories of who you are become uncovered and laid bare, you awake to find your-self where you began and where you have always been.

Truth-telling is a living art. With any type of art, true art, one must surrender the outcome, and there must be a willingness to tell the truth about what is real. Only then will you recognize the real possibility of resting in the deepest truth of yourself, regardless of animal instincts, fears of worthlessness, impulses to cover incompetence, or whatever the strategy may be.

Whatever your features may be, whatever your education or your spiritual experiences may be, you can stand naked before one another as the truth. You can be truly natural, without coverings, without trying to be spiritual, get spiritual, dress spiritual, or eat spiritual. All of that is exhausting anyway, isn't it?

HOW WE LIE

When you wake up to yourself fully, you recognize in an instant that everything is you, and it always has been, as you are everything. So what is it that keeps us from realizing this in any moment?

Many of you have had some glimpse of this truth, some shattering of the illusion of separation. Then following this earth-shattering glimpse, this moment of pure grace, what is it that comes back into play and re-constitutes the illusion? Why is the illusion of separate entities believed or followed ever again?

This is, of course, a mechanism of the mind/body, and there is nothing wrong with it. The body needs enormous protection to survive and so it is wired for protection. The body needs to be fed. It needs to be sheltered. It needs to run, hide, or fight when it's threatened. These are all natural instincts of the body, and there is absolutely nothing wrong with any of them. But in order for these mechanisms to be effective, the mind/body first has to be able to judge what constitutes a threat, and then, very quickly, what is the appropriate response.

We are all familiar with the fight-or-flight response, but protection gets much more subtle than that. In our evolvement as human beings, we have learned to be very subtle in the ways of protection, and our subtlety is in lying.

Did you know that you're a liar? The human animal is a tremendous liar. Since we are wired for protection, we are well-trained in lying. Throughout history, our ancestors have changed their names, moved to different places, or attempted to hide their race so as not to be harmed or killed. A huge amount of lying has been necessary for protection, but then the lies get more and more subtle, and eventually you begin to believe the lies. The cocoon of self-delusion gets woven very tight and has to be maintained. Yet you find it can't be maintained consciously all the time, because there are so many other things to tend to, such as getting enlightened, or getting happier and more successful.

Consequently, all our attempts at protection or attainment begin running just under consciousness. We have flashes of awakening, and we wonder why it doesn't hold, why it doesn't last. We have all kinds of fantasies of what true awakening will be—that we will no longer see separation, we will no longer feel negative emotions, we will perhaps just experience a kind of sweet energy flow. These are all just more lies.

Since our lying has been very useful for survival, and since we have become so accustomed to lying for protection, often the biggest lie, that we are separate from each other, can never really be examined because of all the lies in between. Lies upon lies upon lies. As spiritual seekers, we just want to leap into the belief that we are "one with all," right? I mean, isn't it instinctive to not get into the messy stuff?

Many of you have had these experiences of oneness, and they are beautiful. If the experience lasts, then that's wonderful. There is no problem. If it doesn't last, if you're not someone like Ramana who could wake up and be true to that for the rest of his life; if you are someone who has had glimpses and yet somehow, knowingly or un-knowingly, you have betrayed, trivialized, abandoned, or seemingly lost those glimpses, then it's possible that you can now examine the structure of the mechanisms behind that. Not in an analytical way, because it is very easy to lie analytically. The mind is brilliant at lying. But if you can make this examination in the spirit of real human curiosity, which can be just as strong as the human tendency to lie, then there is a possibility you can begin to expose the lies.

This examination must begin openly, nonjudgmentally, in the spirit of truly innocent curiosity. As the lying begins to be exposed, you can ask to see what's under that lie, and then a little deeper into what's under that. This is not a mental, analytical, or abstract inquiry, but an inquiry regarding your own life and how it has woven itself from conception into a separate bundle that yearns to be united with itself as totality. The totality has not gone away with the lies. It is here, now. It has just been overlooked by the sensed need to maintain the lies.

Our ancestors did whatever they had to do to survive, and they did some horrible things, but now you are being offered an opportunity to begin telling the truth, to actually meet the karma, with the intention of really waking up to the truth. Ask yourself the questions *What am I lying about? Where do I lie? Why do I lie?*

Right now, as you read this, close your eyes and ask yourself this question: *What do I lie about?* In the spirit of innocent, nonjudgmental curiosity, let the answers rise up into your consciousness, with no need to edit the answers with justification or defense. Ask yourself this question repeatedly, letting the answers flow freely: *What do I lie about? What do I lie about? . . .*

Let all that is revealed wash over you. Allow yourself to feel in your body the energy required to maintain the lie, to cover the lie, and then to cover the covering. Experience the weight of the lies. It is possible to experience it without judging it. Simply experience it as it is. Through directly experiencing the energy of the lies, without any story attached, there is the possibility of redemption and the possibility of really beginning to tell the truth.

Maybe now you're seeing even more deeply how easy it is to fabricate lies. Usually it's quite hard to tell the truth. Yet, if you can no longer deny that what you want is the truth, then you are sick of the lies. They don't work. Maybe on some level you thought they were serving you, but when it comes to realizing the truth of the matter, you must stop lying. If you are willing to inquire deeper and deeper, you will get to both the relative truths and the absolute truth, because truth is here. All it takes is for our conscious attention to be turned in that direction rather than turned in the usual direction of protecting, hiding, denying, and then lying about denying.

So now, in the same spirit of open and innocent inquiry, you can ask yourself this question: *What is the truth?* Just as with the last question, ask yourself repeatedly, openly, letting the answers float freely up into conscious awareness: *What is the truth? What is the truth? . . .*

Notice if the truths you are telling are mutable or changeable. Are they true one moment and not true the next moment? Are they halfway true, wholly true, or not true at all? Is the truth something that you decide is the truth? How do you know if that's the truth? What is it based on? Where does it come from? What is it motivated by? Can it stand alone with nothing to support it, nothing under it, nothing above it? If it can, then that's the truth. If it needs a story, characters, a past, or a future, it is a partial truth, a mutable truth, a changeable truth.

Notice the difference in the energy when you're telling the truth, even if it's just a temporary, relative truth. Is there more space? Is there more possibility to actually examine what is even more fully true?

What is the deepest truth of who you are? Is there ever a time, in good times or bad, when this is absent? Is there ever a time when you have not been this?

❖

The truth really wants to be spoken, doesn't it?

Yes, it does. So please, speak it.

I've spent so much time avoiding meeting what's actually here.

We spend entire lifetimes.

There can be an intention to fully meet the truth, and then at the last moment, just a slight little movement away.

What is it that moves away from the truth, even slightly? What is required for that movement?

Some kind of fear.

Not only is fear required, but fear plus a thought, and then a thought following that thought. You can begin to see that there is actually quite a bit of effort involved in moving away from truth.

Yes, it's very draining. And now I see how much energy is actually available through telling the truth. The truth is nourishing; it gives me strength.

Yes, the strength of fearlessness. Fear may be present, but fearlessness is the willingness to tell the deeper and deeper truth, regardless of what is present. It often starts with a relative truth, and telling the relative truths can be very important. They are just not the whole truth. You don't want to dismiss the relative truths, and you don't want to settle for them.

⬖

It seems to me I've been making a mistake. When I'm in the deepest truth, I keep thinking that it will give me all the answers. But it doesn't, necessarily, and I can get very frustrated by this.

Well, I can see two mistakes you're making right away. "When I'm in the truth" is already a mistake because there is not a "you" and "a truth." Truth is not a place that you can "go to" and "get in."

So you're saying that truth is not a place?

That's right. Truth is not a place. I'm also pointing out that you are not a "thing" that can be separate from truth.

So, if truth is not a place and you are not a thing, what does that leave you with?

Not much! (laughing)

It leaves nothing at all! Correct? That's the truth. Yet the moment you make "nothing at all" a thing, it is separate from you, and that's not "nothing at all." Then once again there is a "thing" and there is a "you." This is just how the mind works. "No-thing at all" is not the mind's idea of nothing. It is alive. It is awake. It is vibrant. It is consciousness. And consciousness is truth. Consciousness is not a place. It is not a thing. You can't "find" consciousness and say, "Okay, here is consciousness. I'll put consciousness in this place, and then I'll know where consciousness is if ever I need it again." And this is what the mind attempts to do.

Yes, that's exactly what I do! (laughing)

That's right; it's a good laugh. All that is required is the recognition that this is what you are doing, and then you can stop doing it. You don't have to know what nothing at all is, what truth is, or even what consciousness is. Just notice that your mind is creating objects out of what cannot be objectified, and you are identifying yourself as another object in relationship to these objects. There's nothing wrong with this creating power of mind. It's just not the final truth. For a human child, it may be a very necessary stage of development, but it is also one we get attached to because of the pleasure of creating.

Finally, you realize that the ultimate truth is one you have no power over. It doesn't actually give you what you demand it to give you. Then there can be some recognition—*Wow, I really don't know anything about truth*—and this is wonderful. Then there is actually a possibility for the freshness and the innocence of real inquiry, real curiosity, because you are not approaching it from *what* you want it to give you, or *where* it will be at all times, or *how* you want it to be all the time. Then you are no longer entertained by thoughts of truth as a thing, thoughts of you as a thing, and thoughts about the two of you getting together as two things becoming one.

No wonder I can't get any answers there!

Yes, no wonder! So now, are you simply willing to not have the answer and to rest in the spaciousness of not knowing? You don't have the answer and you don't know where to go for the answer. At least that is telling a relative truth in the moment. That is the beginning, and in that, there is an innocence, an opening, a possibility of seeing.

I am not talking about realizing, "I don't have the answer," and then going into a stupor. I am not talking about, "I don't have the answer, so I'll make up an answer, which is what I've learned to do as a liar and an imitator." It is just simply opening to receive the answer. It is not knowing that you don't know and then thinking you know what it is you don't know. That's already way too crowded, way too complicated. Everything has to be emptied. I am speaking about knowing that you don't know and being willing to not know.

What are you experiencing now?

It's exciting! It's so much less work than trying to get an answer when I can't find an answer, and there isn't any answer, and I don't know any answer.

Exactly. The mind simply opens to see. Don't make the prayer "Tell me; help me," and then start timing the answer.

This is what you've been doing, right?

Yes! (laughing)

Well, that's obviously been a mistake, and you can stop it right now. That's a big bundle of unnecessary suffering. There isn't anything wrong with that. It's just unnecessary. When you're involved in that, you don't even notice when the truth shows up, because you are too busy being furious that it didn't show up five minutes ago or wasn't the truth you were expecting. It's like waiting for the phone to ring and then you don't hear the doorbell.

You now have the choice to stop all of that, to give it a break, to give yourself a break. Be willing to not know. Then have the freedom of not knowing, the innocence of not knowing, and in that, the possibility of discovering the truth for yourself, not secondhand, not what you learned, not what you hope, and not what you decide the right answer is.

The mind can be a vehicle or a conduit for the revelation of truth, but it can't "get" the truth. There is great freedom in the recognition that truth is unknown and unknowable. A life lived in not knowing is an adventure. It is exciting, alive, authentic. Anything that we think we know, in the sense of having captured the truth in knowledge, is subject to change. We can fight that, or we can relax about it and have a good laugh. It's about time for a good laugh!

Yes it is! (laughing)

This is so beautiful. You started by saying how frustrated you felt. That was the relative truth. But could you have expected that the relative truth would take you on this kind of adventure? Who could expect this?

I'm so grateful.

I feel grateful, too. If you will innocently look into your life, you will see that you can even be grateful for the worst of it. Truly. Just the very fact of living is so much to be grateful for, however long it lasts, in whatever state.

Now, in this lifetime, there is the possibility of actually being yourself. You can stop trying to be something you think you should be, something you think you are, or someplace you think you should be getting to.

What a lucky life in which you find yourself! Unimaginable luck. A life where gratitude is present is already a true life. Whenever there is gratitude, there is no story of "poor me, when will I ever get it, how do I keep it, or what should I do next for more of it." You are simply grateful to be, and you can send that gratitude throughout time, past and future, to all being everywhere. Then the gratitude and the blessing can grow endlessly, regardless of circumstances, whether good or bad. What a lucky lifetime! What a blessed life. Thank you.

WHAT DOES YOUR
LIFE STAND FOR?

Many of you are already familiar with various spiritual words and concepts. You are familiar with the many spiritual philosophies, the spiritual lifestyles, and the traditions they may arise from. But do you know the truth? This is the most difficult question of a lifetime. The difficulty arises from the mind's ability to corrupt everything that points to the truth in order to justify living a lie, and we've all lived lies to different degrees. Certainly, if you look at our human ancestry, you see these lies lived to horrible degrees.

At some point in a human lifetime, the mysterious grace of actually wanting to know the truth will appear. One is no longer satisfied with another spiritual philosophy or another sophisticated grouping of spiritual words. Even spiritually blissful feelings, as satisfying as all those might seem, are eventually recognized as not enough—you have to know the truth.

Then, of course, you are drawn to people who speak the truth, and naturally their particular way of expressing the truth gets taken in. Maybe they use new words, and maybe they use words you've heard before, but the words themselves are still not the truth, and you are left with a hunger.

You have heard me speak of self-inquiry and the questions "Who am I?" "Who dies?" These questions are essential and profound. In an · instant, they can lead to the recognition that you are not separate from limitless consciousness. Yet even self-inquiry can be easily corrupted by the mind to become a way of avoiding the lie of one's life. It can become just another spiritual overlay on a life lived in betrayal to truth. The mind is expert at this kind of subterfuge, and so, of course, confusion and suffering continue to arise.

You have to be willing to tell the hard truth about the power of the mind to corrupt the most pure and sublime recognition of truth. Yet this truth-telling also cannot be done through the mind because, as you know, the mind gets very busy with the usual damage control of justifications, excuse making, projections, and blame.

There is another question, however, that you can ask yourself—a question that gives you the opportunity to deeply examine and ruthlessly, often painfully, tell the truth about. That question is, *What does my life stand for?*

So I ask you, what does your life stand for? What has it stood for? What is the deepest call of your life? Look very carefully, ruthlessly, and honestly. You will know if you are speaking words of truth yet still living a lie. You will see it. It can be a painful seeing, and in that pain, the mind will immediately attempt to make the lie into some form of truth.

Answering this question is rigorous truth-telling. What must be examined is often profoundly uncomfortable because in truth there is no separation between ourselves and all that exists. Alive within each of us is the rapist, the murderer, the child molester, the fascist, the abuser of power, the false teacher. If we are willing to face this truth and actually meet it, at whatever level it is being reflected in this lifetime, then there is a possibility of what the Christians have termed "redemption."

True redemption is found in bearing the pain that we as human beings have caused in the name of truth, in the name of love, in the name of service. However long it takes, whether an instant, an hour, a week, a year, or a lifetime, the pain and suffering we have inflicted upon ourselves and each other must be met without indulging it and without repressing it. Only then can the space be revealed for real self-inquiry. Otherwise, inquiry becomes just another way of escaping, another way of feeling good.

You all know these good feelings. You know the nectar of them and the addiction to them. Yet there is a deeper call within you to know the absolute truth or you wouldn't be here, because you know that I am truly not teaching you anything. I am only inviting you to examine, at the deepest level, who you really are. I am inviting you to look where all must look, not, of course, excluding myself.

This examination must begin at the most superficial level, because the willingness to see the most superficial lends the strength and the capacity to see much deeper. Eventually, you are faced with the undeniable recognition that who you *truly* are is nothing at all. This is horrifying to the mind, because the mind's job is to make you something.

As I continue to remind you, this "nothing at all" is not a "something." It is not an enlightened something or an awake something or a happy something. Who you are is truly, unimaginably, nothing at all. Paradoxically, that "nothing" is filled with the most profound bliss, fulfillment, and satisfaction. This is true self-recognition.

Usually, even in the midst of this recognition, the mind will arise and attempt to make claim to being "nothing at all," and this is the "razor's edge" that Papaji often spoke of.

When you recognize the certain possibility that the mind will arise to co-opt whatever true experience appears, then you can tell the deeper truths—*What does my life stand for? What does my life reflect? Where is my allegiance?*

I am not speaking of yet another whip of the superego, such as "you should never speak rudely or have a negative thought." I'm speaking of something much deeper, much closer to the bone. Examining this question is a standing up against the whole tsunami of human conditioning.

The resultant pain or bliss is secondary. It is a willingness to stand up for the absolute truth of oneself, whatever the outcome, whether you are shot, burned, hated, abandoned, adored, or worshipped.

Papaji often said, "All the gods and demons of your past will arise to claim you." He was speaking of the power of the mind. Whatever god realm you may find yourself in, the mind will arise to say, *Yes, this is good . . . but over there it is sweeter, better, nicer, more comfortable.* Whatever your demons are, whether self-doubt, self-hatred, worthlessness, or unlovability, they also will arise to reclaim you.

Self-realization is not for the faint of heart. It can be sweet, yes, but also rough, because what you are really up against is the face of all human conditioning—all human betrayal, human delusion, self-aggrandizement, drama, and abandonment. Self-realization is the willingness to stand as the Buddha, as the Christ, as every great icon we have had throughout time.

These icons have been wonderful examples for us, they have led the way, but if we continue to view them as separate from ourselves, we miss the possibility, as ordinary human beings, living ordinary lives, to stand up in an extraordinary way.

I am happy to meet you in this possibility and to support you in this possibility. I am also happy to be supported by you in this possibility. The truth is, we all need each other. No one stands alone. We are all totally supported in this. As you hear these words, know that they are for you alone, yet at the same time, you are surrounded and supported by all those with the same intent. The same grace is available to all.

In our conversations, you will find yourself with the opportunity to face whatever is present and to discover what holds it all, what bears it all, what recognizes it all. There can be no more excuses. If excuse making begins, which it usually does, it is recognizable in an instant.

I guarantee you will be tested. You are being tested every day, in every relationship, but the possibility is to be conscious of the testing, responsible for your own personal suffering, and at the same time, conscious of the true bliss, radiance, and stillness of your being.

The possibility of awakening, as a regular human being, given this evolved human brain, is very real. You have the capacity to consciously self-reflect, to self-examine, to self-investigate, and to discover an ever-deepening ability to tell the truth. You now have the capacity, the time, and the privilege to honestly inquire into the deepest questions: *What is my life about, really? What do I stand for, really? Where do I rest and take nourishment, really?* Then this human experiment opens to the possibility of something unknowable and unpredictable.

What is possible for us all, everywhere, is no longer limited to the Christ, the Buddha, Ramana, or any of the great saints and sages throughout time. It is available to you now, if you are willing, and it is no small matter. We have each other, all across the planet, in the past, in the future, and in the present.

With that as our intention, let us speak to one another, however that expression emerges. Let us meet one another truly, on whatever level that meeting reveals itself. Always, let us see deeper, broader, higher, with nothing excluded.

❖

Just listening to you, my heart is beating fast, and it feels like I'm on fire. I'm willing and I'm thirsty for the truth.

I have been meeting this truth again and again over the years. For a while, it's so easy to be with it, and it becomes the total priority in my life. Then I start to go to sleep again.

This is very important for everyone to see. The mind is a great power that can be put to use for this. Just as you can rewind the reel of a movie, you can rewind your mind and actually see the choices that you made.

As I reel the movie back, the first thing I am aware of is a fear for survival. I have a strong belief that I have to work and to make work the priority.

Most of us do need to work to survive. So what?

Is it just my attitude around it that gets in the way?

Yes! Your attitude has been that survival comes first, and that is the betrayal.

But the fear is so compelling.

Somewhere in your consciousness, you believe that to stand up and tell the truth means risking your life. You know this because, through some lifeline or another, you have experienced it. You have been shot and burned for speaking the truth. To some people, telling the absolute truth is heresy. People will either love you for it or hate you for it.

Yes, there are people who will feel threatened by the truth. When you stand up out of the herd, you become a target. Even if you don't feel thunderbolts of real lightening, you'll feel them energetically.

The issue of survival is huge. It is the most basic issue. There is nothing wrong with that. Of course our organisms are wired for survival. How could it not be so?

Yes, you must do the work necessary to get the money to feed your body. But you hit it right on the head: your attitude about it is the deeper issue. What you want to be able to track is the moment your attitude shifts to survival being more important than what your life is about.

Can you find that fear right now?

Yes.

Excellent. Fear is not the enemy. It is a vehicle to deeper realization.

Can you let your attention fall into this fear? Can you let yourself *be* this fear, all the way?

I feel myself groping for something, anything, to hang on to.

Excellent. This is the typical movement away from fear. Because we know that if we make a movement to run, hide, or attack, there is still a possibility for our survival. This is very useful in certain circumstances, and there's no need to trivialize that capacity, but finally you can recognize that it's your relationship with fear that shifts your attitude.

You mean my wanting to get away from the fear?

Yes, I'm saying that fear is a natural instinct, but don't stop there.

It comes so quickly, and I'm running before I know it. I can't seem to catch it in the moment.

All right, so you are running, and then you notice you are running. Then what?

Then I think, Damn, it's too late; I've started running again.

It is never too late. That is just another moment of choice.

I may notice that I'm running, but then I don't know how to stop.

The "how" is first to recognize that you are running and that fear is in charge. There are times, of course, when fear is appropriately in charge, such as when you run out of a burning building. You don't have to think; you just run. But in this instance, you are referring to a psychological fear.

All you need to recognize is that you are running. You don't need to know how to stop. The fact that fear is running tells you there is something to be met. Something is calling your attention so strongly that it has you running away from standing in what you know to be true.

Fear can take many forms—fear of survival, fear of image, fear of powerlessness, etc. We all experience these fears. But if you are running away from truth, whatever the reason, justification, or sleepiness, somewhere inside, you know it. Fear is calling you to stand in the truth. You may not know how to stop. You may not know how to meet it. You may not know what made it happen. This is the moment of calling out for help. Have you done that? Have you asked for help?

I have at times.

Well, was help present?

Truthfully, yes.

This is simply the nature of prayer. "Help me get away from this fear" is the usual type of prayer. If, however, your prayer is simply, "Help; I need help," then every aspect of yourself, in every age and every place, is here with you. You truly are not alone. You are supported. But if you spend your time in relationship with the thoughts *How did I get here? How do I stop? What did she say? Meet what?*, your attention is invested in the wrong direction.

Do you see? All of that is just part of the run.

Yes, it's like, "Oh no, not this again!"

That's right. "Not again." "Why me?" "This must mean I'm not enlightened." "How did I lose it again?" All of this is a way of avoiding the help that is here.

A true call for help is a prayer. Arrogance is dropped even in speaking the word. No longer is your attitude, "I can do this myself. What was it I'm supposed to do? I know I've got to stop. How do I do stop?" Just simply say, "Help."

Can you say it?

Help?

No, not like that! (laughter) Really ask for help.

Help!

What a beautiful word this is. This word reverberates out into the cosmos. Haven't you experienced that? Maybe you won't experience the help immediately, but if you ask for it, you will eventually feel it. Help will come. It may not come in the form you thought, or the outcome you imagined, but help is here. Help is the grace of your being. It is your awakened soul. "Ask and ye shall receive" is the truth. Then see what you will do with what you have received.

Be aware that the mind will be right there, ready to make the help its own, claiming, "Okay, I stopped. I met it. I'm free. I'm awake. I'm in charge. Now let me tell *you* what to do."

Personally, I need help every moment. When you lay yourself bare to receive help in every moment, help is here every moment. If you think for one moment that you are doing it yourself, this is hell, right? This is not news. I'm just confirming what you already know, what you've already discovered, and now, I am inviting you to a deeper discovery.

Recently, there was a night of really crying out for help. It was an opening up, like a burning.

Yes, absolute vulnerability.

And the next day, I was so vulnerable and raw, and suddenly this man appeared and gave me a big hug. That hug hasn't ended yet! (laughter)

You met a friend. A friend heard your call, maybe without even knowing he was hearing your call. Now you can really be true friends to each other. Not the normal kind of friendship, but the deepest kind.

You are both very lucky. Now you can support each other in unknowable ways—truly support each other, not just get comfortable and rock each other to sleep.

The full possibility is to tell the deepest truth to each other, and receive the deepest truth from each other, until you recognize without a doubt that your friend is yourself. Your self called out for itself, and what arrived is yourself. Then your lives can be a support for others, an offering of help, whether as individuals or as a couple.

Now, whenever you find yourself running and mentally spinning in some fear-based attitude, you know you can call out for help. This stops you immediately, because to call out for help, you have to stop for a moment. Then all that is needed is the willingness to receive the help.

Just the asking feels good.

Yes. Asking is the opening, and then help is immediately present. Help is always present. It just gets overlooked by the activities of running away from fear or running toward pleasure. Receiving help is not about *doing* anything. It is the willingness to simply be and to stand in being, as being. Asking for help cuts off all past conditioning of independence, until you finally trust that help is always here. There's nothing but help here, in whatever form, because there is no end to the possibility of receiving help.

There are disasters in everyone's life. If they are met in the spirit of asking for help and receiving that help, then disaster is an ally. If it's run from, denied, or lied about, then your life itself is a disaster, and this species has experienced enough of that.

THE FIRE OF SERVICE

The life you are living is giving itself to something. What is your life giving itself to? See what your life serves, and then you have the choice. Do you want to serve suffering, or do you want to serve joy, love, and truth?

What you are serving is where your attention is. Where your attention is reveals what you are supporting with your thoughts, your activities in life, your hopes, your frustrations, and your story.

What are you serving? Check and see. Are you serving some idea of who you think you are, who you think you were, or who you think you should be? Are you serving some idea that your mother, father, or culture has of you? Are you serving some idea that you are the sum total of your good and bad experiences? Or are you serving that which is before all ideas?

Narcissism is the result of serving ideas and images of yourself. Both positive narcissism and negative narcissism are filled with suffering. Suffering can be disguised as pleasure as well as pain.

You must be familiar with narcissism. It is a holdover from when you were two or three years old. In each lifetime of being two or three years old, narcissism is reinforced and then nourished throughout a lifetime as an ideal of freedom and power.

The therapeutic community has identified an "inner child." Inherent in the concept of "inner child" is an image of victimization or power, enslavement or freedom. These are only mental images. If you serve these images, if you bow to these images, whether positive or negative, you must tell the truth about what the results are. Just tell the truth; that is all.

You have the opportunity for your life to be lived beyond subservience to conditioning and beyond rebellion against conditioning. A life freely lived.

See for yourself. Notice in a day or even in an hour what you are attending to, what you are supporting, feeding, or denying. See for yourself.

❖

My whole life I've had feelings of duty and responsibility and a need to be of service. But I also have a massive fear about whether I'm doing it the right way, and this in itself has become a block.

Yes, your idea of responsibility is a burden. True responsibility means the ability to respond. Ability to respond must be free, spontaneous, and intuitive. If it is burdened by the weight of past concepts of what responsibility should look like, feel like, or how it should be received, it is not true responsibility. Any image or imitation of responsibility is a burden.

True responsibility is joyous. It is the willingness to surrender and be who you are, without any idea of what that is. Yes, some fear may arise in that, but if you meet that fear, you will discover it to be nothing. If you serve that fear, then once again you are shouldering some idea of duty or responsibility. To be responsible is to be true only to the deepest command of your being.

There is no way of knowing the effect your response will have. Whether you never move off a couch or whether you travel the globe and never stop speaking, whether you are a public figure or a private figure, all are secondary to responding to that deepest command. If you are willing to meet whatever occurs in your responsibility to that command, life is naturally and joyously served. The burden appears when you ignore that command with ideas of what responsibility should look like. Put your burden down. Stop contributing to the burdens of the world. Be true to who you are, and you will quite mysteriously and miraculously be placed exactly where you must be. Then you will know the deep joy of responsibility.

Some people have expressed fear that they won't take care of their children properly if they serve truth. What better gift can you give your children than your awakening? If you are true to truth, the world can receive awakening from you. If you compromise truth, compromise is what your life is serving.

What is your life serving?

I am not suggesting what the form should be. It honestly doesn't matter. Be a mother, a clerk, or a bum. All forms are included in truth. When you are true to truth, truth is transmitted, whatever the form. If your students are to be bums, fellow shoppers in the grocery store, or your children, what you will transmit is the truth of your responsibility to the deepest command of your being.

Being true means refusing to cling to any idea of what your life should look like. What freedom! Aren't those ideas burdensome? Perhaps some of them are totally in alignment with truth. You cannot know until you are willing to give up all ideas. Then you will see that what is in alignment has no weight, and what is not in alignment is too heavy to fly with you.

Joyous service is not a burden. If it is a burden, stop. Carrying a burden indicates that responsibility is being dictated by some mental concept. In the joy of true responsibility, service is not for an instant separate from surrender, vigilance, self-inquiry, and devotion.

When you see yourself in another form and that form is suffering or confused, what is in the best service of truth?

To be absolutely quiet. Quiet provides the only true help, and from the depths of quietness, either particular action or nonaction will naturally arise. No thought is needed for direction. Anything else is involvement in a particular story of suffering. As long as you are involved in the particular story of suffering, you are overlooking what has never suffered. Recognize what is whole and complete, now and eternally. True recognition is the mother of all acts of compassion.

Quiet holds the whole spectrum of behavior. There is a ruthlessness and relentlessness to compassion, as well as a gentleness and lightness. The whole range of experience can serve truth.

I recognize that what binds me to the world of appearances is a devotion to worrying about the state of the world and hating the violence that characterizes much of human interaction. I have a fear that things will get even more crazy if I and many others let go of protecting what we think of as inalienable rights.

What you are exposing is really a lack of trust. You fear that if you let go of your thoughts and conclusions, you will be irresponsible or not fulfill your service to humankind, the planet, and all species.

Your fear is not based on reality. It is based on your devotion to worrying. It is based on devotion to recounting all the times you have trusted your thoughts, emotions, and interpretations, and they have been proven to be mistaken. In that conclusion, you equate thoughts, emotions, and interpretations with the truth of who you are.

Thoughts, emotions, and interpretations *appear in* who you are. As long as you identify yourself as any thought, grandiose or lowly, or any emotion, sublime or horrible, or any interpretation, profound or mundane, you overlook that which can be totally, completely, absolutely trusted.

You see how unnecessary most of the suffering is, and you desire to put an end to suffering. This is a beautiful and true desire. The mistake comes when you trust your thoughts, emotions, and interpretations about how it should be done, what you should do, how much you should do, and what it should look like. These thoughts, emotions, and interpretations may arise, yet if you place your trust in the unknowable mystery of perfection, you realize a flexibility and openness beyond both responsibility and creativity.

There is no particular formula for how help is given. Look at Gandhi, Martin Luther King, or Mother Teresa, and you see lives of action, commitment, and integrity. Look at the Buddha, Ramana, or Saint Theresa, and you see lives of contemplation and apparent inaction. Who is to say one life is right and another is wrong? As long as you have any idea of what it looks like to serve, you are simply overlooking the opportunity to absolutely trust that the intention to serve reveals the discovery of that which serves. The "how" appears naturally from intention and discovery.

I am familiar with this dilemma. I remember weeping at the impossibility of doing what I saw must be done in the world. I know the worrying. I know the torture and the horror of the way we treat one another. I also know the possibility of surrendering to not knowing, to giving up the idea of how "you" must do it. Let it be done. Let your form be somehow mysteriously used with no idea of how that should be.

If Mother Teresa thought she should stay in a convent and live a life of contemplation, what a waste. If Saint Theresa thought she should be working with lepers, what a waste.

Give up worrying about what you are doing, and discover who you are. Then see if that is not trustworthy. You cannot know by checking your thoughts, emotions, or interpretations. You can know by checking eternal truth. A life lived from the question "How can I be used?" not *knowing* how, but continually *discovering* how, is an open life. It is a life that radiates trust in who you really are. What a life!

Trust is rare, and trust is your opportunity. You are actually in a position to trust. You needn't be concerned every moment with where your next meal is, your shelter is, or if your family is safe. Not having to be concerned with issues of immediate survival is a great privilege, a great opportunity.

See where your concerns are. See if your concern is with something from the past or with being used by the truth.

These are serious questions. They are not casual. Ask yourself what it is you *really* want so that when this lifetime is finished, it is cleanly finished, completely finished, freely finished.

⟡

Last night I had a really powerful dream in which I built a huge bonfire. I would drench one flame with water, and another would pop up, until finally I was totally exhausted. I woke up and I said, "Let it burn." I just surrendered to it, and everything has been so wonderfully different since then. I want to do more for everyone. I pray to heal them.

The healing for everyone is your willingness to experience this fire and not dampen it. This fire is the answer to your prayers. Realize that a shift in the prayer has taken place. Rather than a prayer of supplication, offer a prayer of thanksgiving, a prayer of gratitude, a prayer of service.

Do you mean a prayer of being?

Being is not separate from true prayer. Gratefulness, devotion, and love are not separate from true prayer. As the removal of the mental veil reveals harmony and love, prayer becomes a great song of thanksgiving, and the rest of your life can be lived honoring that. Honor the fire.

Honor the removal of the veil. If you go back again to the old prayer of pleading, you dishonor what has already been revealed.

Let your whole life be prayer. You cried out. You begged for help. Help appeared for you as fire. The spiritual fire burns up suffering. It is the fire of realization. It is the fire of awakening. Live in greatest thanksgiving for what has been revealed. Otherwise, the mind starts its searching activity again.

Don't pick up the old patterns of mind. Your prayer was stronger than the dampening, and all burst into flame, the flame of realization. Honor this fire and let it guide you.

❖

I feel drawn to service like a moth to a flame, but there is fear too.

The fire calls. The fire disintegrates all notions of server and served. If you answer this call with full attention and no idea of what the call should give you, your life will be a reward. Somehow, mysteriously, your life will be of service.

Let the call have you. Let it have your fears, your ideas, and your plans. Let it have all.

Let the fire burn so brightly that it lights up the night.

❖

Christ is sometimes seen with a burning heart. What is the meaning of that?

No amount of talk about it will satisfy you.

Isn't knowledge the greatest purifier?

In this instance, knowledge is the obstacle. Something known, some concept, is the obstacle. Satisfaction comes from direct experience. You have to discover the burning heart within you. You have to peel off the protections of conceptual knowledge so that you can discover what is beyond knowledge. You must discover that in which both knowledge and purification burn.

I guess I'm looking for resolution.

If you are looking for resolution through conceptual knowledge, you are looking in the wrong place.

So just remain in the feeling of the burning heart?

Dive into the center of that feeling. Don't waste any more time on the concept. Then your life is the resolution you have been seeking. You won't be asking anyone about a burning heart. You will be broadcasting your own burning heart, in words or not, in knowledge or not.

Knowledge that is innocent of the past, knowledge that is realized, revealed, alive, is truth.

I guess human nature is to use knowledge to move away from pain.

Yes, always trying to find out how to fix rather than to be. How to fix is called knowledge. For a moment, give up fixing and burn. There is no resolution until you are consumed.

When you are willing to burn, when you are willing to be consumed, when you stop fighting the call of your burning heart and just surrender into that, you realize you are that—not conceptually, but in reality.

⟡

Yesterday was the last day I had with someone who means a lot to me, and I was experiencing a great deal of pain. I went to satsang and just trusted and accepted the encouragement you gave us to surrender absolutely. When I looked into the pain, the peace was really there! I hope to serve that peace with my life.

You do serve that. Your report serves that. The willingness to surrender and to ask "Is this true?" is already service. Then you see for yourself. Recognize that truth is being given freely and completely, everywhere you look, and the more you give it, the more you discover it. It cannot be hoarded. It cannot be saved. If you give it to everything you see in every moment, you discover something unspeakable.

True Meaning of Vigilance

Is it essential to maintain vigilance? Can you give us some guidelines?

Yes, vigilance is essential. The problem with the word "vigilance" is that it is misunderstood to mean a strenuous imposition of discipline. Vigilance is discipline, but it is the discipline of surrender.

If you pull your attention even slightly from what is free, from what is boundless and endless, suffering is experienced. When suffering is experienced, the habitual tendency of mind arises to deny truth. By being vigilant, the capacity of thought to deny truth is acknowledged and seen through.

If effort is used to maintain vigilance, sooner or later you become exhausted. However, if you relax your mind, your individual mindstream is already naturally aligned with the ocean of pure awareness. Then alertness, vigilance, surrender, and discipline are all effortless.

Being still reveals non-identified awareness, pure intelligence aware of itself. If the impulse to effort appears, and it may because efforting is a strong tendency, recognize that this very effort assumes you are not that awareness. Check, has pure awareness moved? In truth, is there any separation between you and pure awareness?

Self-inquiry is vigilance. If in any moment you feel pulled toward identification with suffering, ask yourself *who* is suffering.

The belief *I am not divine, radiant, eternal consciousness*, and the resulting suffering, must be faced. Direct experience is self-inquiry. "*Who* is not that? *Who* is suffering?" In self-inquiry, one uncovers self-denial through fabrication of thought. Belief in fabricated thought as reality leads to suffering. In the moment of directly experiencing the fabrication, the lie is exposed and annihilated.

What do I do when I am totally hooked into the drama that is going on?

Drop the story instantly! To be hooked, you must be feeding the story line with more commentary, or searching for release through a different story line. Drama might appear from past feedings, but it cannot continue without present feeding.

Be very aware of how you maintain past, present, and future. Vigilance breaks the imaginary bonds called "me and my drama."

Do you always have a choice, in any moment, to not keep feeding energy to the drama that's happening?

Yes, you always have the choice.

My suggestion is that you direct all power of choice toward recognizing the truth of who you are in every moment. Surrender the power of choice to deny truth. Give it up. Declare that you will no longer choose to believe that you are separate from truth itself, even in suffering, in drama, in grief, in adverse circumstances of all kinds.

The usual choice is to overlook pure, radiant awareness. Surrender that choice on the altar of truth. You may be tested, but if you have really given up the choice to deny truth, you will not be tempted.

Declare yourself married to truth, and be faithful, regardless of whichever old lovers come and ask you to play. Declare that you have chosen truth, and nothing can separate you from that. Old lovers may appear. Let them appear. If they are not entertained, they disappear.

Few people have the courage for this divine marriage, because it is imagined that pleasure comes from playing around with old habits.

Playing around is normal in a certain stage of immaturity. With maturity, you realize that you have played around enough. There has been enough going from this thing to that thing.

In silence, the true Beloved reveals itself. Then you have the possibility of choosing the Beloved and giving up all other choices—*all* others.

This is the potential. Satsang is the wedding invitation. Recognize that the Beloved is here. Regardless of busyness, pain, or pleasure, it is here. It has been waiting patiently, lovingly, for you to finish your playing around.

Love of truth is mature love, but if you are fixated on adolescent fantasies, it can seem terrifying. It is feared that in mature love something will be lost. Yes, it will; and that loss is the gain of realization.

Choosing truth demands giving up flirting with egocentric arrogance and egocentric self-denial. Be willing to give up both egocentric pleasure and egocentric pain for the Beloved, and then tell me what you have given up.

❖

I can discover freedom in silence, but to discover it in action is difficult.

The distinction you make between silence and action is artificial. Silence does not go anywhere when action appears. There is no action separate from silence.

Have you found the boundary of silence?

The boundary is that as soon as I find myself in mental activity, then I'm lost.

What does "I am lost" mean?

Days or weeks can go by before I notice the silence again.

In these days and weeks, does awareness go anywhere?

The awareness was not aware of itself.

But it was aware?

There was awareness in every moment.

Is awareness separate from silence?

I've never looked at that.

Well, look. There is always more to see.

Events happen in awareness. Your individual mindstream may be consciously aware of an event or subconsciously aware of an event. In this moment, turn your individual mindstream toward the ocean of awareness that is aware of your individual mindstream as an event.

Conscious and subconscious awareness dissolve in the ocean of pure awareness. Events remembered and events forgotten dissolve here. Here you are—purely *I*.

I am lost. *I* am found. *I* am in meditation. *I* am at work. *I* am having a good time. *I* am having a bad time. *I* am ignorant. *I* am enlightened. There is still *I*, just *I*. The true *I* does not go anywhere.

So focus on the *I* in every moment?

Focus on the *I* right now and tell me, what do you find?

There is only awareness.

Thank you. Do you see?

Yes!

It is wonderful that you recognize this in an instant in satsang. This is the halfway point. To complete your journey, begin to explore if awareness ever goes anywhere. Is true *I* ever lost?

When you think *I am lost,* check. *Who* has gone? Has awareness gone anywhere? Experience of lostness has appeared in awareness, but has awareness been affected?

Recognize directly what is always present and cannot be other than present. Then stop looking for particular states to confirm that.

Once you have experienced this confirmation directly, every state is a reconfirmation. Experiences of loss, bliss, sadness, good events, bad events, are all recognized to appear in awareness. Finally, totality of experience is the reconfirmation *I am That!* Before and after any thought of what I am or how I am or where I am, *I AM.*

❖

Following an instant of realizing pure silent awareness, a great rush of many physiological and emotional effects occurs. The tendency is to become attached to these byproducts. When the byproducts are finished or change or transform, the thought may arise, *Oh, I lost myself.* Do you hear the absurdity of this thought? Where can you go? Only *thoughts* of you go.

Events come and go. Thoughts come and go. Moods come and go. Good times come and go. Bad times come and go. Awareness is always present. You are awareness.

Awareness, your own true self, is vast beyond measure. Awareness has no problem with anything appearing or disappearing in it. Everything is included.

Whatever seems to pull you away from silence, when experienced directly, is also discovered to be a confirmation of eternal, silent presence of awareness. Without awareness, how can imagination of past appear?

See for yourself.

In every moment?

Yes, in every moment. Now we are speaking of vigilance!

❖

I had an image of climbing a ladder, and it seemed that every rung of the ladder was a realization or an accomplishment. Then all of a sudden, the ladder turned into a greased pole. At first, it felt like I was falling down and backward. Now there's just no direction to it at all, and it's a delightful ride.

The first step is in giving up your defeats. Give up your hell, your insanity, your personal suffering. Next, give up your victories, accomplishments, and self-importance. Really fall. Free-fall.

Give up the old ladder of accomplishments. Whatever is acquired must be defended. This defense fraudulently uses the name of vigilance. Defending is not vigilance. Vigilance is the willingness to free-fall through all illusion.

The moment the identification *I am somebody* arises, directly inquire into its reality. Then falling is not falling. In direct self-inquiry, rising and falling are not separate. Truth and you are not separate. Life and you are not separate.

❖

I notice that when my mind is quiet, it is very easy to be aware of myself, to see what arises and to not touch it. But throughout the day I forget, and I have to keep myself coming back to vigilance. I feel that vigilance takes effort.

The effort arises from the misunderstanding that vigilance means to capture some particular state. Stop all attempts to capture. Do not make vigilance an exercise. Be vigilant by surrendering every effort to define yourself according to mental or emotional states.

Effort is not needed to *be*. If you trust being and begin to explore being, *as being,* then can you find any activity separate from yourself?

Vigilance is attention. Attention gets its attentiveness from pure awareness, which is who you are. Self-definition only keeps you fixated on waves while yearning to find the deep. The ocean has no problem with waves. Never for a moment does the ocean imagine the waves as separate from itself. Never for a moment does the ocean imagine its depths as separate from itself. Never for a moment does the ocean imagine any separation between wave and depth.

Be the ocean. This is vigilance.

SELF-DOUBT:
THE LAST OBSTACLE

Self-doubt and self-distrust are impostors of true questioning. They have been used for socialization throughout time. To truly question all preconceived assumptions, your own and those of your culture, of history, of religions, governments, and politics of all kinds, is an act of reflective intelligence.

To doubt the perfection of your personality, the power of your body, or the wisdom of your thinking process is legitimate and even wise. To doubt who you are, to doubt the truth of eternal truth, is a waste of time at best. A waste of time that is a proven formula for suffering.

Ramana said that self-doubt is the last obstacle. It is the final play of the mind. The mind is a great and wondrous power. It has the power to say no, the power to doubt, the power to deny. Now I am asking you to put that power aside, to not know, to not doubt, to be still.

Self-doubt is based on belief in your image of yourself as reality. Attached to that image is an idea that right and wrong look a certain way. Living bound to this image and evaluation of self is conditioned existence. You fear that without your ideas of yourself, you will certainly do it wrong. You believe that at your core, you really *are* wrong.

Right and wrong as moral codes have an important place. Images of right and wrong have an important place. But finally, when you are called to know the truth of who you are, you cannot look to any image. You cannot look to anyone else's evaluation. If you have some picture of what enlightenment or freedom or right or wrong looks like, then you are duped by conditioned existence. All these images are present in your mind only as you refer to the historical past. Horrible events occurred in the past, as did wondrous events. There is much to learn from history. History is a long, continuing story of the arrogance of mind, the horror that is the result of that arrogance, the release from that arrogance, and the humbling and peace that follow. End your long story with the humbling of the mind before truth.

Doubt the power of the mind, but do not doubt your true self. Do not give your mind such absolute power. The mind does not know how to make good use of such power. It just spins with it. The mind, with illusions of absolute power, is a tyrant. We can certainly see that throughout history, without a doubt! The mind is a beautiful servant. All of the intellect and all your life experiences can be, and potentially are, in service to truth and true self. But first, doubt must be obliterated.

If you doubt yourself, you will suffer and search for release from this suffering through thought, emotion, and physical circumstance.

Do you understand this? I am not saying don't doubt your circumstances. I am saying don't doubt the truth of who you are. You are bigger than any circumstance. Your are bigger than any thought, be it of grandiosity or worthlessness. You are before any emotion, after any emotion, and finally, as you will see, during every thought, emotion, and circumstance.

What a release when the old structures of mind fall. All the conditioning is like scaffolding, but the purpose of scaffolding is to not be left standing. When the individual consciousness is at a certain point, the scaffolding naturally needs to come down. Tear the scaffolding down. It is time, or you would not be attracted to satsang. If you are not attracted to satsang, it is perhaps not time. That is fine. Keep your scaffolding. When you are on fire, when there is true desire to awaken, everything that has come before must be torn down.

You may like or dislike whatever image you have of yourself, whatever body you have, whatever personality you have, whatever accomplishments you have, but to discover the truth of who you are is to discover self-love. Self-love is not anything that has to be maintained. It is inherent in self-discovery. Self-love can never be taken away. Self-love is self-knowledge, self-discovery, self-realization. Not who you think you are, but who you truly are. True self is not discovered in any thought. Thoughts may arise, *I am woman, I am man, I am human, I am wonderful, I am horrible,* but these thoughts have nothing to do with self. When you discover yourself, you will find no gender, no species, no qualification.

This is the truth: at the core, you are pure goodness. You are inconceivably lucky to discover this core of goodness. This discovery is your homecoming.

You are welcomed home. Receive the nectar of home. It is the nectar of self-recognition. Drink it. Allow it to be received in your being, and the disease of self-doubt is cured. If you turn from it, if you put it on a shelf, if you make plans to drink it some other day, then you are liable to imagine you have lost it.

Drink the nectar of yourself now. Just check inside and you will see that it is being offered. Check in the core of your being, and receive the mystery being offered there. Drink! When you have drunk your fill, you will overflow with nectar. You will offer it to any who come. This is Holy Communion. You and truth are one.

YOU ARE THAT

ou will never be satisfied until you realize who you are.
The time is now.

How do I remove the clouds obstructing the sun of realization?

Clouds that seemingly obstruct the sun have to be removed only if you
imagine you are not the sun. If you are the sun, what can it matter that
clouds pass by? Do they block your own light from yourself?

If your point of view is that you are separate from the light, then
anything that appears has the potential to come between you and that
light. Recognize that the core of your being radiates light. What can
separate you from that?

You are even more than the sun. You are the sky. By sky, I don't mean
the upper atmosphere of our planet. I am speaking of endless, limitless,
spacious consciousness. The power that gives rise to clouds and the
power that gives rise to dissipation of clouds is in the sky.

This power cannot be imagined. It is too big to be thought. The sky
of consciousness is inclusive of all, blocked by nothing.

You are the sky. The sun is an image that arises in you. The image of light exists in the sky of consciousness. The sky is infinitely larger than any image.

In your mind you may imagine that consciousness, God, truth, or sky is up there somewhere. But really, where does it begin? Where does it end? When is it ever absent? Even if you close yourself into a closet, is the sky of consciousness absent? No, it is never absent.

Clouds are born in you and die in you. If you begin to identify yourself with phenomena, such as clouds, there is unnecessary suffering. If you identify yourself with the cloud called the body, you will experience separation from the eternal sky of consciousness.

The true sky is endless. It is both forever beyond and immediately present. It is forever here. There are different realms, different universes, and different solar systems, yes, but all exist within the sky of consciousness. In true identification you recognize yourself as that. Recognize yourself truly, and there is no problem with any cloud, any sunset, or even an eclipse. Different climatic events are just phenomena. Atmospheric weather, emotional weather, and mental weather do not affect the sky of consciousness.

Early astronomy once imagined that the sun and planets revolved around the Earth. This type of primitive thinking is still within our psyche. Misidentification must be realized to be old thinking that is useless, and must now be discarded.

This philosophy of the sky as self is easy to talk about, but it is hard to realize.

You are partially right. It is easy to talk, but it is even easier to realize. Ease is the secret. Books, teachers, parents, friends, and enemies have told you, "It is hard; it is difficult." Now this cloud—*It is difficult*—has become a part of your primitive belief system. You walk around thinking, *Awakening is hard; realization is difficult.*

With the thought of difficulty, awakening is experienced as hard; realization is experienced as difficult. I am telling you that awakening is inherently easy. You are already that which you are seeking in awakening. Put aside your commentary and see.

Is it easy to stay in that state of mind all the time?

No state of mind is present all the time. States of mind are like clouds, appearing and disappearing.

And the good feelings that can arise?

Feelings come and go. You are the sky that feelings and states come and go in. *You Are That*

It is not a question of, if you feel you are that, then you are that. You *are* that, whatever the feeling.

What about life?

Life is that! *You are life!*

So all is self-realization?

All is true self. There is no separation anywhere.

Suffering comes while imagining separation from self. Fear arises around whatever it is you imagine you are separate from. You wonder, *Is this enemy or is this friend?* Fear-based relating is very ancient. Dogs and pigs and even protoplasm in a petri dish relate in protective, fear-based ways. Somehow, with a human birth, a gateway through that fear opens up.

The gateway is the call and the promise of all who have awakened. This is the good news of the Buddha, the good news of Christ, the good news of Mohammed—*Consciousness is one; God and I are one; Allah is one.* Whoever awakens declares the possibility of realizing, *I am that oneness.*

What you are telling me is very familiar.

I am telling you what you already know.

Now trust what you know beyond what has been told to you. Trust deeper than what you have read or believed or followed.

✦

I feel very serious about this, and it also makes me fall into desperateness. I feel it is so important.

It is important. It is the most important, and you must be absolutely serious. However, if by serious you mean rigid, then your seriousness is absurd.

I think the rigidity is the problem.

True seriousness is resolve. True resolve must be immovable. Resolve is serious sometimes, and lighthearted and joyful at other times. Resolve uses all faces.

The tide of conditioning, temptation, and self-doubt is very large, isn't it?

Oh, yes!

Without serious resolve, satsang would be just another experience in your mental bundle of experiences. I applaud your resolve. I bow to your resolve.

You must strap yourself to this resolve, this bodhi tree, this mountain peak, this cave, and not be moved.

There will be tests of your resolve. Tests reveal the depth of resolve. Let the whole world come to try to move you, including God itself. Be immovable.

Whenever I feel my resolve isn't great enough, I get angry with myself, and I want to let that anger go.

You do not have to let go of anger. Just keep full attention on the truth of who you are. Anger may arise. All emotions and states arise and pass. If you fix attention on the story of anger, then you are back into the old, sordid relationship with it, and attention is pulled from the truth of who you are.

Many tendencies arise to be burned. In resolve, if you have one tendency left or thirty-five million tendencies, it does not matter because that is not where your attention is.

Let whatever arises arise. In letting it arise, you let it go. It is only when you pull your attention away from the truth of who you are that you get into the story of what should or should not arise.

Be prepared for everything to arise. Be prepared for nothing to arise. It is the same, really, and this is the great secret.

Enormous feelings of suffering may arise. In the moment that you are willing for everything to arise, while your attention is firmly, resolutely, attached to that in which all arises, suffering cannot continue.

If you call some state, emotion, or event suffering, then as awareness itself, meet suffering. Then it is conscious suffering. Running from suffering only perpetuates suffering. In your willingness to directly experience whatever arises, then suffering is not suffering.

Jesus is reported to have said, "If you know how to suffer, you do not suffer."

How to suffer? By willingly, completely, and unsentimentally experiencing the suffering all the way through to the core to discover *who,* in reality, is really suffering.

⬦

This week at massage school, when I was being worked on, I had a feeling of going into a different space that was really happy and blissful, but there was nothing there.

Yes!

My teacher kept trying to lead me back.

Leading you back to known reality is the normal teaching. Luckily you are not a normal student.

I looked around at the surroundings, and it felt like I had been beamed somewhere. Then I ran into confusion as to why I'm even in a body. Why can't I just be in that other place all the time?

You are. Your body is in that all the time. Your body is never separate from that.

But it is.

No, it's not.

Are they both just as real as one another?

There is that which is permanently real, and there are experiences in that which seem real, look real, and feel real, but are limited in duration. Your body is an example of limited, impermanent experience. In satsang, the word "real" refers to what is permanently present, not what appears real and then disappears.

People sometimes do not want the body to continue, and people sometimes want the body to continue forever. Both desires reflect the same misidentification. Some get the idea that the only way to return to final truth is to get rid of the body. You must recognize that truth is here now. It is the animating force of all bodies, and it exists independently of any body. Only when the body is either worshipped or reviled is it a problem. In either worshipping or reviling what is limited, the limitless source is overlooked.

So why do bodies feel so separate from one another?

They feel separate because they appear to be separate, and we are trained to accept our perceptions as reality. There is deep conditioning that you are a particular body. Then for an instant you glimpse the freedom of no body present. This glimpse is the cut in the knot of misidentification.

Directly experience the body, and you will see. At its core, at the core of every cell, at the core of every phenomenon, is that limitlessness which is bound by no body.

◈

Can you speak further on a word you've touched on at other satsangs, "unborn"?

When you own nothing—not your body, your name, your history, your fear, your courage, or your conclusions—then you recognize yourself to be that which is forever unborn. Even deeper than unborn—*that which is forever unconceived.*

The moment that conception arises, stop. What is before that? Purity before and beyond all conception is the truth of who you are. This purity does not go away during conception or after conception. It is immovable. It is untouched by anything conceived.

What is unborn and unconceived has nowhere to go. In this moment, discover within yourself that peace which has nowhere to go. It is forever unborn, and yet all that is born is born of it.

◈

Satsang is not limited to something read or heard. Satsang is the potential context for every moment of your life.

You are not separate from any awakening that has ever occurred. You are not separate from Buddha's awakening, Christ's awakening, Ramana's awakening, Poonjaji's awakening, or any other awakening. It is the same awakening, the same self awakening to itself, crossing all lines of religion and culture, boundaries and horizons, crossing all lines of perceived differences and separation, recognizing itself totally and without limit. Each of us has some exquisite role to play, an unknown, mysterious role. The possibility in satsang is to be inspired to play that role fully. To play a role fully, recognize that any role is just a role, and that who you truly are is beyond all roles.

If you end mental fixation on personal problems, awakening of self to itself is served. Your life is then naturally used to facilitate the awakening of all being, and service to awakening is discovered to be the deepest bliss.

❖

Now is the time to recognize the core of peace that exists within you. *You Are That*

Yes, now is the time.

ABOUT THE
GANGAJI FOUNDATION

The Gangaji Foundation offers public meetings and retreats with Gangaji, as well as books, audios, and videos. To receive a complete catalog and schedule of programs, please visit www.gangaji.org, email info@gangaji.org, or call 800.267.9205.

ABOUT SOUNDS TRUE

Sounds True was founded in 1985 with a clear vision: to disseminate spiritual wisdom. Located in Boulder, Colorado, Sounds True publishes teaching programs that are designed to educate, uplift, and inspire. We work with many of the leading spiritual teachers, thinkers, healers, and visionary artists of our time.

To receive a free catalog of tools and teachings for personal and spiritual transformation, please visit www.soundstrue.com, call toll-free 800-333-9185, or write to us at the address below.

SOUNDS TRUE
PO Box 8010 / Boulder CO 80306